The Permanent War Economy

T. N. Vance & Walter J. Oakes
_____

THE PERMANENT WAR ECONOMY

Copyright ©2008
Center for Socialist History
All Rights reserved

PO Box 626
Alameda CA 94501
Tel: 510 601-6460
www.socialisthistory.org
info@socialisthistory.org

ISBN 0–916695–16-6
Editor: E Haberkern

TABLE OF CONTENTS

Introduction   i

The Permanent War Economy   1951

     Part I — Its Basic Characteristics   1

     Part II — Declining Standards of Living   27

     Part III — Increasing State Intervention   65

     Part IV — Military-Economic Imperialism   107

     Part V — Some Significant Trends   137

     Part VI — Taxation and the Class Struggle   163

Commentary

     A. A. Berle's Capitalist Revolution   205

     An Amalgam of Marx and Keynes   217

     The Myth of America's Social Revolution   233

Appendix

     Towards a Permanent War Economy? *Politics*   1944   243

     After Korea — What?   263

     For the Common Defense,
         A Plea for a Continuing Program Industrial Preparedness   271

Index   283

Introduction

When I went looking for the quote from Dwight Eisenhower that appears on the cover of this book, I remembered his use of the phrase "military-industrial complex" as a simple warning against another set of lobbyists. But, as you can see, it is much more serious than that, especially in the paragraphs where Eisenhower describes the transformation of the American University from a center of "intellectual curiosity" into a seeker of "government contracts."

> Akin to, and largely responsible for the sweeping changes in our industrial-military posture, has been the technological revolution during recent decades.
>
> In this revolution, research has become central, it also becomes more formalized, complex, and costly. A steadily increasing share is conducted for, by, or at the direction of, the Federal government.
>
> Today, the solitary inventor, tinkering in his shop, has been overshadowed by task forces of scientists in laboratories and testing fields. In the same fashion, the free university, historically the fountainhead of free ideas and scientific discovery, has experienced a revolution in the conduct of research. Partly because of the huge costs involved, a government contract becomes virtually a substitute for intellectual curiosity. For every old blackboard there are now hundreds of new electronic computers.

There is another passage from this farewell address, delivered on January 17, 1961, in which Eisenhower refers to the military's role in the development of the computer industry. In fact, the original IBM computer, using, not silicon chips but vacuum tubes, would have been inconceivably expensive and, for that matter, not of much practical use for even the largest corporation. The list could be expanded. The Interstate Freeway system, begun during Eisenhower's own administration; the Internet, originally ARAPnet which linked University and military research systems; the system of space satellites on which the Internet and other forms of international communications depend; nuclear power stations;

The Permanent War Economy

all not only depended on, but were initiated by government funding for military purposes and under military control.

Interestingly enough, almost twenty years before Eisenhower's farewell address Charles E. (Edward) Wilson, then vice chairman of the War Production Board and former chairman of General Electric (hence "Electric Charlie"), gave a speech to the Twenty-Fifth Anniversary Dinner of the Army Ordnance Association on January 19, 1944 which was published in *Army Ordnance* (Vol. XXVI, No. 143, March-April, 1944) under the title "For the Common Defense, A Plea for a Continuing Program of Industrial Preparedness" in which he argued the necessity of a "permanent war economy."* Although he did not use the phrase, as has often been claimed, the concept is certainly there. In particular, Wilson emphasized the role of military research as an engine of scientific progress.** He did not, however, argue that a permanent war economy was an economic necessity if postwar capitalism was to avoid collapse. And that is the main argument in the essays that follow.

The essays in this collection also predated Eisenhower's address by almost twenty years. The first of them appeared in February 1944 in the magazine *Politics* edited by Dwight MacDonald. While roughly contemporaneous with Wilson's speech it is unlikely that either author was familiar with the other's work. They traveled in different circles. But both reflect the anxiety of the immediate postwar period.

The period of economic prosperity and relative social peace that characterized the 50s and 60s relegated concerns about what was happening to contemporary capitalist economies to the back-burner. But in the 70s the disillusionment following the Vietnam war and the first economic effects of "globalization" led to renewed interest in the question. Professor Seymour Melman wrote a number of studies of the question which are now, unfortunately, out of print, although used copies are still available. More recently Professor Chalmers Johnson has devoted a three volume series to the subject.

---

* This speech is reproduced in the appendix to this collection.

** The author of these lines is often confused with Charles E. (Erwin) Wilson, Eisenhower's Secretary of Defense and former chairman of General motors ("Engine Charlie"). The confusion is understandable since "Engine Charlie" is well-known for his testimony before a congressional committee that "what is good for General Motors is good for the country and vice versa." The Permanent War Economy was certainly good for General Motors. If not for the country.

Introduction

The author of the essays in this book (the two authors cited on the cover are, in fact, pen names of Edward Sard about whom little else is known) differs from other critics of the "military-industrial complex" in a number of ways.

He was a product of the left wing socialist youth movement in the 1930s whose members became increasingly disillusioned with the Soviet Union and the official Communist parties. They were attracted to Trotsky's attack on the new bureaucratic class/caste that grew up in the economic and social chaos that followed the civil war in Russia. During the 30s and 40s they were involved in a very interesting, if occasionally acrimonious, discussion of what this new phenomenon augured for the future of the socialist and working class movements.

By 1944 most had come to the conclusion that the bureaucracy was a new class whose control of the statified economy made it an opponent both of private capital and the organized working class. * But this analysis also opened up another question. What was the significance of "socialistic" measures adopted by the New Deal such as the Tennessee Valley Authority or the sweeping nationalizations carried out by the Labour government under Clement Atlee? Sard's 1944 article in *Politics* was a contribution to this discussion. By 1948 the political organization that published *The New International* in which the remainder of Sard's articles appeared had adopted the position that:

> In proportion as production for war purposes becomes the accepted and determining end of economic activity, the role of the bureaucracy ceases to be that of a political superstructure and tends to become an integral part of the economy itself. This bureaucratization of economy in the capitalist countries leads to the growth of the state bureaucracy in size, in the importance of its role for the regulation of the economy, and in its relative independence from the direct control of the capitalist class. (*The New International*, April 1949, 116.)

---

* For a small selection of essays from this debate see the Center for Socialist History's anthology *Neither Capitalism nor Socialism* available from Amazon.com.

The Permanent War Economy

What followed from this proposition, and Sard's articles were essentially an elaboration on this thesis, was that capitalism was not only turning into another version of its arch-enemy Stalinism but that this transformation was the only way that the capitalist class could survive. The thesis put forward by Melman, Johnson and other critics of the war economy was that this development was an economic disaster for the average American which is undoubtedly true. The question that Sard raises is: is this transformation, however great a disaster it may be for the working and middle classes, necessary to preserve capitalism itself? He also emphasizes that the Permanent War Economy is a transitional stage in the development of modern capitalism. It prepares the way for state intervention in the economy not directly tied to arms and war preparation.

Like other economic prognoses, Marxist and non-Marxist, Sard's tended to telescope events. For one thing, like practically everyone else at the time he expected the US/Soviet rivalry to lead to a Third World War in the near future. In his 1944 article he predicts this war to break out around 1960. As we now know this did not happen despite John F. Kennedy's best efforts. Sard also expected the negative economic impact of the Permanent War Economy to begin more or less immediately. In fact, the economic dominance of the US during the 50s and 60s forestalled these effects. By the 70s, however, the decline began to set in. Some of the statistics cited by Sard and some of his predictions read like the business section of this morning's newspaper.

In addition to Sard's six part series which is the main section of this work we have included three book reviews which touch on the topic and an appendix which contains his 1944 *Politics* article and an article titled *After Korea — What?* both of which are referred to in the first article of the main series. We conclude with "Electric Charlie's" speech to the Army Ordnance Association.

The Center would like to thank the www.marxists.org web site for allowing us to use its transcriptions of the Vance articles which are included in its extensive online library of materials on the socialist movement. It made the job of producing this anthology much easier

E. Haberkern
Center for Socialist History

The Permanent War Economy

Part I – Its Basic Characteristics

With the beginning of World War II, both American and world capitalism entered a new epoch – the era of the Permanent War Economy. This was not easily discernible in the immediate postwar period and it is only now, after the outbreak of the Korean war, that there is growing awareness that capitalism has entered a new stage. Its political basis of "neither peace nor war" was demonstrated in "After Korea – What?" in the previous issue of *The New International*.* Whether American armed forces are continuously engaged in active combat is immaterial to the *nature* of the new period in which we live. That is merely a *tactical* aspect in the current struggle for world supremacy between American and Stalinist imperialisms. In fact, the character of the Permanent War Economy, because it operates in either "peace" or "war," is most clearly delineated precisely when American armed forces are *not* engaged in open hostilities.

In the same article, by analyzing the gigantic growth in output during the war and the maintenance of this high level of production since the war, together with the huge accumulation of capital, we have really provided the key data underlying the economic basis of the Permanent War Economy. Its essential features can be seen by examining the entire period since 1939, remembering that never before in the history of the United States have expenditures for war or "national defense" purposes in peacetime exceeded one or one and one-half per cent of total output. In other words, prior to the advent of the Permanent War Economy the end-purpose of economic activity, other than in wartime, was to satisfy consumers' wants through the production and distribution of commodities that yielded a profit or other form of surplus value to the capitalist. War outlays were so negligible in peacetime that they could be ignored in any analysis of the economy for they had no real measurable impact.

During the century and more of the development of modern capitalism, since the first industrial crisis of 1825, the capitalist sought his profit in the marketplace through the production of consumer goods and services. Some capitalists, of course, made a profit through the production of means of production (fixed capital) but such machinery was intended for the use of other capitalists who, in turn, would employ the machines

---

* See the second chapter in the appendix to this work (EH)

The Permanent War Economy

to produce consumer commodities more profitably than could otherwise be done. This was the typical *modus operandi* of capitalism up to and into the period of its decline, except in wartime, until the beginning of the Permanent War Economy. It governed all phases of the business cycle.

To be sure, relatively small standing armies and navies were accepted. Even in European countries that practice conscription, however, these armed forces were distinguished by their smallness. With only a handful of exceptions, the bourgeoisie did not look to government war orders or "defense contracts" as an important source of business or profit. When a war came, it was universally regarded as an interruption of normal activity, even if it yielded imperialist profits and markets. When a war ended, it was the bourgeoisie who took the lead in resuming production of peacetime commodities and who, for the most part, resented any governmental attempt to maintain a larger armed force than had previously existed in peacetime. While war was normal in the sense that it occurred every so often, and was an acceptable instrument of national policy, it was abnormal in that large expenditures for war purposes in peacetime were not socially acceptable and that morally war and war outlays were to be avoided if at all possible.

THE DOMINANT CHARACTERISTIC OF THE PERMANENT WAR ECONOMY is that war output becomes a legitimate end-purpose of economic activity. This development and its basic significance were analyzed by Walter J. Oakes in an article in the February 1944 issue of *Politics*, entitled "Toward a Permanent War Economy?"* Oakes' definition remains perfectly valid to this day:

> A war economy . . . is not determined by the expenditure of a given percentage of a nation's resources and productive energies for military purposes. This determines only the *kind* of war economy; good, bad, or indifferent from the point of view of efficiency in war-making. The question of amount, however, is obviously relevant. At all times, there are *some* expenditures for war or 'national defense.' How much must the

---

* See the first chapter in the appendix.

Basic Characteristics

government spend for such purposes before we can say a war economy exists? In general terms, the problem can be answered as follows: *a war economy exists whenever the government's expenditures for war (or 'national defense') become a legitimate and significant end-purpose of economic activity.* The degree of war expenditures required before such activities become *significant* obviously varies with the size and composition of the national income and the stock of accumulated capital. Nevertheless, the problem is capable of theoretical analysis and statistical measurement. (Italics in original.)

We shall return to Oakes, both his contributions and his mistakes. We now have, however, a large body of factual data from 1939 to 1950. We can also project our data through 1953 with a fair amount of accuracy on the basis of what is currently known regarding Washington's plans. Only one major assumption is required; namely, that large-scale global hostilities involving the armed forces of the United States will not take place before 1954. We shall then have a period of fifteen years to analyze. With the rapid movement of history in the twentieth century this is sufficient to isolate the major features of the Permanent War Economy, to discover its basic laws of motion and to propose what now appear to be proper strategy and tactics for the independent socialist movement.

It is clear that we must begin with the relationship between war outlays and total output. As a first step, we can take the government's official figures for "national defense and related activities" as a percentage of gross national product, net national product and national income. These data for 1939-1953 are shown in Table A on the following page.

The use of either gross national product, net national product, or national income as a measure of total output does not alter the basic relationships or trends involved. The definition of war outlays, and therefore the choice of series selected, is, however, of some significance. Inasmuch as it is desirable to use official government figures wherever possible, without distorting the picture that emerges, we have selected the series called "national defense and related activities" as our measure of direct war outlays. We could have used the Federal war component of gross national product, as estimated by the National Income Division of the Department of Commerce. Aside from the fact that Commerce has not published the breakdown between Federal war and non war purchases

The Permanent War Economy

TABLE A:
RELATIONSHIP OF WAR OUTLAYS TO TOTAL OUTPUT, 1939-1953
(Dollar Figures in Millions)

Year	Gross National Product (1)	Net National Product (2)	National Income (3)	War Outlays (4)	Col.(4) As % of Col.(1) (5)	Col.(4) As % of Col.(2) (6)	Col.(4) As % of Col.(3) (7)
1939	$91,339	$83,238	$72,532	$1,356	1.5%	1.6%	1.9%
1940	101443	93003	81347	2772	2.7	3	3.4
1941	126417	117123	103834	12708	10.1	10.9	12.2
1942	161551	151570	137119	50892	31.5	33.6	37.1
1943	194338	183658	169686	83172	42.8	45.3	49
1944	213688	201801	183838	90888	42.5	45	49.4
1945	215210	202800	182691	78756	36.6	38.8	43.1
1946	211110	198947	180286	24087	11.4	12.1	13.4
1947	233264	218419	198688	14541	6.2	6.7	7.3
1948	259071	241676	223466	11201	4.3	4.6	5
1949	255578	236806	216831	12847	6	5.4	5.9
1950*	278000	257000	234000	15922	5.7	6.2	6.8
1951*	300240	279359	251550	40095	13.3	14.4	15.9
1952*	315252	293327	263373	46920	14.9	16	17.8
1953*	321557	299194	268377	54255	16.9	18.1	20.2

*Data for 1950-1953 are estimated, as explained in the text; 1950 national income and product data are based on Department of Commerce figures for the first half of the year, with 1950 war outlays based on expenditures for "national defense and related activities" as reported by the Treasury Department for the first eight months of the year.

Basic Characteristics

since 1946, this latter series, although based on Treasury classifications of expenditures, runs at a somewhat lower level than the former, apparently being more closely confined to the heart of war expenditures as represented by the Department of Defense.

Under the Commerce concept, for example, the peak of war outlays in 1944 is $88,615,000,000 against the $90,888,000,000 shown in the table. While this is a difference of more than $2 billion, the percentage of resources devoted to direct war output at the peak of the war effort is only reduced from 42.5 per cent to 41.5 per cent of a gross national product or, in the case of a net national product, from 45 per cent to 43.9 per cent. A shift of one or two percentage points in the ratio of war output to total production is of little consequence to our analysis and well within the margin of error than the Treasury series. This discrepancy may be due to arithmetical error or, more probably, to different procedures in allocating war expenditures by years.

At any rate, as explained in the 1949 statistical supplement to the *Survey of Current Business*, expenditures for 'national defense and related activities' currently include those of the Departments of the Air Force, the Army, and the Navy; payments under Armed Forces Leave Act; Expenditures of the US Maritime Commission, UNRRA, surplus property disposal agencies, and the Reconstruction Finance Corporation (after July 1, 1947, expenditures of RFC for national defense and related activities were not segregated from other expenditures of the Corporation and its affiliates, which are included under 'other' expenditures).

Conceptually, this appears to represent a fairly good measure of direct war outlays and is, in any case, the best available. It permits a relatively accurate analysis of the impact of direct war outlays on the economy.

WAR OUTLAYS, AS THUS DEFINED, were projected for the last four months of 1950 and for 1951-1953 on a fairly crude basis, in the absence of any detailed public information on military requirements and related programs. The method used was to assume an armed force manpower trend from the latest published figures, including such information as is available on the draft, and the announced goal of reaching an armed force of three million by mid-1951. A "salary" ratio for average military personnel was then developed on the basis of published data for military wages and salaries, which assumes only a very modest increase from 1949 to 1953 in the cost of maintaining

The Permanent War Economy

average military personnel. While this factor is subject to some margin of error, it is necessarily small. A more serious difficulty was encountered in the second step of the projection, which was to develop an "equipment" ratio to relate total expenditures of the Department of Defense to total military wage and salary payments. Here the assumption of increasing fire power and mechanization, although based on past experience, is essentially arbitrary. To compensate for any possible overstatement inherent in the method, or for any lag in military procurement, the projection excludes any attempt to forecast the trend in the "related activities" portion of our war outlays series. Expenditures for direct war outlays of $40.1 billion in 1951, $46.9 billion in 1952 and $54.3 billion, in 1953 were obtained, as can be seen from a column (4) in the table on Relationship of War Outlays to Total Output. These results conform rather closely to the guarded public statements of leading officials in the Department of Defense. If anything, our figures appear to be on the conservative side.*

The projections of the total output measures, gross national product, net national product and national income, were based on fairly straightforward extrapolations of existing trends. Allowance was made for increasing indirect business tax liabilities, thus accountings for the somewhat smaller rate of an increase in national income as compared with a national product, both gross and net. With the exception of 1951, when it is assumed that many defense plants idle since the end of the war will be reactivated, constant rates of capital consumption have been assumed. Virtually identical trends in both gross and net a national product thus result. It should be kept in mind that the method employed makes rather full allowance for rising prices in 1950, but only partially anticipates the inflation that is bound to occur in 1951 and makes virtually no allowance for rising prices in 1952 and 1953. This, however, is entirely consistent with the method used to project war outlays, which likewise largely ignored the effects of inflation on military salaries and procurement, thereby permitting fairly accurate measurement of the relationships involved.

---

*Editor's Note: (*New International*) The President's budget message recommends an expenditure of $41.4 billion for military services during the coming fiscal year, corresponding rather closely to the author's forecasts.

Basic Characteristics

It is recognized that more accurate results would be obtained if the relationship between war outlays and total output were expressed in constant rather than in current dollars, for it may be safely assumed that price rises in the war sector *during a major war* outstrip price rises in the civilian sector. It should be emphasized, however, that this would be noticeable in columns (5), (6) and (7) only for the years 1942-1945. Inasmuch as the difference would not be significant (at the peak of the war effort in 1943-1944, war outlays would still take at least 40 per cent of gross national product in real terms as compared with 42.8 per cent or 42.5 per cent) and the statistical measure could only be the crudest sort of approximation, we accordingly sacrifice theoretical to practical considerations and make no attempt to express our data in constant dollars.

In view of the fact that war outlays are gross (that is, they make no allowance for the consumption of capital in the war sector), it may be wondered why the relationship between war outlays and total output is not confined exclusively to gross national product. In theory, this would indubitably be a sounder procedure. In practice, however, this would tend to understate the impact of war and the Permanent War Economy, for the definition of war outlays is relatively narrow and restricted. It is confined exclusively to the Federal government, and hardly covers all direct war-induced outlays in this sphere. It omits all private expenditures that may directly or indirectly result from war or war preparations.

If, for example, we posit an economy in which war and war preparations are nonexistent, think of all the expenditures in the private sector that would be abandoned, thereby freeing these resources for the satisfaction of consumer wants. Included would be such matters as all private expenditures for civil defense, an unknown percentage of the output of the chemical, aviation and other industries that is not financed by the government, an unknown percentage of various aspects of privately-financed research, and without question a significant portion of the outlay for all forms of transportation. Moreover, the consumption of capital in the war sector is relatively small compared with the civilian sector. In view of all these considerations, not to mention certain conceptual and statistical limitations in the measurement of gross national product, we are of the opinion that the relationship between war outlays and net national product, as shown in column (6), is the best single measure available of the impact of direct war

The Permanent War Economy

preparations and production and that the range of probable error in the estimates is adequately shown by columns (5) and (7).

WHILE TOTAL REAL OUTPUT ROSE steadily during the war, with relatively minor fluctuations since the end of the war, it will now be further increased until by 1953 production will approximate the peak achieved during the last war. Meanwhile, war outlays rose much faster than total output during World War II, thereby reflecting both the increase in total output and the shift of resources from civilian to war production. In percentage terms, the 1.6 per cent of total output devoted to war outlays in 1939 represents, insignificant as it may be, an extremely high level for a peacetime year before the development of the Permanent War Economy. The economy of the United States was for the last time to lag behind the rest of the *capitalist* world in conforming to the requirements of the Permanent War Economy. By 1940, with three per cent of production devoted to war purposes, American imperialism began in rather hesitating fashion, while war was engulfing the world, to develop its own war economy. With war outlays taking about 11 per cent of total output in 1941, the percentage then rose more than fourfold to about 45 per cent in 1943-1944 as American imperialism crushed the challenge of German and Japanese imperialisms, aided of course by the Allies.

There then occurred a sharp decline, until Korea, in the ratio of war outlays to total output. It is most significant, however, that the decrease in war outlays or in the ratio between war outlays and total output did not approach the low levels of 1939 or even of 1940. Here is the first real evidence of the change ushered in by the Permanent War Economy. Even at their low point in 1948, direct war outlays of more than $11 billion, representing almost 5 per cent of total output, are hardly insignificant. They will now rise sharply, although not as rapidly as during World War II. Nevertheless, there will immediately be a threefold rise in direct war outlays and, by 1952-1953, a threefold increase in the ratio of war outlays to total output.

We are, so to speak, in a situation comparable to 1941. This does not mean that 1942 has to follow immediately. On the contrary, as already explained, there is every reason to believe that all-out shooting war will not take place for several years. It does mean, however, that war expenditures have indeed become both a *legitimate* and *significant* end-purpose of economic activity. As a consequence, economic theory (both bourgeois

Basic Characteristics

and Marxist) will have to be modified in several important respects. Consider, for example, the following statement of Simon Kuznets, the outstanding pioneer in the field of national income in the United States, in his book, *National Product in Wartime*, published in 1945:

> In conclusion, we stress the dependence of the concept and the estimates upon the definition of the purpose of economic activity. National product cannot be measured for the years of a major war as it is in peacetime because the customary long-run assumptions concerning the goals of economic activity are not basic.

It is precisely the goals of economic activity that the Permanent War Economy has changed. *Sizable outlays for "defense" are now normal and socially acceptable.* It may even be suspected that these war outlays play an important role in sustaining a generally high level of economic activity. This appears to be clear when the ratio of war outlays to total output exceeds 10 per cent but what about the period from 1947-1950 when the percentage hovered around five and six per cent? Direct war outlays may have been below the "critical" point in these years, but the picture is considerably altered when indirect war outlays are included in our analysis.

ASIDE FROM THE EXPENDITURES of the Department of Defense and the relatively minor additional outlays included in the series on "national defense and related activities," our measure of direct war outlays, there are a whole host of programs in which the Federal government is engaged that stem directly or indirectly from previous wars or are an integral part of American imperialism's preparations for World War III. These fall into two broad categories: foreign economic and military aid, whose essential purpose is to obtain allies and markets for American imperialism; and certain domestic programs, such as all the expenditures of the Veterans Administration, that are imposed on the national state as the only feasible method of carrying them out. While some of these expenditures, although from different motives and with different results, would have to be incurred by a workers' state, they are clearly a product of the Permanent War

The Permanent War Economy

Economy. Failure to include them in our analysis would distort the entire nature and impact of the new stage in the history of capitalism.

Indirect war outlays are really a new phenomenon in the sense that they first become sizable in the post-World War II period, as can be seen from Table B on the following page, which also permits a comparison of the relative importance of direct and indirect war outlays and an analysis of their combined impact on total output.

Our estimates of indirect war outlays have been built up by analyzing in detail each program that it appeared proper to include in our classification and by projecting those programs that appear reasonably certain to continue on as conservative and realistic a basis as possible. If anything, our figures understate the true magnitude of indirect war outlays. In keeping with our entire approach, only government programs have been considered. The exclusion of all indirect private war outlays leaves out such febrile activities as building of atomic bomb shelters and preservation of records in bomb-proof vaults, to mention only the obvious. Then, we have made only token allowance for state and local government expenditures for civil defense and related matters. Moreover, we have failed to identify all the Federal programs that should be included under the classification, "indirect war outlays." For example, no attempt has been made to include RFC loans for "defense" purposes, which have been excluded since July 1, 1947 from direct war outlays. In addition, propaganda activities of the Federal government, such as the "Voice of America," are excluded from our figures, but are clearly part and parcel of war preparations, at least in large measure.

Our projections of the major programs comprising indirect war outlays have assumed that the Republican gains in Congress will be reflected in a more careful scrutiny of all such expenditures, although no fundamental change in policy is anticipated. Dollar-wise, the most important program is represented by the Veterans Administration, which reached a peak of $7.1 billion in 1947 and remained at $6.8 billion during 1948 and 1949. Although current expenditures of the Veterans Administration are running at the rate of $6 billion annually, we have reduced this item to $5 billion in 1951 and only subsequently do we project a modest increase in view of the expanding size of the armed forces.

Basic Characteristics

TABLE B:
DIRECT AND INDIRECT WAR OUTLAYS. 1939-1953
AND THEIR RELATIONSHIP TO TOTAL OUTPUT
(Dollar Figures In Billions)

Year	Net National Product* (1)	WAR OUTLAYS Direct* (2)	WAR OUTLAYS Indirect (3)	WAR OUTLAYS Total (4)	Col.(2) As % of Col.(1)* (5)	Col.(4) As % of Col.(1) (6)
1939	$83.2	$1.4	$0.6	$2.0	1.6%	2.4%
1940	93	2.8	0.8	3.6	3	3.9
1941	117.1	12.7	1.2	13.9	10.9	11.9
1942	151.6	50.9	0.9	51.8	33.6	34.2
1943	183.7	83.2	0.9	84.1	45.3	45.8
1944	201.8	90.9	1.3	92.2	45	45.7
1945	202.8	78.8	4	82.8	38.8	40.8
1946	198.9	24.1	9.5	33.6	12.1	16.9
1947	218.4	14.5	15.4	29.9	6.7	13.7
1948	241.7	11.2	12.4	23.6	4.6	9.8
1949	236.8	12.8	12.2	25	5.4	10.6
1950 est.	257	15.9	12	27.9	6.2	10.9
1951 est.	279.4	40.1	15.9	56	14.4	20
1952 est.	293.3	46.9	15	61.9	16	21.1
1953 est.	299.2	54.3	16.2	70.5	18.1	23.6

* Taken from Table A.

The Permanent War Economy

With regard to the so-called Mutual Defense Assistance Program, which covers all forms of military aid to Atlantic Pact nations, Greece, Turkey, etc., it is difficult to see how this can be less than the $5 billion projected in 1952 and 1953. If any serious attempt is made to contain Stalinist imperialism in Asia, this type of expenditure may be expected to increase markedly above present insignificant levels. Despite the Gray report, our projections for the Marshall Plan, Point Four and Export-Import bank loans have been extremely modest. They total $2.7 billion in 1951, $2 billion in 1952 and only $1.5 billion in 1953. In the case of the Point Four program, for which the Gray report recommends an annual expenditure of 500 million dollars, our peak projection reaches only $200 million. All remaining foreign aid programs are inconsequential in magnitude. Our analysis remains unaffected even if they were to be completely eliminated, but such cannot be the case since they include Korean aid and other programs that will be operated mainly through the United Nations. Because a portion of the data was obtained on a fiscal year basis, there may be certain adjustments required in the allocations by calendar year, but these are unlikely to be serious. The only place where there is any possible overstatement of indirect war outlays is in our assignment of total expenditures by the Atomic Energy Commission to this category. There is no basis, however, for allocating any portion of such activities to civilian output and the safest procedure seemed to be to assign total appropriations, as reported in the Federal Budget, to indirect war outlays. The fact that AEC procurement now carries a "D.O." priority rating indicates that the government considers this program an integral part of the "defense" program.

We have deliberately omitted inclusion of net interest on the national debt, now running well over $5 billion a year, from our concept of war outlays because the Department of Commerce in its basic revision of 1947 eliminated such payments from the national income and product. It may well be that government interest payments "do not represent currently produced goods and services or the current use of economic resources," as Commerce contends, although even this would be true only when the government is operating at a deficit which exceeds total net interest payments on the national debt. We find most unconvincing, however, the statement in the July 1947 *National Income Supplement to Survey of Current Business* that "it seems sensible that a

Basic Characteristics

comparison of the prewar and "postwar volume of production should not be distorted by the continuing interest on the national debt that arose during the war." On the contrary, the rise in the national debt and the enormous interest burden thereby created are basic characteristics of the Permanent War Economy and should be considered in any analysis of production or its distribution. While this is particularly true of the relationship between war outlays and total output, we refrain from making the adjustment in order to avoid any theoretical controversies, but we feel that this omission is an added reason for believing that our ratios of war output to total production are conservative.

THE RISE OF INDIRECT WAR OUTLAYS in the postwar period to a point where five per cent or more of total output is siphoned off by the government programs included under this concept is one of the basic characteristics of the Permanent War Economy. For American imperialism this represents an indefinite and apparently permanent burden. As the table shows, in the years 1947-1950 inclusive, indirect war outlays were virtually as important as direct war outlays with the former totaling $52 billion for the four-year period and the latter $54.4 billion. As a result, total war outlays even at their postwar nadir in 1948 amounted to $23.6 billion and took about 10 per cent of total output.

Naturally, the projected rise in indirect war outlays is dwarfed by comparison with the anticipated increase in direct war outlays. In fact, it is the precipitate growth in direct war outlays that imposes such a careful screening of, and relative curtailment in, indirect war outlays, for there is a limit to the economic strength of American imperialism.

Total war outlays, as shown in column (4), and their ratio to total output, as shown in column (6) of the above table, become the key instruments of analysis. It is only when these figures are examined that the true character of the Permanent War Economy emerges. Enormous production and enormous waste go hand-in-hand. They are both cause and effect of the huge volume of capital accumulation described in the previous article. We showed that total private gross capital formation averaged $39 billion annually in the five postwar years from 1946 to 1950 inclusive. During the same period, total war outlays averaged $28 billion a year. Imagine what would have happened to capital accumulation and to production if war outlays had returned to the negligible

The Permanent War Economy

level of 1939 or before! In one sentence, the prophets of postwar depression would have been correct. By the same token, because of the inherent nature of capitalist production, total output could not be entirely devoted to civilian purposes without rapidly glutting the market and ushering in the previously typical capitalist crisis.

A corollary and yet basic feature of the Permanent War Economy is both the size and nature of state intervention in the economy, as revealed by the magnitude of total war outlays. Federal budgets of $40 billion and more become a permanent feature of the new stage of capitalism, with war outlays, direct and indirect, taking the bulk of Federal expenditures. This role of the "balancing" expenditures by the state was anticipated by Oakes, and we shall return to it in a subsequent article.

The peaks and valleys in the proportion of total output devoted to paying for wars, past, present and future, are not quite so extreme in variation once indirect war outlays have been added to direct war outlays. Nevertheless, the changes are rapid and qualitative in nature, which is another characteristic of the Permanent War Economy stage of capitalism. The figures suggest that about 10 per cent of total output must be spent in the form of war outlays before the latter become significant in their impact. This is quite reminiscent of the 10 per cent export level that characterized American imperialism prior to 1929. Its significance is comparable and for essentially the same reason. In those former days, without exporting 10 per cent of its output, the profitability of the remaining 90 per cent of the output of American capitalism that went to the domestic market would have been jeopardized. Similarly, today, without 10 per cent of its output going to war outlays, the profitability of civilian output would be endangered. We shall likewise elaborate on this point at another time.

What is most important for the development of the class struggle is what happens as the percentage of total war outlays to total output declines from 45 per cent to 10 per cent and then rises again to 20 per cent and more. Let us not forget that the ratio of war outlays to total output has become the prime mover of the economy! As the ratio rises above 10 per cent, production controls become necessary. The capitalist market loses its effectiveness as an allocator of resources. At or about the 20 per cent level, judging from past experience, the inflationary and class pressures become intolerable and distribution controls (rationing and price control) have to be instituted. At the 30 per cent level or

Basic Characteristics

thereabouts, large-scale war has already broken out and manpower controls are invoked to the extent the bourgeoisie considers feasible. At the 40 per cent level or above, total war has engulfed society and precious little remains of the normal functioning of capitalism.

BEFORE CONSIDERING THE PRACTICAL consequences of the Permanent War Economy, it is helpful to examine its theoretical foundations.

Under the heading *The Problem of Unpaid Labor*, Oakes analyzed the basic contradiction of capitalist society and showed why the "'balancing' expenditures on the part of government must take the form of war outlays rather than public works." This, in essence, provides the theoretical foundation of the Permanent War Economy, and we summarize what he wrote on this subject.

> The root of all economic difficulties in a class society," states Oakes, "lies in the fact that the ruling class appropriates (in accordance with the particular laws of motion of the given society) a portion of the labor expended by the working class or classes in the form of unpaid labor. The expropriation of this surplus labor presents its own set of problems; generally, however, they do not become crucial for the ruling class until the point is reached where it is necessary to pile up accumulations of unpaid labor. When these accumulations in turn beget new accumulations, then the stage of 'primitive accumulation' . . . ceases and the stability of the society is threatened.

In other words, it is the accumulation of capital that at bottom endangers the rule of the capitalists. Oakes continues:

> The ruling class is impaled on the horns of a most serious dilemma: to allow these growing and mature accumulations to enter into economic circulation means to undermine the very foundations of existing society (in modern terms, depression); to reduce or eliminate these expanding accumulations of unpaid labor requires the ruling class or sections of it

The Permanent War Economy

> to commit *hara-kiri* (in modern terms, the capitalist must cease being a capitalist or enter into bankruptcy). The latter solution is like asking capitalists to accept a 0 per cent rate of profit, because if they make 6 or 10 per cent they . . . destroy the economic equilibrium. This is too perturbing a prospect; consequently, society as a whole must suffer the fate of economic disequilibrium *unless the ruling class can bring its State to intervene in such a manner as to resolve this basic dilemma.* (Italics in original.)

Oakes then discusses the necessity for state intervention to immobilize *excess* accumulations of unpaid labor and how this problem was solved in Ancient Egypt by pyramid-building and in feudal times by the building of elaborate monasteries and shrines.

> Capitalist society, has had its own pyramids. These ostentatious expenditures, however, have failed to keep pace with the accumulation of capital. In recent times, the best examples have been the public works program of the New Deal and the road building program of Nazi Germany. Both have been accomplished through what is termed 'deficit financing.' That is, the state has borrowed capital (accumulated surplus labor for which there is no opportunity for profitable private investment) and consumed it by employing a portion of the unemployed millions, thus achieving a rough but temporarily workable equilibrium.
> While the Roosevelt and Hitler prewar 'recovery' programs had much in common, there is an important difference. The latter was clearly a military program . . . In the United States, only a minor portion of the W.P.A. and P.W.A. programs possessed potential military usefulness. Consequently, as such expenditures increased, the opposition of the capitalist class rose . . . The more money the state spent, the more these expenditures circumscribed and limited the opportunity for profitable private investment. The New Deal was dead before the war; the war merely resuscitated its political expression and was, in reality, an historical necessity.

War expenditures accomplish the same purpose as public works, but in a manner that is decidedly more effective and more acceptable (from the capitalist point of view). In this, capitalism is again borrowing from the techniques employed by the more static class societies of slavery and feudalism. War outlays, in fact, have become the modern substitute for pyramids. They do not compete with private industry and they easily permit the employment of all those whom it is considered necessary to employ. True, this type of consumption (waste) of surplus labor brings with it a series of difficult political and economic problems. These, however, appear to be solvable; in any case, they can be *postponed*.

Thus, the continued preservation of the capitalist mode of production, a system that has long outlived its historical usefulness, demands ever-increasing state intervention which must take the form of the Permanent War Economy. We need not concern ourselves with the many rationalizations whereby increasing war outlays are justified and accepted socially by all classes, although it is worth noting that: it is the propaganda of the bourgeoisie that penetrates all social layers and it is the bourgeoisie which decides what proportion war outlays shall be of total output. The Permanent War Economy, however, is a form of capitalism. The process of converting unpaid or surplus labor into surplus value, of which profits are but one form, still continues. Above all, capital is still accumulated and, as previously, it is the size, composition and rate of capital accumulation that provides the basic laws of motion of capitalism.

These laws, which were thoroughly analyzed by Marx, have been altered by the development of the Permanent War Economy, some quantitatively and some qualitatively. As Oakes puts it:

> The Marxian general law of capitalist accumulation may, for convenience, be expressed as two laws: namely, the inevitable tendencies toward the polarization of classes and the increase in unemployment. Today, however, this analysis no longer holds good without certain modifications.

The Permanent War Economy

We do not entirely share Oakes' conclusion concerning the slowing up of the rate of class polarization, but there is little doubt that he was correct in forecasting the relative elimination of unemployment.

> THE GREATER THE SOCIAL WEALTH, the functioning capital, the extent and energy of its growth, and, therefore, also the absolute mass of the proletariat and the productiveness of its labor the greater is the industrial reserve-army. The same causes which develop the expansive power of capital, develop also the labor-power at its disposal. The relative mass of the industrial reserve-army increases therefore with the potential energy of wealth. But the greater this reserve-army in proportion to the active labor-army, the greater is the mass of a consolidated surplus-population, whose misery is in inverse ratio to its torment of labor. The more extensive, finally, the lazarus-layers of the working class, and the industrial reserve-army, the greater is official pauperism. *This is the absolute general law of capitalist accumulation.* Marx in *Capital* (Kerr edition, Volume I, p.707)

Without entering into all its ramifications, the decisive point for Marx was that as capitalism evolved, capital constantly accumulated and brought with it an increase in unemployment. Naturally, Marx was well aware that his statement had to be modified in many ways, especially in relation to the fluctuations of the business cycle. Yet, prior to the Permanent War Economy, this fundamental of Marxism was perhaps the most impressive characteristic of capitalism. That it no longer holds true may be seen by referring to the official figures on unemployment.

TABLE C											
UNEMPLOYMENT, 1939-1950 (In Thousands)											
1939	1940	1941	1942	1943	1944	1945	1946	1947	1948	1949	1950
9480	8120	5560	2660	1070	670	1040	2270	2142	2064	3395	3100

Basic Characteristics

The data on unemployment are compiled by the Bureau of the Census and include those fourteen years of age and over who are either looking for work or are on public emergency work projects. This official measure of unemployment refers to the non-institutional population and is based on a sample of 25,000 households in 68 areas. As such, it is admittedly subject to a wide margin of error, with the maximum difference between actual and estimated unemployment calculated at 18 per cent. While the series may not properly evaluate the level of unemployment, and actually conceals the millions of changes that occur monthly from the status of employed to unemployed or vice versa, as well as the changes into and out of the labor force, there is little doubt that it reflects the trend in unemployment.

In 1939 there were on the average almost 9,500,000 unemployed. This is typical of the decade of the 1930's, for the peak year of unemployment was in 1933 when the average was 12,830,000. As the ratio of war outlays to total output increased, unemployment declined until in 1944 it fell to an average of 670,000. This is even below the so-called minimum "frictional" level of unemployment, representing those who are merely in process of changing from one job to another, which is usually placed at one million persons at a minimum. Then, as the ratio of war outlays to total output began to decline, unemployment increased until in 1949 it averaged almost 3,400,000. For the first half of 1950, unemployment averaged almost 3,900,000. With hostilities beginning in Korea came an increase in war outlays. Immediately, unemployment began to drop and by September was about two million. We may expect that in 1951 unemployment will average about one and one-half million and in 1952 and 1953, for all practical purposes, unemployment will be non-existent.

Thus, a 20 per cent ratio of war outlays to total output will now have the same effect on unemployment as a 40 per cent ratio had during the war. The reason is, of course, that the present increase in war outlays starts with the economy operating virtually at capacity. In other words, there is a close relationship between a high level of production and low unemployment, but the relationship is even closer in the case of the ratio of war outlays to total output, for war expenditures are the prime mover in bringing about capacity or near capacity production. Consider that at the peak of its pre-Permanent War Economy prosperity, in 1929, there was an average of 1,550,000

The Permanent War Economy

unemployed and one can readily see the tremendous impact of the Permanent War Economy on American capitalism!

The negligible character of unemployment under the Permanent War Economy, which is vital to the maintenance of a stable and safe economic equilibrium for the bourgeoisie, becomes even more apparent when we compare the level of unemployment with the size of the total labor force, as is done in Table D on the following page.

The volume of unemployment has particular relevance when related to the total labor force, for with the growth in population there are on the average several hundred thousand persons each year who seek employment as new entrants into the labor force. According to Marx, the greater the size of the proletariat, the greater the industrial reserve army. While pressures still operate in this direction, they are overcome (even if our figures were restricted to factory employment) by the ability of the Permanent War Economy to find "employment" for millions in the armed forces and in munitions industries. For example, in 1944 about 22,400,000 persons on the average were employed as workers in munitions industries, civilian employees in Federal war agencies and members of the armed forces. More than one-third of the total labor force at the peak of the war was thus completely unproductive in providing consumer goods and services.

The 32 per cent rise in civilian employment in a little more than a decade of the Permanent War Economy furnishes dramatic proof of the impact of war outlays on the productive capacity of the economy. The size of the armed forces (derived by subtracting the total civilian labor force from the total labor force, including the armed forces) naturally follows very closely the movement of war outlays and is further evidence of the highly volatile nature of the Permanent War Economy. Some question may be raised concerning the propriety of measuring the "unemployment ratio" in terms of the total labor force, including the armed forces, rather than by comparison with the total civilian labor force. The resulting pattern, however, would not be fundamentally different and the relatively large size of the armed forces is one of the basic characteristics of the Permanent War Economy. More than one person in every six was unemployed in 1939 against one in every four in 1933. The limited and precarious character of the recovery

Basic Characteristics

	TABLE D: RATIO OF UNEMPLOYMENT TO TOTAL LABOR FORCE, 1939-1950 (In Thousands)			
Year	Civilian Employment	Total Civilian Labor Force*	Total Labor Force, incl. Armed Forces	Ratio of Unemployment to Total Labor Force, incl. Armed Forces
1939	45,750	55,230	65,600	17.1%
1940	47,520	55,640	56,030	14.6
1941	50,350	55.910	57,380	9.7
1942	53,760	50,410	60,230	4.4
1943	54,470	55,540	64,410	1.7
1944	53,960	54,030	65,890	1.0
1945	52,820	53,860	65,140	1.6
1946	55,250	67,520	60,820	3.7
1947	68,027	60,168	61,608	3.5
1948	59,378	61,442	62,748	3.3
1949	68,710	62,105	63,571	5.3
1950	60,300	63,400	64,900	4.8

* Includes unemployment as shown in the previous table.
† Estimated on the basis of the data for the first nine months

The Permanent War Economy

under the New Deal is thus apparent. The unemployment ratio then declined from 17.1 per cent in 1939 to the fantastically low figure of one per cent in 1944. This compares with an unemployment ratio of 3.1 per cent in 1929. Even with the curtailment of war outlays following 1944, the unemployment ratio does not become much greater than in 1929. We can now expect a further sharp decline in the unemployment ratio to 2.5 per cent in 1951, 1.5 per cent in 1952 and less than one per cent in 1953. No wonder Washington is reported to be considering the drafting of women if and when the plunge is made to conscript all manpower!

THE BASIC CHARACTERISTICS of the Permanent War Economy are the permanence of the sizable level of war outlays, which have become a legitimate expression of growing state intervention in the economy, and the high rates of capital accumulation and production accompanied by insignificant levels of unemployment. If there were no other consequences, aside from the danger of mortal defeat in battle, it might be assumed that the capitalist system had acquired a new lease on life. While it is true, as Lenin was fond of stressing, that "there is no absolutely hopeless situation for the bourgeoisie"; thereby implying the necessity of the conscious intervention of the proletariat in leading mankind on the road toward the socialist emancipation of society, the development of the Permanent War Economy does give rise to new problems, and aggravates old problems, that continually threaten to undermine the foundations of capitalism. We shall comment briefly on the more important differences from "normal" capitalist operation and, in subsequent articles, develop at some length those aspects of the Permanent War Economy that are of particular significance to the working class.

1. *Standards of living decline.* To quote Oakes:

> If the Permanent War Economy succeeds in stabilizing the economy at a high level, unemployment will be eliminated, but only through employment in lines that are economically unproductive. *Thus capitalist accumulation instead of bringing about an increase in unemployment, will have as its major consequence a decline in the standard of living.* (Italics in original.) . . . At first, of course, there may be a rise in the average standard of living if [there is an increase in real national income] and if,

> simultaneously, there is a sharp reduction in total military outlays [from the wartime peak] ... Within a relatively short period, however, assuming that the economy is stabilized at the desired level with a minimum of unproductive governmental expenditures, the maintenance of economic equilibrium will require a steadily rising curve of military outlays. The decline in the average standard of living of the workers, at first relative, will then become absolute – particularly on a world scale as all nations adapt their internal economies to conform with the requirements of the new order based on an international Permanent War Economy. Naturally, the decline will not be a descending straight line; it will have its ups and downs, but the long-term trend will definitely be downward.

It follows, of course, that with the economy operating at capacity an increase in war output requires a corresponding decrease in civilian output. Therefore, the average standard of living must decline, but the burden of declining standards of living will be disproportionately heavy on the low-income groups, especially the working class.

2. *State intervention increases.* The market mechanism cannot be relied upon to allocate resources in accordance with the new, dual end-purposes of economic activity. Accordingly, to meet the requirements of the war sector *and ultimately of the civilian sector,* more and more state controls are imposed upon the body economic. There is a permanent growth in the state bureaucracy, with the state, in effect, guaranteeing the profits of the bourgeoisie. Both profits and production remain at very high levels, as does employment. In this connection Oakes made his most serious mistake, as he apparently did not fully take into account the implications of his own theory and therefore understated future levels of both production and employment.

3. *Capital accumulates rapidly.* Not only do private capital accumulations remain at extremely high levels, but state capital accumulations increase with the growth in the ratio of war outlays to total output. The large demand for capital rapidly exhausts the supplies of idle capital and an overall shortage of capital develops. Accordingly, normal pressures to increase the rate of surplus value are reinforced by the insatiable appetite of the state to dispose of the fruits of past and present labor. Through increased taxation and related fiscal policies, the state consumes a relatively larger portion of total output. The natural tendency toward a declining standard of living is therefore accelerated.

The Permanent War Economy

4. *Bonapartist tendencies develop*. The proletariat increases in size both absolutely and relatively to the growth in the working population. The greater economic strength of the American proletariat is in sharp contrast to the weakness of its political strength, and the danger of the class struggle erupting and seriously interfering with the ability of the state to carry out all the individual programs that add up to the Permanent War Economy is ever present. At the same time, the bourgeoisie increasingly penetrates the organs of the state. On both counts, it therefore becomes necessary for the state to give the appearance of being "above classes" and to "freeze" the class struggle in the role of "impartial" umpire. The growing executive power of the state and the interlocking directorates between big business and the higher military echelons will ultimately spell the doom of bourgeois democracy.

5. *Military-economic imperialism grows*. Increasingly, the state must finance and guarantee international trade and investments. Exports of private finance capital, hitherto the traditional mode of operation of "democratic" imperialism, steadily diminish in importance despite all efforts to revive them. The American state enters permanently into the foreign economic field through various types of "relief and rehabilitation" programs. These programs, in turn, are subordinated to military aid as American imperialism seeks to overcome its relative deficiency in manpower by seeking allies in the struggle to contain and eventually to eliminate Stalinist imperialism. The nationalist revolutions of colonial areas, especially in Asia, present virtually an insoluble problem for American imperialism and are compelled by the desire to survive to move in the direction of third campism.

6. *Inflation is irresistible*. The greater the percentage of war outlays to total output, the greater the inflationary pressure on the economy. This general law of the Permanent War Economy operates at all stages, but becomes more apparent when the economy is running at full capacity. Anti-inflationary techniques cannot halt the inflation, which arises from the relative excess of consumer spending power in comparison with the available supply of consumer goods and services, but can only slow it down and modify its class impact. The major battles of the class struggle, in fact, will arise over the question of who shall pay for the increase in war outlays and which class shall bear the major burden of inflation.

The Permanent War Economy, in brief, offers no hope of solving the basic problems of humanity. It represents a further stage on the road to barbarism and is the inevitable price the world proletariat must pay for its failure to put an end to both capitalism and Stalinism.

Basic Characteristics

It does, however, exist and only fools and demagogues will base their politics on the assumption that nothing has changed. We must find ways and means of coping with the problems of living under the Permanent War Economy or resign ourselves to defending the slaves of totalitarianism and ultimately to the atomization of most of organized society.

The New International November 1950 – T. N. VANCE

Part II – Declining Standards of Living

The general law of accumulation of capital under the Permanent War Economy (see January-February issue, *Basic Characteristics of the Permanent War Economy*) is that an increase in capital, instead of causing an increase in unemployment, is accompanied by relatively full employment and declining standards of living. This new and fundamental law of motion increasingly governs all human and class relations under this latest stage in the decline of capitalist society. Because of its tremendous significance we shall attempt to develop the key quantitative measures, however rough and approximate, so as to permit analysis of the various factors underlying the decline in living standards.

Having already obtained total war outlays, both direct and indirect, and the net value of current production, in order to measure the relationship between war outlays, and total output, our starting point in deriving a measure of the average standard of living is clearly to subtract total war outlays from net national product. The difference between the two series, by definition, represents the net output of civilian goods and services. If, from this result, we then subtract net private (civilian) capital formation – a necessary step since net private capital investment is included in total production, and capital in any of its forms does not directly satisfy human wants – we then have a measure of total civilian output of consumer goods and services as produced by both private and government sources.

It is only from this portion of total output, equivalent conceptually to the summation of personal consumption expenditures and government nonwar purchases, that the ingredients comprising the standard of living can come. For, aside from conceptual and statistical limitations inherent in many of the components of gross national product, especially as calculated by the Department of Commerce, the total output of consumer goods and services (shown in column five of Table I) theoretically expresses the market value of all commodities consumed by consumers. Unless food, clothing, housing, consumer durables, etc., etc. are purchased by consumers and, it must be assumed, thereby consumed, production does not currently and directly satisfy human wants and is therefore outside our definition of standard of living.

In other words, we make a sharp distinction between personal wealth and standard of living. The former indicates possession or ownership that may ultimately be converted into consumption of want-satisfying commodities. But savings, factories, stores, real estate, and other forms of capital or property, including money, cannot be eaten or worn or utilized to satisfy human wants unless they are first transformed from exchange values into use values

Permanent War Economy

or employed to produce use values capable of directly entering into the process of human consumption. It is true that the greater one's personal wealth, the higher his standard of living. This, however, does not follow because personal wealth is directly consumed by its owner, except in the rare case where a capitalist lives by using up his principal, but rather as a result of high personal incomes which simultaneously permit high consumption and accumulation of personal wealth or claims upon capital. The true gauge, therefore, of relative standards of living is the amount of commodities and services, both material and intangible, economic and cultural, actually consumed.

Table I on the following page portrays civilian output of consumer goods and services from 1939 to 1953, the first step in computing standards of living under the Permanent War Economy.

Net private capital formation was obtained by taking gross investment, as reported by the Department of Commerce, and subtracting from it Commerce's figures for capital consumption allowances. The projections were based on a study of the individual components and are consistent, both as to understatement of price inflation and the magnitude of war outlays and their impact on capital accumulation, with the methods used to forecast war outlays and total output.

If anything, our forecasts minimizes the quantity of components and are consistent, both as to understatement of price inflation and the magnitude of war outlays and their impact on capital accumulation, with the methods used to forecast war outlays and total output. If anything, our forecast minimizes the quantity of private capital that may be expected to be accumulated during 1951-1953, thus maximizing the volume of consumer goods and services that will be available for civilian consumption. This was deliberately done in order to present the trend in the average standard of living in as favorable a light as possible.

Declining Standards of Living

TABLE I:
CIVILIAN OUTPUT OF CONSUMER GOODS AND SERVICES. 1939-1953
(Billions of Current Dollars)

Year	Net National Product (1)	Total War Outlays (2)	Civilian Output (Col.1-Col.2) (3)	Net Private Capital Formation (4)	Civilian Output of Consumer Goods and Services (Col.3 -Col.4) (5)
1939	$83.2	$2.0	$81.2	$2.7	$78.6
1940	93	3.6	89.4	7	82.4
1941	117.1	13.9	103.2	10.1	93.1
1942	151.6	51.8	99.8	0.7	99.1
1943	183.7	84.1	99.6	-7.2	106.8
1944	201.8	92.2	109.6	-6.3	116.9
1946	202.8	82.8	120	-3.1	123.1
1946	198.9	33.6	166.3	21.1	144.2
1947	218.4	29.9	188.5	24.2	164.3
1948	241.7	23.6	218.1	27.7	190.4
1949	236.8	25	211.8	14.7	197.1
1950	267	27.9	229.1	23	206.1
1951	279.4	66	223.4	19.1	204.3
1952	293.3	61.9	231.4	14.1	217.3
1953	299.2	70.5	228.7	11.6	217.1

* Estimated, with 1950 data based on first half actual. Projections of net national product and total war outlays were explained in the previous article.

Permanent War Economy

THAT CIVILIAN STANDARDS HAVE lagged well behind total output can readily be seen by comparing columns five and one in Table I. Over the entire period, from 1939 to 1953, the net value of production will have increased 3.6 times in current dollars, while the portion available for civilian consumption will have risen less than 2.8 times. It is axiomatic that production for war purposes cannot contribute to civilian standards of living. During the first fifteen years of the Permanent War Economy a total of almost $659 billion will have been spent on direct and indirect war outlays, an average of $44 billion each year. Even if full allowance is made for the production of food, clothing and other consumer goods for the armed forces, and granting as much validity as possible to the socially necessary character of certain indirect war outlays, it is still impossible to escape the conclusion that approximately three years total production has been completely wasted.

Had it been possible for a rational economic system to have prevailed, producing and distributing an equivalent amount of commodities to consumers, the national debt of $257 billion could be completely retired and a dividend of $10,000 could be allotted to each family! It may be wondered why we have not confined our measure of the average standard of living to personal consumption expenditures expressed in constant dollars on a per capita basis. Such an approach, usually without considering the growth in population, is generally adopted by those who seek to depict the "benefits of a free enterprise economy." This could provide a first approximation provided that proper allowance was made for changes in the price level, but it would entirely omit from consideration the contribution made by the various levels of government to the average standard of living. Government nonwar purchases of goods and services, especially expenditures by state and local governments for education, utilities, transportation, and similar services, including the net postal deficit, are supported by taxes (except when government operates at a deficit) and presumably benefit more or less equally the entire population. While there may always be room for improvement, it must be assumed that such expenditures are an integral part of the average individual's total want satisfactions and therefore of his standard of living. As a matter of fact, to the extent that such government services are provided free of charge and therefore excluded from personal consumption expenditures or simultaneously included in capital formation as part of new public construction activity (school buildings, public hospital buildings, highways, etc.), the contribution of government to the average standard of living is understated.

Nevertheless, we could have added government nonwar purchases to personal consumption expenditures and theoretically obtained an identical result for civilian output of consumer goods and services. There are two major reasons why this procedure was not followed, aside from the minor inconvenience that would be caused by the failure of Commerce to publish the breakdown between Federal war and nonwar purchases since 1946: (1) our estimate of total war outlays is higher than that of Commerce chiefly, as explained in the previous article, because of our inclusion of the concept of "indirect" war outlays; and (2) while, on balance, the official figures for total output, as represented by the national product series, appear to be reasonable, we take exception to the inclusion and exclusion of certain items and to the classification of owner-occupied residential construction as a capital expenditure.

Thus, for example, we see no justification for the inclusion of imputed rent (of owner-occupied houses), imputed interest, or payments in kind in a national product series that is attempting to estimate the market value of current production. One might just as logically include the imputed value of housewives' services. This type of inclusion tends to overstate both total output and consumer outlay. On the other hand, exclusion of virtually all the expenditures of the Veterans Administration, net government interest payments and government subsidies tends to understate total output (to the extent that such activities, like any other government activity, are supported by taxes) and total war outlays. The exclusions, in general, ought to be reflected in total output but not in consumer output, as for the most part they belong to the war sector. To treat residential construction (except when it is income-producing property) as part of capital formation is to identify wealth with capital and to betray a lack of understanding of the nature and functioning of capital. One might just as well include any other consumer durable possessed of a relatively long lifetime, such as personal passenger cars, radios, television sets, furniture, etc. Owner-occupied residential construction, therefore, ought to be shifted from gross private domestic investment to personal consumption expenditures.

Permanent War Economy

In short, we feel that the official figures for personal consumption expenditures are overstated by approximately the same amount as total war outlays are understated. This is particularly true for 1946, where our biggest difference of more than $12 billion occurs. Consequently, the method used to obtain civilian output of consumer goods and services maintains a proper aggregate for total production while at the same time assuring a more realistic apportionment between the war and civilian sectors of the economy. It also enjoys the additional merit of facilitating the projection of Civilian output of consumer goods and services. The residual method employed does, it is true, understate the level of government nonwar purchases, particularly since 1915, but *we* prefer to maintain the official series for personal consumption expenditures rather than to make all the adjustments that would be required to conform with our criticisms. There is no difference in the average standard of living and the differences in per capita standards of living by classes would be negligible.

It may be helpful at this point to present the figures for personal consumption expenditures, both because they are by far the largest component in the formation of the average standard of living and because we subsequently base our class analysis of trends in living standards on a class breakdown of the official data for personal consumption expenditures. What consumers are officially reported to have spent in current dollars from 1939-1949, together with our projections for 1950-1953, is shown in Table II on the following page, which also expresses consumer outlay in constant dollars by using the BLS Consumers' Price Index as deflator.

It will be noted that the trend in personal consumption expenditures is not too dissimilar from that shown by civilian output of consumer goods and services, with the noteworthy exception of 1945-1947. As a matter of over-all comparison, during the entire period from 1939 to 1953, personal consumption expenditures will increase almost three times on a current dollar basis, whereas our series for civilian output of consumer goods and services rises 2.8 times, hardly a significant difference. Far more important in evaluating what has happened to the average standard of living is the allowance made for the increase in consumer prices.

Declining Standards of Living

TABLE II
PERSONAL CONSUMPTION EXPENDITURES. 1939-1953
(Current and Constant Dollar Figures in Billions)

Year	Personal Consumption Expenditures (1)	BLS Consumers' Price Index (2)	BLS Cons. Price Index (1939=100) (3)	Personal Consumption Expenditures in 1939 Dollars (4)	Index of Personal Consumption Expenditures in Constant Dollars (5)
1939	$67.5	99.4	100	$67.5	100
1940	72.1	100.2	100.8	71.5	105.9
1941	82.3	105.2	105.8	77.8	115.2
1942	91.2	116.5	117.2	77.8	115.2
1943	102.2	123.6	124.3	82.2	121.8
1944	111.6	125.5	126.3	88.4	130.9
1945	123.1	128.4	129.2	95.2	141
1946	146.9	139.3	140.1	104.9	155.4
1947	165.6	159.2	160.2	103.4	153.1
1948	177.4	171.2	172.2	103	152.5
1949	178.8	169.1	170.1	105.1	155.6
1950*	192.6	171.1	172.1	111.9	165.7
1951*	189.3	177.4	178.5	106.1	157.1
1952*	201.3	180.1	181.2	111.1	164.5
1953*	200.1	180.3	181.4	110.3	163.3

* Estimated with 1950 based on first nine months actuals. A report of the Department of Commerce, published in *The New York Times* of December 31, 1950 indicates that personal consumption expenditures for 1950 are estimated at "about $190 billion." The projections are consistent with the methods used to forecast output and make only partial allowance for rising prices in 1951 and almost none in 1952 and 1953.

Permanent War Economy

The Chamber of Commerce of the United States, for example, in a recent pamphlet entitled *Policies and Controls in a War-Burdened Economy*, obviously uses the BLS Consumers' Price Index as its measure of changes in prices paid by consumers and thus is able to conclude that "real consumer purchasing power also increased (during the war)!" While there was a slight increase during the war, to indicate that there was a 41 per cent rise in real consumer purchasing power or the average standard of living between 1939 and 1945 is highly misleading, just as much as to indicate that the average consumer in 1950 was more than 65 per cent better off than in 1939.

The Consumers' Price Index for Moderate Income Families in Large Cities of the Bureau of Labor Statistics, despite its widespread use by trade unions in collective bargaining contracts as a measure of the rise in the cost of living to which wage rates are linked, is not an accurate indicator of changes in the average cost of living, especially of factory workers. It may record fairly accurately typical consumer price trends in a period when government controls and inflationary shortages are non-existent, but in the epoch of the Permanent War Economy it is extremely insensitive to quality depreciation, evasions of controls, changes in controls, and the disappearance or relative disappearance of basic consumer commodities from the market. Moreover, it fails utterly to take into account changes in consumer buying habits and consumption patterns. Since 1941 it has markedly understated the rise in the average cost of living, with the deviations from reality becoming cumulative. Accordingly, any attempt to assess changes in living standards by the use of the Consumers' Price Index necessarily lacks validity.

It is obvious, however, that analysis of standards of living cannot be intelligently undertaken on the basis of current dollars and that we must discuss in terms of dollars possessing constant purchasing power. We therefore need a price index that reflects as accurately as possible the changes in average prices paid by average consumers. Unfortunately, no such index exists and we are reluctantly compelled to devise one arbitrarily. This has been done by calculating the arithmetic average between the Consumers' Price Index and the BLS Wholesale Price Index, on the theory that the former represents the minimum change in consumer price levels and the latter the maximum possible change due to the well-known greater flexibility of wholesale prices compared with retail prices. The arbitrary part of the

Declining Standards of Living

approach consists in giving equal weight to both indexes, whereas it may well be that one should weigh more heavily than the other in trying to achieve our objective. We are aware of no evidence, however, that would warrant unequal weighting.*

It is necessary to emphasize that the selection of a price index far outweighs any other factor in analyzing living standards. If, for example, we had applied the Consumers' Price Index to our series on civilian output of consumer goods and services, the results would not differ too greatly from the picture shown in Table II on the following page. For 1950, the growth in the consumption sector of the economy would be 52.6 per cent over 1939 instead of 65.7 per cent. Our thesis that the workers have suffered a decline in their living standards as a result of the Permanent War Economy would be greatly weakened, even though a relative decline compared with the growth in total output is apparent.

WE NOW PROCEED TO THE SECOND basic step in our analysis, which is to develop an index of the output of the consumption sector of the economy, by which term we distinguish from the war sector and the capital sector. The results are shown in Table III on the following page.

While the wholesale price index evidences the same difficulty in surmounting official failure to recognize the prevalence of black markets during price control as does the Consumers' Price Index, it is a much more comprehensive and more sensitive index. Our derived average price index, except for the later stages of the war, is probably as satisfactory a measure of price changes in the consumption sector as can be obtained. A 35 per cent rise in the output of the consumption sector from 1939 to 1950 is certainly more plausible than a 65 per cent rise.

---

* Since this was written, the Department of Commerce has announced (*The New York Times* of January 22, 1951) gross national product figures in 1939 dollars. The Implicit Price Index thus derived was published for selected years and yields the comparison with our average price index in the table on the right.

The two indexes apparently correspond quite closely, being identical for 1941 and only three per cent apart in 1949. The Commerce Index, however, indicates a price rise of less than two per cent from 1949 to 1950, whereas our index shows an increase of more than four per cent during the same period.

Year	Average Price Index	Commerce Implicit Price Index
	(1939 = 100)	
1941	110	110
1949	186	180
1950	194	183 (preliminary)

TABLE III

INDEX OF CONSUMPTION OUTPUT. 1939-1953

(Dollar Figures In Billions)

Year	Output of Consumer Goods and Services (1)*	BLS Wholesale Price Index (1939=100) (2)†	Average Price Index (1939=100) (3)‡	Consumption Output in 1939 Dollars (Col.1÷Col.3) (4)	Index of Consumption Output in 1939 Dollars (5)
1939	$78.5	100.0	100.0	$78.5	100.0
1940	82.4	101.9	101.4	81.3	103.6
1941	93.1	113.2	109.5	85.0	108.3
1942	99.1	128.1	122.7	80.8	102.9
1943	106.8	133.7	129.0	82.8	105.5
1944	115.9	134.9	130.6	88.7	113.0
1945	123.1	137.2	133.2	92.4	117.7
1946	144.2	157.1	148.6	97.0	123.6
1947	164.3	197.3	178.8	91.9	117.1
1948	190.4	213.9	193.1	98.6	125.6
1949	197.1	201	185.6	106.2	135.3
1950	206.1	215.3	193.7	106.4	135.6
1951	204.3	223.5	201.0	101.6	129.4
1952	217.3	226.8	204.0	106.5	135.7
1953	217.1	227.1	204.3	106.3	135.4

* Taken from column five of Table I.

† Estimates for 1950 and subsequent years are calculated in a manner identical with the projection of the Consumers' Price Index.

‡ Average of column two above and column three of Table II.

Declining Standards of Living

Moreover, our series now shows a decline in consumption output from 1941 to 1942-43, as well as a decline from 1946 to 1947, both movements conforming far more closely to common experience than the highly misleading series represented by personal consumption expenditures deflated by the Consumers' Price Index.

It is thus apparent that the rise in output of consumer goods and services, from both private and government sources, rose very modestly indeed during the war. With the exception of 1947, which was a year of unbridled inflation following the abandonment of price control in 1946, there was then a further steady growth until the outbreak of the Korean war. Now, we can expect a noticeable decline in 1951 followed by a leveling off at about the 1950 rates in 1952-53 – this, on the basic assumption stipulated in the projection of war outlays that the armed forces of the United States will not be engaged in any major conflict prior to 1954. It will be noted that the movement of real consumption output (the basis of all living standards) follows the trends in the ratio of war outlays to total output – but in reverse. This is only natural inasmuch as war output must take place at the expense of civilian output unless there is a corresponding increase in total output, which is never possible and which at the present historic juncture is severely limited in its potential by a whole host of factors.

The relative decline in standards of living is beyond dispute, regardless of the figures chosen or statistical methods used. Even if one were to deflate total output by the wholesale price index, on the ground that price inflation in the war and capital sectors of the economy is more severe under the Permanent War Economy than in the consumption sector, the contrast is obvious and dramatic in its implications. Consider the following brief tabulation, which deflates total output as reflected by net national product (column one of Table I) by the BLS wholesale price index (column two of Table III) in comparison with our index of consumption output in 1939 dollars for the key historical years in our fifteen-year period:

Permanent War Economy

	RELATIVE DECLINE IN CONSUMPTION OUTPUT COMPARED WITH TOTAL OUTPUT (In Index Numbers)	
Year	*Total Output*	*Consumption Output*
1939	100	100
1945	178	118
1950	144	136
1953	158	135

From 1939 to 1945, or during World War II, total real output in the United States rose 78 per cent, while the output of the consumption sector increased but 18 per cent. Had such a phenomenal increase in production been possible without the stimulus provided by the war or, in other words, had the rise in consumption kept pace with the upsurge in production, there would have been a further 50 per cent increase in the output of consumer goods and services from both private and government sources! In spite of the idle resources that existed at the outbreak of the war, the expansion of the war sector necessitated an actual decline in certain types of consumer production such as automobiles, radios, refrigerators, most consumer durables, and even some types of clothing and food, not to mention many services, especially those made available by government. Had the war lasted much longer, it is highly probable that the great lag in consumption output compared with total output would have been followed by an absolute decline in the output of consumer goods and services. History under the Permanent War Economy has so far been very kind to the American capitalist class. The major turns have occurred at just the right time. World War II lasted long enough, but not too long. Sharp class dissensions were thus avoided. In the postwar period from 1945 to 1950, there was a further growth in consumption output of 15 per cent. The rate of growth in the production of consumer goods and services was thus maintained at about 3 per cent per annum. Since, at the same time, there was a decline of 19 per cent in total output, by 1950 output in the consumption sector had almost caught up with

Declining Standards of Living

total production, the relative lag in growth being only 6 per cent. Maintenance of these trends for another year would have resulted in a reversal of position, with the growth in consumption output exceeding the increase in total production. Under capitalist conditions of production, a first-rate crisis would have developed by the end of 1951, thereby revealing that a 10 per cent ratio of war outlays to total output is inadequate to sustain economic equilibrium at a high level for more than a limited number of years. As we have previously indicated, the outbreak of the Korean war came in the nick of time. The threatened crisis due to relative overproduction of consumer goods was averted and the dominance of the Permanent War Economy guaranteed.

The current increase in the ratio of war outlays to total output will bring to a halt the steadily rising trend in the output of consumer goods and services. While we expect a leveling off to take place until such time as American imperialism is engaged in full-scale war, there will actually be a decline of almost 5 per cent from 1950 to 1951 in the output of consumer goods and services. From 1950 to 1953, a period of mobilization for World War III according to our assumption, we have projected a modest increase of 10 per cent in total real output. If certain bottlenecks to increased production are removed and if war outlays prove to be larger than we have forecast, the increase in total output may be somewhat larger. None of it, however, would go to the consumption sector, so that the relative decline in production for consumer account compared with the increase in total output would be even greater than we have projected. If 1953 be considered representative of a typical year under the Permanent War Economy, with total war outlays taking almost 24 per cent of current production, the relative decline in consumption output compared with total output for the entire period since the advent of the Permanent War Economy is accurately measured by the 35 per cent increase in consumption output compared with the 58 per cent increase in total output. This is merely another way of saying that had the growth in consumption paralleled the rise in total output, which is the minimum performance to be expected from a satisfactory economic system once the basic productive forces are fairly well developed, there would have been a further increase of 17 per cent in the output of consumer goods and services.

Permanent War Economy

PRODUCTION FIGURES BY THEMSELVES, although the basis of living standards, cannot accurately portray what has happened to individual standards of living for they ignore any changes that may have occurred in the size of the population. Since there has historically been a steady growth in the American population, for the average individual merely to be as well off as at the beginning of any period of years under analysis the growth in consumption output must at least equal the growth in population. In other words, we cannot intelligently talk about trends in average living standards unless we have first obtained a measure of per capita consumption output. This brings us to the third basic step in our analysis, which consists of deriving population figures representing the average total population for each year from 1939 to 1953 and applying them to the annual series for consumption output. The results, summarized in Table IV on the following page, provide per capita consumption output in both current and constant dollars and enable us to see what has happened from 1939 to 1953 in the *average* standard of living.

The growth in the American population has been substantial, far in excess of most predictions, especially since the end of World War II. We calculate an average increase of 2,000,000 annually for the fourteen-year period from mid-1939 to mid-1953, or a total of about 28 million. Merely to support this increase in population in the style to which the average person is accustomed requires an annual increment on the average in the consumption sector of the economy of more than 1.5 per cent, or a total of more than 21 per cent from 1939 to 1953. Thus, by 1953, about two-thirds of the growth in consumption output will have been devoted to satisfying the wants of the net increase in population, assuming that there is no marked variation in the living standards of net additions to the population compared with old members of the population. The entire picture of what has happened to the average American standard of living under the Permanent War Economy is obviously altered to a significant extent by the introduction of the per capita concept in our analysis.

The American standard of living may be the highest in the world, but it is a complete delusion to claim any marked expansion in average living standards since the beginning of the Permanent War Economy in 1939, or for that matter since American capitalism entered the permanent world crisis of capitalism in 1929. *So far as average*

Declining Standards of Living

standards of living are concerned, the vaunted economy of American capitalism has been virtually stagnant for more than two decades. In this fact are reflected all the ills and contradictions of American imperialism. Now, as the Permanent War Economy becomes more thoroughly entrenched, it is good-bye to the New Deal and to the Fair Deal and to all significant attempts to raise average living standards. Is any more dramatic confirmation required of the Marxian thesis that capitalism cannot be reformed into a rational and workable economic system?

Constant reference to the "growth in consumption," as mirrored by the indisputable and very sizable increase in personal consumption expenditures or in our series on consumption output, on the completely acceptable theory that consumer outlay represents actual consumption, is of no avail in appraising trends in the average standard of living. There can be no growth in real consumption or living standards unless the increase in dollar expenditures by consumers and government for consumer goods and services exceeds the loss in the purchasing power of the dollar and the growth in the population. It may be comforting to defenders of capitalism to be able to state that average per capita consumption has exceeded $1,300 since 1948, which is equivalent to almost $5,000 per family, but this is meaningless by itself. Only per capita consumption output in constant dollars, the index of which is shown in column six of Table IV on the following page, can be used to discover what has happened to *average* living standards.

THE AVERAGE AMERICAN has experienced a slight improvement in his standard of living since 1939, but the lag behind the increase in total production has been enormous. For the entire period from 1939 to 1953, our analysis indicates only an 11½ per cent betterment in the per capita average real standard of living, or less than one per cent a year. The various ups and downs within this over-all picture are most revealing. From 1939 to 1941, as idle resources were put to work under the stimulus of increasing war outlays, the average consumer experienced a 6 per cent rise in his standard of living.

Then, in 1942-1943, as rapidly increasing war expenditures caused an actual curtailment in many lines of civilian production, the average standard of living reverted back to approximately the 1939 level. From 1944 to 1946, as war outlays reached their peak and then declined as the war ended, there was a rapid increase of almost 5 per cent a year in the

Permanent War Economy

TABLE IV						
PER CAPITA AVERAGE STANDARD OF LIVING. 1939-1953						
Year	Consumption Output (Billions of Current Dollars) (1)*	Consumption Output (Billions of 1939 Dollars) (2)*	Population (Millions) (3)†	Per Capita Consumption Output in Current Dollars (4)	Per Capita Consumption Output In 1939 Dollars (5)	Index of Per Capita Average Real Standard of Living (1939=100) (6)
1939	$78.5	$78.5	130.9	$600	$600	100
1940	82.4	81.3	132	624	616	102.7
1941	93.1	85	133.2	699	638	106.3
1942	99.1	80.8	134.7	736	600	100
1943	106.8	82.8	136.5	782	607	101.2
1944	115.9	88.7	138.1	839	642	107
1945	123.1	92.4	139.6	882	662	110.3
1946	144.2	97	141	1023	688	114.7
1947	164.3	91.9	143.4	1146	641	106.8
1948	190.4	98.6	146.1	1303	675	112.5
1949	197.1	106.2	148.7	1325	714	119
1950	206.1	106.4	151.5	1360	702	117
1961	204.3	101.6	154	1327	660	110
1952	217.3	106.5	156.4	1389	681	113.5
1953	217.1	106.3	158.8	1367	669	111.5

* From Table III
.† Based on Bureau of the Census data for continental United States, with an attempt made to include all armed forces except that small portion considered to be permanently stationed overseas. Data are as of July 1 or mid-year to represent average population for the year. Projections for 1951-1953 assume maintenance of present rate of growth of about 200,000 per month.

average standard of living as the economy continued to operate at or near capacity levels. However, from 1946 to 1947 the average American suffered a 7 per cent decline in his standard of living as the increase in prices together with the decline in total

Declining Standards of Living

output outstripped the reduction in war outlays. There then followed from 1947 to 1949 a rise of more than 11 per cent, bringing the average standard of living in 1949 to 19 per cent above the 1939 level, which was the highwater mark under the Permanent War Economy and will undoubtedly remain so. The slight decline in 1950 will be followed by a substantial decline of more than 6 per cent in 1951 as, once again, an actual curtailment in certain industries producing consumer goods and services will be experienced. A leveling off may then be expected at slightly above 1951 levels which may be expected to last until such time as there is a pronounced change in the ratio of war outlays to total output

It is recognized that many other factors should be taken into consideration in evaluating trends in living standards, such as changes in the length of the working day and the working week, the intensity of labor, the impact of new methods of satisfying consumer wants, the disappearance of existing methods of satisfying consumer wants, especially in the field of consumer durables, and the changing character of distribution – to mention the most obvious. Nevertheless, the index of per capita average real standards of living is both conceptually sound and statistically accurate, at least sufficiently so as to permit confidence in the results. We must stress, however, that all -we have succeeded in accomplishing at this point is to obtain a relatively precise view of what has happened and what may be expected to happen to the *average* American.

It goes without saying that we do not live in a classless society and that there is consequently a sharp differentiation in actual levels of living among the various classes and, equally important, in trends in class standards of living. This brings us to the fourth and final step in our analysis of declining standards of living under the Permanent War Economy. Without some indication of the differences among classes, no matter how tentative the figures must necessarily be, it is impossible to complete our analysis or to understand the most significant causal relationships affecting living standards under the Permanent War Economy.

THEORETICALLY, THE PROBLEM OF analyzing changes in the living standards of the major classes in capitalist society is not too difficult. All that is required is workable definitions, delimiting each of the major functional classes in terms of their relationship to the productive forces, together with a distribution of their respective claims upon the available supply of consumer goods and services. Statistically, however, we are confronted with the impossibility of measuring per capita standards of living by classes with any real degree of accuracy. Despite the libraries of statistical data relating to the economic system and its functioning, which are so voluminous that no single individual can hope to master all the sources of information in an ordinary lifetime, the unfortunate and highly significant fact is that the data collected and published are not designed to disclose the precise inner workings of an exploitative society. On the contrary, specific information may jeopardize the competitive position, real or fancied, of a firm or an industry or may penetrate the cloak of moral sanctity which a venal ruling class uses to justify many of its actions. There is, consequently, not only a running battle between industry and government over the types of reports necessary for policy formation, especially when economic, controls become mandatory, but also an inherent bias against the full truth in such data as are collected.

The choice, then, is one of halting our analysis of standards of living under the Permanent War Economy at a point where only classless conclusions can be reached, or of pioneering in an uncharted field in the hope that tentative conclusions will be helpful. We have chosen the latter course because there is sufficient empirical evidence that the impact of the Permanent War Economy has not been borne equally by all classes. "Equality of sacrifice" may be an attractive political slogan, but it is largely confined to pious resolutions. Consider, for example, this typical motivation for "equality of sacrifice" from the President's Economic Message to Congress of the unemployed of January 12, 1951:

> It is essential that the sacrifices which are necessary in these critical times be shared fairly by all groups. Business men will be more cooperative in sacrificing peacetime profit objectives and paying more taxes, if it is clear that this is not being done just so farmers and workers can have more income.
>
> Farmers will be more cooperative in sacrificing peacetime farm income objectives, if it is clear that this is not being done just so workers can get

more wages and business men can get more profits. Workers will be more cooperative in sacrificing peacetime wage objectives, if it is clear that this is not being done just to provide more profits for business or more farm income.

Professional people, civil servants, office workers and those living on fixed incomes, will be willing to accept their share of necessary sacrifices, to the extent that it is clear that this is not being done just to provide for other people more profits or wages or farm income. All will be willing to make far more sacrifices for national defense and to keep our economy strong, if the burden is shared on a fair and equitable basis.

The classless approach, plausible as it may appear to some, freezes all the inequities that existed at the beginning of the Permanent War Economy or of any specific mobilization, even assuming that the policy of "equality of sacrifice" is rigorously enforced. Just what the record has been and is likely to be becomes apparent only on the basis of a class analysis.

It must be emphasized that while the class data which follow are experimental yet we believe that the broad conclusions which emerge possess general validity.

OUR CLASS BREAKDOWN IS CONFINED to the four major economic classes, working classes, middle classes, farming classes, and bourgeoisie, each concealing within its fairly broad limits rather distinct income and class variations. The bourgeoisie covers the various sections of the capitalist class, that is those who own or control the production and distribution of commodities and services, other than farmers, whose substantial incomes are derived from capital, although in certain cases they may take the form of salaries as corporation officers or managers. It is this numerically inconsequential class of barely more than one per cent of the population that exercises effective control over the economy of the United States. The variation in personal income within the bourgeoisie is greater, percentage wise, than within any other class as it ranges from the moderately well-to-do receiving $20,000 a year to the millionaire and multi-millionaire.

Permanent War Economy

The farming classes cover all those who live or work on farms, whose incomes, whether they be agricultural migratory laborers, tenant farmers, small independent farmers, or large commercial farmers organized as single entrepreneurs, cooperatives or corporations, are derived principally from agriculture. The class differentiations within this group are as obvious as the contrast between the Farmers Union and the Farm Bureau. Although the farming classes currently compromise almost 20 per cent of the population, the income variations are extreme, extending from the poor itinerant laborer and poverty-stricken self-sufficient farmer who barely see any cash at all during the year to the wealthy landowner in California's lush Imperial Valley or other large-scale farm capitalist whose income and living standard are hardly distinguishable from the millionaire.

The middle classes are much harder to define, as at the lower limit they may overlap the working classes and at the upper limit the bourgeoisie. They include the small shopkeepers, the independent tradesmen and artisans, the independent professionals, and those salaried officials of government and private business who clearly belong to management, especially in relation to the power to hire and fire. Regarding salaried members of the middle classes, we have arbitrarily used as income limits to assist our functional analysis a range of $4,700 to $20,000 for 1948, the latest year for which family income distributions are available. In short, the bulk of single entrepreneurs and partnerships together with a minimum portion of salaried individuals in medium income brackets are numbered among the middle classes. Altogether, we currently place the middle classes at about 12 per cent of the population. If a strict income approach were to be used, the figure would be larger. The decisive criterion, however, is not income but relationship to production. All teachers and most government employees, for example, may think of themselves as middle class, but we have classified them as members of the working classes.

The working classes, consequently, compromise about two-thirds of the population and are much broader in scope than the factory proletariat. All those nonfarm workers who must sell their labor power in order to support themselves and their families, except for the relatively small portion of salaried employees included in the middle classes and the bourgeoisie, are subsumed under the heading "working classes." In addition to factory wage earners, the overwhelming majority of white collar employees is considered to be part of the working classes. What may be interpreted as an upward bias in the size of the working classes is enhanced by our decision to place all the unemployed and their families in the working classes. This was done not so much for theoretical reasons, although it could be amply justified on these grounds alone, but for the very practical reason that there is no basis whatsoever for assigning any portion of the unemployed to the middle classes, in spite of the fact that members of the middle classes do experience unemployment from time to time and then find employment in a position enabling them to preserve their middle class status. Income variations among the working classes thus range from virtually zero to approximately $5,000 a year, with certain salaried individuals employed by government or organizations receiving considerably more.

Our broad functional, class approach corresponds to the relative fluidity of class lines in the United States. It is interesting to note that even the most patriotic classless appeals for national unity are constrained to recognize the existence of these broad economic classes. Having arrived at these definitions of the four major economic classes, it was then necessary to distribute the population, personal consumption expenditures and government nonwar purchases in accordance with our definitions. Distributing the population by classes did not present any insurmountable obstacles, as we begin with the existence of relatively good data on the farm population compiled by the Bureau of Agricultural Economics. The only significant manipulation required here was to allow for those members of the armed forces drawn from agriculture. The recent development of new series on the compensation of corporate officers, together with family income statistics and an arbitrary small percentage of the number of active proprietors of unincorporated enterprises, facilitated the derivation of the size of the bourgeoisie. The extent of the middle classes was based on the number of active non-agricultural proprietors, together with a portion of salaried employees adjusted for functional status and family income data. In effect, therefore, the calculation of the population of the working classes could be derived as a residual, except that the results were checked by using data on the number of non-agricultural employees together with fragmentary information on the number of employees per family and the number of individuals per family by income levels. We believe that the results are fairly consistent with our definitions.

Permanent War Economy

To distribute personal consumption expenditures by classes required a more elaborate technique starting with the relationship between total personal income and total personal consumption expenditures, the overall data, including projections, being shown in Table V below.

TABLE V:
TOTAL PERSONAL INCOME, PERSONAL TAX AND NON TAX PAYMENTS, PERSONAL SAVINGS, AND PERSONAL CONSUMPTION EXPENDITURES. 1939-1953
(Billions of Dollars

Year	Personal Income	Personal Tax and Nontax Payments	Personal Savings	Personal Consumption Expenditures*
1939	$72.6	$2.4	$2.7	$67.5
1940	78.3	2.6	3.6	72.1
1941	95.3	3.3	9.7	82.3
1942	122.7	6	25.5	91.2
1943	150.3	17.9	30.2	102.2
1944	165.9	18.9	35.4	111.6
1945	171.9	20.9	27.9	123.1
1946	177.7	18.8	12	146.9
1947	191	21.5	3.9	165.6
1948	209.5	21.2	10.9	177.4
1949	206.1	18.7	8.6	178.8
1950†	221.5	19	10	192.5
1951†	236.3	22	25	189.3
1952†	247.2	23.5	22.4	201.3
1953†	248.7	24.5	24.1	200.1

* Identical with the series shown in Table II, column one.
† Projections, with 1950 data based on actuals for first nine months, comparable to methods used for all output figures, with assumptions regarding increases in personal income taxes necessarily arbitrary.

Declining Standards of Living

Personal income, as the name implies, delineates all income payments received by individuals and is presented by Commerce under these major heads: wage and salary receipts, other labor income, proprietors' and rental income, dividends, personal interest income, and transfer payments.

Certain types of income payments, such as net interest paid by government and transfer payments are excluded from national income and product. When personal tax and nontax payments by individuals to government, excluding purchases from government enterprises and consisting chiefly of personal income taxes, are subtracted from personal income the result is equal to disposable personal income which must either be spent or saved. Personal income minus personal tax and nontax payments minus personal savings therefore equals personal consumption expenditures, although the technique used by Commerce measures personal consumption expenditures independently and obtains personal savings as a residual. By analyzing the components of personal income separately, it was possible to break them down by classes in a manner consistent with the class distribution of the population. In certain cases, as for example rent, the distribution is admittedly arbitrary, but the resulting pattern appears to be plausible. Limitations of space prevent us from showing any of the class derivations. The distribution of personal tax and nontax payments was weighted entirely by the distribution of individual income taxes, as revealed by Treasury data through 1946, an OPA study on *Civilian Spending and Saving, 1941 and 1942*, and selected TNEC data for 1939. Apportionment of personal savings was based on the aforementioned OPA and TNEC studies, a farm study by the Department of Agriculture for 1946 and, above all, a sample interview survey by the Federal Reserve Board showing the distribution of family liquid assets and savings in 1946 by income groups. We have no brief for the projections except that they seem to be reasonable. If there is any bias it is in the direction of minimizing personal taxes and savings of the working classes so as to maximize their personal consumption expenditures in order to set their standards of living at as high a level as possible.

Personal consumption expenditures by classes were then divided by the respective class populations in order to obtain per capita personal consumption expenditures by classes. To these results were then added per capita government nonwar purchases for the entire population on the assumption, already stated, that each person benefits equally from

Permanent War Economy

these contributions of government to the average standard of living. The maximum sum involved was $123 for 1949. The aggregate of per capita personal consumption expenditures by classes and per capita government nonwar purchases yields per capita standards of living by classes, the data for which in both current and constant dollars are presented in Table VI on the following page.

We have, of course, used the average price index developed in Table III to translate the current dollar figures into 1939 dollars, although a case can be made that the prices paid for commodities and services are not uniform in their rates of change for the various classes. Aside from the lack of evidence, it is unlikely that any attempt to adjust for such variations in price changes would materially affect the picture that emerges. Even in current dollars, the working classes have clearly lagged behind the rest of society. Merely on the basis of what has happened, as revealed by the increase in per capita standards of living in current dollars from 1939 to 1950, the myth of "equality of sacrifice" vanishes into thin air when confronted by facts. While the working classes were experiencing an increase from $596 to $1,139, a rise of 91 per cent, the middle classes went from $635 to $1,619, a rise of 155 per cent, the farming classes climbed from $295 to $779, a rise of 164 per cent, and the bourgeoisie soared from $7,546 to $21,384, a rise of 183 per cent. Now, as our data for 1951-1953 demonstrate, the disparity between the working classes and the other major classes will become even greater.

The gross average weekly earnings of production workers in manufacturing industries of the BLS, commonly used to describe changes in the status of the average worker, shows a rise from $23.86 in 1939 to about $59 in 1950, or an increase of 148 per cent. This is still below the increase in consumption for other classes and it must be remembered that "take-home" pay is a much better indicator of spending power than gross earnings. It is probable, however, that the factory proletariat enjoys a higher standard of living than most sections of the working classes.

Declining Standards of Living

	TABLE VI: PER CAPITA STANDARDS OF LIVING BY CLASSES IN CURRENT AND 1939 DOLLARS, 1939-1953							
	Working Classes		Farming Classes		Middle Classes		Bourgeoisie	
Year	Current Dollars	1939 Dollars	Current Dollars	1939 Dollars	Current Dollars	1939 Dollars	Current Dollars	1939 Dollars
1939	$596	$596	$295	$295	$635	$635	$7,546	$7,546
1940	617	608	301	297	679	670	7847	7739
1941	688	628	368	336	736	672	8466	7732
1942	723	589	402	328	736	600	8828	7195
1943	773	599	402	312	790	612	8748	6781
1944	825	632	430	329	862	660	9317	7134
1945	862	647	420	315	884	664	10533	7908
1946	875	589	546	367	1215	818	14981	10081
1947	949	531	641	359	1324	740	18579	10391
1948	1066	552	802	415	1559	807	20442	10586
1949	1103	594	771	415	1615	870	20299	10937
1950	1139	588	779	402	1619	836	21384	11040
1951	1073	534	809	402	1646	819	20764	10330
1952	1136	557	842	413	1708	837	21546	10562
1953	1087	532	876	429	1749	856	22051	10793

TO VIEW THE REAL IMPACT OF the Permanent War Economy on the standards of living of the various classes, it is helpful to express the per capita data in 1939 dollars contained in Table VI as index numbers. This is done in Table VII below and in the accompanying chart on the following page, which graphically shows the trends in average and class per capita standards of living.

Permanent War Economy

		TABLE VII:			
		INDEXES OF AVERAGE & CLASS PER CAPITA STANDARDS OF LIVING, 1939-1953			
		(1939=100)			
Year	Working Classes	Farming Classes	Middle Classes	Bourgeoisie	Average all Classes*
1939	100	100	100	100	100
1940	102	100.7	105.5	102.6	102.7
1941	105.4	113.9	105.8	102.5	106.3
1942	98.8	111.2	94.5	95.3	100
1943	100.5	105.8	96.4	89.9	101.2
1944	106	111.5	103.9	94.5	107
1945	108.6	106.8	104.6	104.8	110.3
1946	98.8	124.3	128.8	133.6	114.7
1947	89.1	121.7	116.5	137.7	106.8
1948	92.6	140.7	127.1	140.3	112.5
1949	99.7	140.7	137	144.9	119
1950	98.7	136.3	131.7	146.3	117
1951	89.6	136.3	129	136.9	110
1952	93.5	140	131.8	140	113.5
1953	89.3	145.4	134.8	143	111.5
		*Taken from Table IV, column six.			

Declining Standards of Living

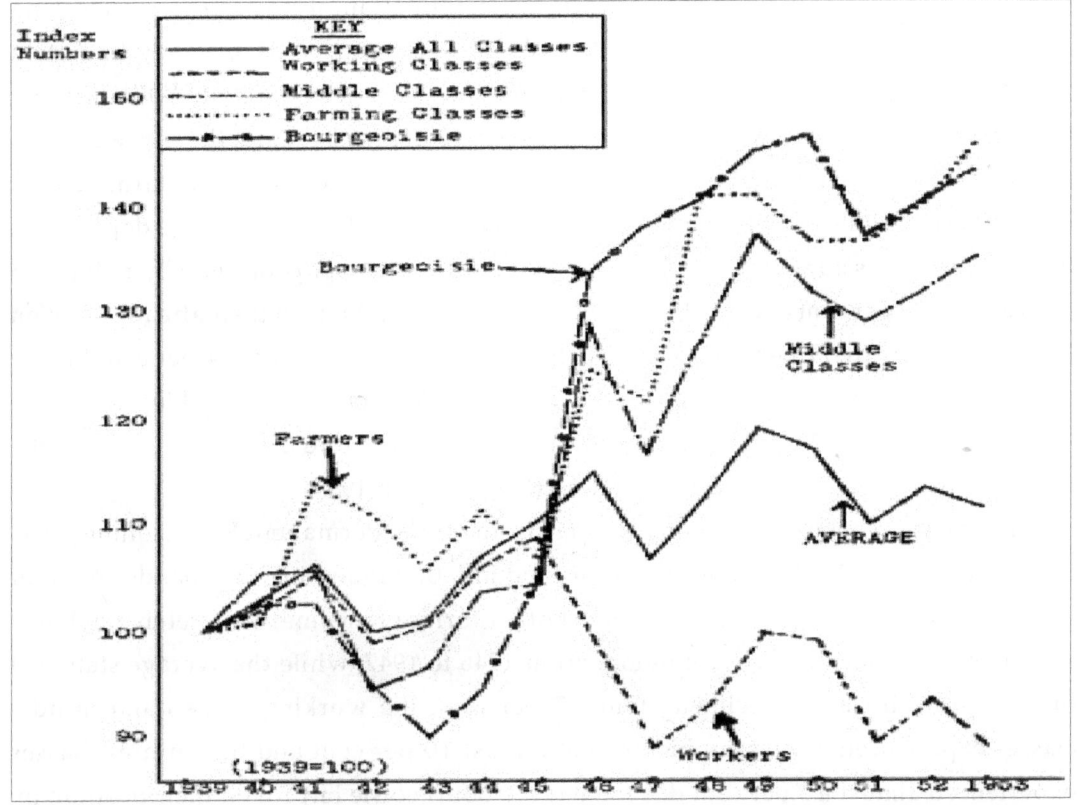

During the war there was a rough sort of equality among the classes, although it is clear that the farmers considerably improved their position. The rise in farm prices, aided by the preferred legislation successfully introduced by the farm bloc, made the farmers the one class whose standard of living exceeded the average. The workers roughly maintained their standard of living at the average as war outlays increased and the increased earnings due to overtime pay. The middle classes lagged slightly behind the average as many individual proprietors had to abandon their businesses due to the draft and the difficulty in obtaining supplies. The bourgeoisie lagged most, reaching their low point in 1943 when the first sharp increase in taxes took effect. In terms of comparative levels of living, however, the bourgeoisie maintained their overwhelming superiority over all other classes. The year 1946 marked the transition from a period of relative freezing of class inequities to one where the working classes suffer both an absolute and relative decline in their living standards. From 1945 to 1946, as overtime

Permanent War Economy

ceased and unemployment increased with the termination of hostilities, the working classes underwent a decline of 9 per cent in their living standards, bringing them to a level below 1939. At the same time, as business opportunities expanded, the farming classes increased their living standards by 16 per cent, thus bringing them to a level 24 per cent above 1939 and more than compensating for any inequities that farmers may have experienced in 1939 due to their slow recovery from the depths of the depression; the middle classes augmented their living standards by 23 per cent, thereby rising to a level almost 29 per cent above 1939; and the bourgeoisie enhanced their already swollen living standards by 27 per cent, resulting in a level of living almost 34 per cent higher than in 1939. While these unprecedented divergent movements were taking place, the average per capita standard of living for all classes rose some 4 per cent, making the mythical average individual 15 per cent better off than in 1939.

The fate of working class living standards under the Permanent War Economy was irrevocably sealed in 1947, a year of unbridled inflation following the abandonment of price control with wages, contrary to most other forms of income, completely unable to keep pace with the rising cost of living. From 1946 to 1947, while the average standard of living for all classes declined almost 7 per cent, the working classes and middle classes experienced a catastrophic drop of almost 10 per cent and the farming classes experienced almost a 2 per cent decline but the bourgeoisie improved their position by 3 per cent. This meant that the average worker in 1947 was 11 per cent worse off than in 1939, but the average farmer was 22 per cent better off, the average member of the middle classes was 16.5 per cent better off, and the average member of the ruling class was 38 per cent better off. The fact that the average member of American society was 7 per cent better off was of little consolation to the workers who, as usual, bore the brunt of inflation.

Despite strike action and other attempts to improve their situation, the working classes could not show any significant recovery in their living standards by 1950. They still remained worse off than in 1939, while the farming classes were 36 per cent better off, the middle classes 32 per cent better off and the bourgeoisie 46 per cent better off, with the result that our mythical average American was 17 per cent better off. The fact that the average worker, including members of his family, received $1,139 worth of consumer goods and services in 1950 might indicate to the uninformed that the average member of the working classes enjoyed an extremely high standard of living. This is undoubtedly true compared with workers in other countries, but it is not true when compared with the situation of the average American worker in 1939 or of the average member of other classes. It is not even true that the average worker is better off than the average farmer, for in addition to the $779 that the average member of the farming classes received in 1950 he consumed a great many commodities raised on his farm that are not fully reflected in personal consumption expenditures. Certainly, the average member of the middle classes, who received more than $1,600 worth of consumer goods and services, was clearly in a better position than the average worker; and the average member of the bourgeoisie, whose consumption exceeded $21,000 in 1950, enjoyed such a luxurious standard of living that comparison with the average worker is like the position of a Stalinist or feudal lord contrasted with that of a modern or ancient serf. Now, as the ratio of war outlays to total output increases sharply and controls are introduced, we can expect all classes except farmers to undergo a decline in their living standards in 1951. While the average for all classes is expected to decline 6 per cent, the farming classes will hold their own, the middle classes will experience a 2 per cent decline, the bourgeoisie a decline of less than 7 per cent, and the working classes a decline exceeding 9 per cent. A slight improvement in 1952 should then be followed by a further attack on working class living standards in 1953. If our analysis is reasonably valid, and we believe that it is, the disparity between the working classes and other classes will be greater by 1953 than ever before in recent history. A deterioration of almost 11 per cent in the standard of living of the average worker from 1939 to 1953 will be accompanied by a more than 45 per cent improvement in the position of the average farmer, an almost 35 per cent betterment in the status of the average member of the middle classes, and a 43 per cent enrichment in the well-being of the average member of the bourgeoisie. For the working classes the fact that the average member of society will still be 11.5 per cent better off than in 1939 only makes more poignant the general law that as capital accumulates under the Permanent War Economy, there is both a relative and absolute decline in living standards.

There can be little doubt concerning the general picture of living standards shown by the chart. Following the end of the war the working classes have suffered substantially in comparison with all other major economic classes. Inasmuch as the

Permanent War Economy

present increase in the ratio of war outlays to total output is taking place at a time when there is relatively little room for further expansion of civilian and total output, the possibility of duplicating the rough equality of World War II is virtually non-existent. There must be a decline in average real standards of living and, under capitalist conditions, the working classes can expect to bear the brunt of this inevitable diversion of resources from civilian to war output. It is indeed a sad commentary on the functioning of a capitalist war economy that the working classes appear to achieve a "more just" share of such consumer goods and services as are produced under an all-out mobilization, when the ratio of war outlays to total output is between 40 and 45 per cent, than under a semi-mobilization, when the ratio of war outlays to total output runs between 20 and 25 per cent.

It is, of course, politically much easier to achieve rough equality when there is very little to share than when more of the things that make life pleasanter are available for distribution. This is virtually a universal law applicable to all class societies. The situation in the United States since 1939, however, has been complicated by a number of factors whose impact, as the years unfold, is seen to be disproportionately heavier on the working classes than on the other major economic classes. We have reference to such elements in the economic equation as the incidence of the growth in population, the incidence of increased taxation, the concentration of net savings, the unequal burdens imposed by the temporary disappearance of certain consumer commodities from the market, the greater intensity of labor as manpower shortages develop, and the peculiarly chronic character of inflation under the Permanent War Economy.

AS HAS BEEN INDICATED, the growth in population from 1939 to 1953 has been sizable, amounting to 21 per cent. But Marx's law concerning the polarization of classes has still been operating. Our tentative data reveal that for the fourteen years under analysis the farming classes will have experienced a decline of 3,600,000, more than enough to offset an increase of 2,000,000 among the middle classes and a growth of 500,000 in the bourgeoisie. Thus the size of the working classes will have expanded by 1,100,000 more than the increase in total population, or an augmentation of 29 million in the working classes. This is tantamount to a working class rate of growth of 35 per cent, with two-thirds of the increase occurring since the end of World War II, in large part due to the rapidly accelerating birthrate. Accordingly, we calculate the working classes as defined represented 63 per cent of the total population in 1939, but the proportion will have risen to 70 per cent by 1953! The pressure of increasing population is therefore almost exclusively in the direction of reducing the living standards of the working classes.

The incidence of taxation falls with increasing severity on the working classes as taxes are increased. We exclude reference to corporation taxes, for corporation profits after taxes have increased far more rapidly than wages after taxes and, in a good many, cases, corporations have been able to pass higher taxes on to their customers in the form of higher prices. Regarding solely personal tax and nontax payments, the working classes paid less than 10 per cent of the total prior to 1943. With the first big increase in the individual income tax, accomplished more by a lowering of exemptions than an increase in tax rates, the working classes immediately jumped to about 35 per cent of total personal tax and nontax payments. Since 1943, the working classes have borne from one-third to two-fifths of this burden. Naturally, other classes have witnessed an increase in the *amount* of their personal tax and nontax payments, but their personal incomes have increased at a much faster pace than those of the working classes. Thus, the increase in taxation *rates* for the non-working classes has been relatively negligible. We shall return to this subject at a later date, particularly in relation to the current drive to impose a universal sales tax. That taxation, however, has been a potent weapon in reducing the standards of living of the working classes is beyond dispute.

SAVINGS OCCUPY A UNIQUE ROLE in any discussion of standards of living. Possession of sizable savings, for example, can readily lead to a higher rate of consumer expenditure than would otherwise take place. This, in turn, would lead to a higher standard of living and, more importantly, to a competitive bidding up of prices where goods are in short supply, thereby depriving those without savings of commodities they would normally be able to obtain if not for the existence of large savings in relatively few hands. The Federal Reserve study previously cited indicates that in 1946 79 per cent of all net savings occurred among those groups with $4,000 or more income. This would indicate that the working classes account for approximately 20 per cent of net savings.

It may be objected that 1946 is not a typical year, inasmuch as personal savings are estimated at only $12 billion, while in the peak year of 1944 personal savings exceeded $35 billion. As a matter of fact, for the fifteen years under consideration personal savings, as can be seen from Table V, are estimated to total $252 billion, an average of

Permanent War Economy

almost $17 billion annually in spite of the low levels of 1939-1941. Our estimates indicate that the working classes increase their personal savings very sharply when the decline in the supply of consumption goods is noticeable, and that for the entire period they account for 32 per cent of the total. Thus, two-thirds of the population are responsible for less than one-third of personal savings, while one-third of the population accumulates more than two-thirds of personal savings, a per capita differential against the working classes of more than four to one.

Although personal spending and savings habits vary widely, class differences are the decisive factor in explaining why the average non-worker saves four dollars for every dollar saved by the average worker. By and large, working class savings are fortuitous and temporary, as witness the current decline in the net volume of E bonds outstanding. This is not because workers lack a "sense of thrift" compared with other classes, but because they lack the opportunity to accumulate large savings. Low incomes are hardly conducive to high rates of savings. Given the widespread use of credit, the lower one's income and therefore one's savings, the more restricted is the opportunity to obtain credit. Conversely, a person with large savings is a better "risk" than one with little or no savings and therefore more apt to receive credit in any of its various forms. Savings, consequently, have both a psychological and indirect effect on living standards and cannot be entirely ignored in any appraisal of relative standards of living, especially among the major economic classes.

It is clear that no set of statistics can adequately measure the impact on living standards of the disappearance, or relative disappearance, of entire classes of commodities from the market due to the imposition of government controls. If an extreme situation be considered, such as during the war, when the production of certain consumer durables like automobiles, refrigerators, radios, etc., ceased as a result of governmental edict, it may at first glance be thought that the disparity among class living standards is reduced. The living standards of the bourgeoisie, for example, suffer greatly, while those of the working classes are barely affected. There is the rough equality of the ration card. There is also, however, the gross inequality of the black market where "money talks." Likewise, the big hoarders can never be found among those whose incomes are too low to permit such unpatriotic actions, except on a very small scale. It is frequently stated that "anyone can buy anything for a price." To the extent that this is true, it tends to offset the declines in the levels of living of the upper classes in a period of actual reduction or elimination of certain types of civilian output. Although it is not susceptible of statistical proof, we suspect that the absolute or relative disappearance of consumer commodities from the legitimate market creates a heavier burden on the standards of living of the working classes than of any other class.

The lengthening of the work week and the payment of premium rates for overtime were important factors in explaining the rapid rise in the personal income of the average worker during the war. There are other methods, however, of increasing the intensity of labor. Speed-up can and does take place, especially where assembly-line methods of production prevail, and it is rarely accompanied by adequate compensation. Again, we are in a field where statistics are conspicuous by their absence. Nevertheless, it can be accepted as a universal law that the greater the shortage of manpower, the greater the intensity of labor. This is a burden that falls almost exclusively on the working classes. It has a most important bearing on real standards of living, for in a very real sense the capacity to enjoy leisure time is as important a measure of true living standards as the ability to purchase consumer goods and services. A worker whose leisure time has been reduced or who is physically exhausted by an inhuman speed-up of the assembly line and therefore in no position to enjoy such leisure time as he may theoretically possess has suffered a decline in his standard of living just as surely as if he experienced a reduction in his real income. This entire problem, in turn, is related to incidence of illness, length of productive working life, income at retirement, and average longevity. There can be little doubt that all these factors adversely affect working class living standards to a marked, if not readily measurable, extent.

THE CHRONIC CHARACTER OF INFLATION under the Permanent War Economy is apparent to anyone with eyes to see. Whether the degree of inflation from 1939 to 1950 be measured by the Consumers' Price Index, which shows a rise of 72 per cent, or the newly announced implicit price index affecting gross output of the Department of Commerce, which reveals a rise of 83 per cent (preliminary), or our own average price index, which displays a rise of 94 per cent, the fact remains that the price level has increased on the average by seven or eight per cent annually over the first eleven years of the Permanent War Economy. This rate of increase in the price level will continue to be maintained, regardless of controls, because inflation is unceasing and permanent.

Permanent War Economy

The higher the ratio of war outlays to total output, the greater the degree of inflation. There is no method under capitalism whereby the creation of purchasing power through waste (war) production can be so controlled and absorbed that inflation is eliminated. The value and therefore the price of civilian output is necessarily augmented as the war sector of the economy increases in size and scope. A worker in an aluminum plant, for example, must receive the same wage whether the product of his labor goes into pots and pans or bombers and fighter planes. In the former case, however, he can through the market exchange the labor time expended in the production of pots and pans for food, clothing and other commodities and services needed to provide subsistence and constant reproduction of the value of his labor power. This is possible only because pots and pans possess a use value to other workers. If, on the other hand, he is producing warplanes these are of no interest to the workers who produce food and clothing and, in fact, are not distributed through the market mechanism but by government direct purchase or requisition. The inflation is inevitable because munitions production does not satisfy human wants and therefore cannot contribute to the reproduction or the expansion of the variable portion of capital.

The most that controls can do under capitalism is to slow down the rate of inflation and, if fairly devised and executed, distribute the burden equitably among all classes. It is precisely in this regard, however, that the naked class character of capitalism is most clearly revealed. The per capita output of consumer goods and services from both private and government sources, as was shown in Table VII, has increased, but the living standards of the working classes have declined. Inflation is one of the chief factors in the constant gnawing away at the living standards of the working classes under the Permanent War Economy. Just as taxes are designed to lighten the burden on business, so are inflation controls geared to bear most heavily on wages and to tread lightly on profits. By and large, the profits of the bourgeoisie are in effect guaranteed by the state, while wages rapidly depreciate under the full impact of inflation and controls – but this is a subject for another article.

TO A MARXIST, OF COURSE, standards of living are a function of the rate of surplus value. If the living standards of the working classes have declined, both relatively and absolutely, then there must have been an increase in the rate of surplus value. That this has indeed been the case can readily be seen from Table VIII on the following page

Declining Standards of Living

	TABLE VIII: RATE OF SURPLUS VALUE. 1939-1953 (Dollar Figures In Billions)		
Year	v(Variable Capital)	s(Surplus Value)	s/v (Rate of Surplus Value)
1939	$43.3	$39.9	92%
1940	46.7	46.3	99
1941	56.6	60.5	107
1942	72.3	79.3	110
1943	89.7	94	105
1944	98.8	103	104
1945	98.1	104.7	107
1946	92.6	106.3	115
1947	98.8	119.6	121
1948	105.4	136.3	129
1949	105.6	131.2	124
1950*	115	142	123
1951*	124.2	155.2	125
1952*	129.9	163.4	126
1953*	131.1	168.1	128
* Estimated			

The absolute levels of surplus value and variable capital are necessarily tentative inasmuch as they are based on the class distribution of income data. Variable capital has been developed as the sum of wages and salaries of the working classes, wages and salaries of farm employees, other labor income (mainly employer contributions to private pension and welfare funds and compensation for injuries), employee contributions for social insurance, and employer that net national product actually represents the net value of current production or the total values created by labor power

61

in the process of production, we have subtracted variable capital from net national product in order to obtain the magnitude of surplus value. The rate of surplus value is calculated as in Marx by dividing the mass of surplus value by the mass of variable capital.

The projections for employee and employer contributions for social insurance are arbitrary, although based on the anticipated effect of the revisions in the Social Security Act and our previously developed projections for the various income and output measures. These represent shares in current production even if they can only be spent in the future. A more serious objection to the simplified method used is the inherent assumption that the entire income of the non-working classes is derived from the surplus values created by the working classes, whereas it is clear that a portion of the income of some farmers, some single entrepreneurs and even some members of the bourgeoisie represents productive labor. It is felt, however, that this is substantially offset by the broad definition of the working classes, which includes many unproductive workers (in the Marxian sense), such as government employees, certain types of white collar workers as salesmen, insurance agents, etc., the unemployed and retired workers. Moreover, the bourgeoisie and middle classes are heavy beneficiaries of employer contributions to private pension and welfare funds.

The calculated amount of surplus value appears to be reasonable and the rate of surplus value coincides with everyday observation and what one would expect to find from a more detailed study. Even if exception be taken to the magnitudes of s and v, the rising trend in the rate of surplus value is clearly established. From 1939 to 1953, the rate of surplus value will have increased almost 40 per cent. Eschewing our projections, this sizable increase in the rate of exploitation was already reached by 1948. It is only since then, and belatedly, that the trade union movement has made some slight progress in reducing the rate of surplus value. The conclusion is inescapable that the enormous growth in the productivity of labor since 1939 has not redounded to the benefit of the working classes.

The rise in the rate of surplus value from 92 per cent in 1939 to 129 per cent in 1948 and to an estimated 123 per cent in 1950 provides an incontestable refutation to the puerile argument of the apologists for the status quo that "labor has fared as well as anyone else, for wages and salaries remain fairly constant at about two-thirds of the national income." What these gentlemen conveniently overlook is the fact that wages and salaries constitutes a completely misleading income classification, concealing within its broad cover the six-digit salaries of corporation executives, Hollywood actors and leading public entertainers, not to mention the salaries of all types of people in managerial and semi-managerial positions. To lump together the salary of a Charles E. Wilson (General Motors or General Electric) with the $50 or $65 weekly wage of a typical factory worker is simply to render impossible any type of scientific analysis concerning standards of living or the real workings of the economic system. And the evidence is clear that compensation of corporate officers, for example, has increased faster than the wages and salaries of other corporation employees.

It is no longer possible to arrive at an approximation of the magnitude of surplus value, as Marx did, by adding the shares of income admittedly paid out in the form of profits, interest, rent and royalties. It is equally necessary to include a large portion of wages and salaries, representing currently at least all salaries in excess of $10,000 annually. Such an adjustment, obviously required if the true position of the working classes is to be realistically examined, results in an increase in the mass of surplus value of about one-third and almost doubles the rate of surplus value!

Reducing the rate of surplus value does not arrest inflation, but it would help to make the burdens of inflation and declining standards of living more equitable. These are the immediate and central tasks of the working classes on the economic front. The longer they are delayed the more likely is the new environment of the Permanent War Economy to entrench itself and to condemn the mass of humanity to an existence devoid of hope for escape from the threats or reality of misery, war and totalitarianism.

The New International January 1951 — T.N. VANCE

Part III – Increasing State Intervention

"When we are sick we do not let nature take its course, but send for a doctor or surgeon . . . As in the physical world, so in the economic world." Thus spoke R.C. Leffingwell of J.P. Morgan & Co. in a speech reported in the New York Times of March 22, 1934, making it amply clear that the doctor in the economic world is the Federal government, i.e., the state. Not all sections of the American bourgeoisie supported state intervention as the remedy for the depression, but decisive support was forthcoming for the essential features of Roosevelt's "Dr. New Deal." Capitalism was seriously ill, to the point of prostration. Traditional methods of recovery, relying upon the "automatic" forces of the market had been tried and failed. Only state intervention could pump blood (profits) into the arteriosclerotic veins of a desperately sick economy.

The depression has been succeeded by the Permanent War Economy, but state intervention in the economy remains. In fact, it has increased until *state monopoly capitalism* provides an alternative description for the new stage of capitalism. Inasmuch as some degree of state intervention has obtained ever since the existence of national states, the nature, purposes and consequences of state intervention require somewhat detailed analysis to reveal precisely what is new in the situation.

The growing state intervention in the capitalist economy, which distinguishes it from the traditional or laissez-faire phase of capitalism, is an outgrowth of financial imperialism. This was clearly perceived by Lenin (*Imperialism: The Highest Stage of Capitalism*, p.25) when he wrote:

> Capitalism in its imperialist stage arrives at the threshold of the most complete socialization of production. In spite of themselves, the capitalists are dragged, as it were, into a new social order, a transitional social order from complete free competition to complete socialization. Production becomes social, but appropriation remains private. The social means of production remain the private property of a few. The general framework of formally recognized free competition remains, but the yoke of a few monopolists on the rest of the population becomes a hundred times heavier, more burdensome and intolerable.

The Permanent War Economy

The intercorporate arrangements that caused production to be come social at the turn of the twentieth century have first been regularized and then controlled by the state as the twentieth century has unfolded. The preservation of "the yoke of a few monopolists" is now inconceivable without the direct and indirect support of the state, whose ubiquitous interference in daily life manifests itself in a thousand and one ways. At first, as Lenin indicates, ". . . state monopoly in capitalist society is nothing more than a means of increasing and guaranteeing the income of millionaires on the verge of bankruptcy in one branch of industry or another." (*Imperialism*, p.39) State intervention in the Great Depression of the 1930's was characterized exclusively by the objective of restoring the profits of the millionaires, and in this it was largely successful.

Events have a logic of their own. The restoration of the rate of profit could not be followed by an abandonment of state intervention. On the contrary, like a patient who has recovered from an almost fatal illness solely through taking medicine containing habit-forming drugs, the enduring "health" of capitalism demands the continuation of "habit-forming drug" of state intervention. This becomes obvious as the economy of depression is followed by the Permanent War Economy. There are differences, however. Not only is state intervention more extensive, but it is no longer confined to restoring the profitability of "sick" industries. The most decisive sections of capital are subjected to state control and direction, but the reward is the virtual guarantee of the profits of the bourgeoisie as a class.

THE GROWTH OF THE STATE BUREAUCRACY and the increasing consumption of surplus value by the state in the form of increasing taxes are both evidence of increasing state intervention and we shall examine the facts below. Increasing domination of the apparatus of state control by representatives of monopoly capital is an even more impressive feature of the new capitalism. Lenin, with his remarkable insight into the function of capitalism in its imperialist stage, also anticipated this development. Referring to finance capital as the "personal union" between banking and industrial capital, he states (*Imperialism*, p.42): "The 'personal union' between the banks and industry is *completed by the 'personal union' between both and the state.*" (Italics mine – T.N.V.) And the union between finance capital and its state is of the most personal nature possible through the appointment of outstanding representatives of "big business" to positions of authority in the administration of virtually all state controls affecting production, distribution and prices – and therefore profits.

The rationalization for state intervention in the depression was provided by John Maynard Keynes, who showed why traditional wage-cutting methods could not restore effective demand and the rate of profit. According to Keynes, restoration of effective demand could not be left to private control of investment decisions. "I conclude," says Keynes in *The General Theory of Employment, Interest, and Money* (p.320), "that the duty of ordering the current volume of investment cannot safely be left in private hands." Thus, the role of the state is a steadily increasing one: "I expect to see the State . . . taking an ever greater responsibility for directly organizing investment." (*The General Theory*, p.164)

Despite certain of his critics, especially the unreconstructed advocates of laissez-faire, the purpose of state intervention in the Keynesian system is to preserve capitalism. A perfectly fair and thoroughly valid appraisal of Keynes is provided by the American Keynesian, Seymour E. Harris, in his introduction to *The New Economics: Keynes' Influence on Theory and Public Policy* (p.5):

> . . . it may be well to insist that Keynes was essentially a defender of capitalism. Only the stupidity of those whom he supports can account for any other interpretation. *Keynes indeed offers government a larger degree of control over the economic process and a larger degree of operation than the old-fashioned classical economist; but his motive is to save capitalism, not destroy it . . . Keynes wanted government to assume responsibility for demand, because otherwise the system would not survive.* [My Italics – T.N.V.] It was possible to have both more government activity and more private activity – if unemployment could only be excluded. And above all, Keynes would not remove the foundations of capitalism: free choice, the driving force of the quest for profits, the allocation of resources in response to the price incentive.

The Permanent War Economy

Keynes' own appraisal of his role accords quite closely with that of Harris. In the concluding notes to *The General Theory* (pp.380-381), he writes:

> Whilst, therefore, the enlargement of the functions of government, involved in the task of adjusting to one another the propensity to consume and the inducement to invest, would seem to a nineteenth-century publicist or to a contemporary American financier to be a terrific encroachment on individualism, I defend it, on the contrary, both as the *only practicable means of avoiding the destruction of existing economic forms in their entirety* and as the condition of the successful functioning of individual initiative. [Italics mine – T.N.V.]
>
> For if effective demand is deficient, not only is the public scandal of wasted resources intolerable, but the individual enterpriser who seeks to bring these resources into action is operating with the odds loaded against him. The game of hazard which he plays is furnished with many zeros, so that the players *as a whole* will lose if they have the energy and hope to deal all the cards. Hitherto the increment of the world's wealth has fallen short of the aggregate of positive individual savings; and the difference has been made up by the losses of those whose courage and initiative have not been supplemented by exceptional skill or unusual good fortune. But if effective demand is adequate, average skill and average good fortune will be enough.
>
> The authoritarian state systems of today seem to solve the problem of unemployment at the expense of efficiency and of freedom. *It is certain that the world will not much longer tolerate the unemployment* which, apart from brief intervals of excitement, is associated – and, in my opinion, *inevitably associated with present-day capitalistic individualism*. But it may be possible by a right analysis of the problem to cure the disease whilst preserving efficiency and freedom. [Italics mine – T.N.V.]

Increasing State Intervention

Under the Permanent War Economy, state intervention in the capitalist economy not only expands, but also takes on added functions. The problem is no longer one of buttressing effective demand to eliminate unemployment. From an economy being undermined by deflationary forces, there has occurred a complete shift to one in which inflationary forces predominate. State intervention must therefore, in the first instance, now be concerned with controlling production and prices. Demand has become too effective and must be curbed; the state must also take such measures as are necessary to allocate supplies so as to achieve the desired balance between the war and civilian sectors of the economy.

The increase in state functions, accompanied by a loss in the effectiveness of the capitalist market, has meant a colossal expansion in government expenditures, which, in turn, has necessitated a phenomenal increase in taxes. The relationship of government income to current production and surplus value from 1939 to 1950 is shown in Table I on page 71.

In 1939, at the beginning of the Permanent War Economy, total government receipts were $15.4 billion, with Federal government receipts two billion dollars less than State and local government receipts. Starting in 1941, Federal government receipts rise sharply, dwarfing the relatively modest increase in State and local government receipts. By 1950, while the latter had more than doubled compared with 1939, the former had increased more than six times, with the result that total government receipts had more than quadrupled.

Even after government receipts of social insurance contributions, which have virtually tripled since 1939, are subtracted from total government receipts, total government receipts of taxes of all forms, including certain fees and related payments, have increased from $13.3 billion in 1939 to an estimated $56.5 billion in 1950. In other words, the cessation of hostilities, aside from minor declines in 1946 and 1949, has not been accompanied by any diminution in the state's appetite for surplus value. This becomes crystal clear when we examine columns seven and nine in Table I on page 71, portraying the share of government income in both total production and surplus value.

The Permanent War Economy

The passage is remarkable, both for its typical expression of Keynes' fundamental thesis that only state intervention can save capitalism from destroying itself through mass unemployment and, for an otherwise first-rate economist, his complete inability to understand the origin and nature of profits. Why "effective demand" periodically is "deficient" requires an insight into the inner workings of capitalism impossible to attain without such basic Marxian tools as the labor theory of value, the laws of capital accumulation and the falling average rate of profit. Of this Keynes is incapable for, with all his emancipation from the fetishism of Marshallian economics, he still attributes the ability of capital to increase its magnitude (profits) to its "scarcity." Thus (*The General Theory*, p.213), "the only reason why an asset offers a prospect of yielding during its life services having an aggregate value greater than its initial supply price is because it is scarce; and it is kept scarce because of the competition of the rate of interest on money."

While Keynes' "theory" of profits is, of course, sheer nonsense, it does not detract from his role as chief theoretician justifying state intervention. To quote the leading American Keynesian, Alvin H. Hansen, in an essay entitled, *The General Theory*, contained in Harris' book previously cited

> David McCord Wright, in a recent article on the "Future of Keynesian Economies" (*American Economic Review*, June, 1945), put his finger quite accurately on the basic change in outlook effected by the 'Keynesian Revolution.' We cannot follow, he says, the main lines of Keynes' argument and say that the capitalist system, left to itself, will automatically bring forth sufficient effective demand. Keynes' ideas 'derive much of their unpopularity because they form the most widely known arguments for intervention even though such intervention may be quite capitalist in nature.' It is the analysis of the problem of aggregate demand, together with the implications of this analysis for practical policy, which challenges the old orthodoxy.

TABLE 1
RELATIONSHIP OF GOVERNMENT INCOME TO CURRENT PRODUCTION AND SURPLUS VALUE, 1939-1950 (Dollar Figures in Billions)

Year	Total Gov't. Receipts (1)	Federal Gov't. Receipts (2)	State and Local Gov't. Receipts (3)	Total Gov't. Receipts of Social Insurance Cont. (4)	Total Gov't. Receipts of Taxes (Col.1-Col.4) (5)*	Net National Product (6)**	Taxes as % of Prod. (Col.5/Col.6) (7)	Surplus Value (8)†	Taxes as % of Surplus Value (Col.5/Col.8) (9)
1939	$15.4	$6.7	$8.7	$2.1	$13.3	$83.2	16.0	$39.9	33.3
1940	17.8	8.7	9.1	2.3	15.5	93.0	16.7	46.3	33.5
1941	25.2	15.7	9.5	2.8	22.4	117.1	19.1	60.5	37.0
1942	32.9	23.2	9.7	3.5	29.4	151.6	19.4	79.3	37.1
1943	49.5	39.6	9.9	4.5	45.0	183.7	24.5	94.0	47.9
1944	51.8	41.6	10.2	5.2	46.6	201.8	23.1	103.0	45.2
1945	53.7	43.0	10.7	6.1	47.6	202.8	23.5	104.7	45.5
1946	51.7	39.7	12.0	6.0	45.7	198.9	23.0	106.3	43.0
1947	57.8	44.0	13.8	5.7	52.1	218.4	23.9	119.6	43.6
1948	59.8	43.9	15.9	5.2	54.6	241.7	22.6	136.3	40.1
1949	56.2	39.2	17.0	5.6	50.6	236.8	21.4	131.2	38.6
1950‡	62.2	42.7	19.5	5.7	56.5	257.0	22.0	142.0	39.8

* Includes gross tax receipts plus minor amounts of nontax income.
** From Table I of Part I
† From Table VIII of Part I
‡ State and local government receipts and receipts of social insurance contributions are estimated. The official figure for net national product in 1950. when released, will probably be about $2 billion higher than our estimate.

In 1939, one-sixth of current production and one-third of surplus value went to the state (all branches). This represented, so to speak, the fruits of state intervention in the

The Permanent War Economy

depression. Under the impetus of the rapid increase in war outlays and increasing government controls, these proportions rose rapidly until in 1943 almost one-fourth of current production and nearly one-half of surplus value went to the state. In spite of steady declines from 1943 to 1949, there has been no question of restoring pre-war relationships. Even in 1949, the state consumed 21.4 per cent of current output and 38.6 per cent of surplus value. In 1950, these percentages increased to an estimated 22 and almost 40 per cent, respectively. With the present rapid increase in war outlays and Federal tax rates, it is obvious that these ratios will climb rapidly toward their wartime peaks.

ALTHOUGH IT IS TRUE, as shown in the last chapter on *Declining Standards of Living*, that a sizeable portion of taxes comes from the working classes, the bourgeoisie contribute the major share to the upkeep of the state. Hence, the loud hue and cry from all sections of the capitalist press for "elimination of government waste." This is quite understandable when roughly two out of every five dollars accruing to the bourgeoisie go to support its state. Admittedly, there is considerable room for numerous savings in government operations without in any way impairing the functions of the state. Yet, before we shed tears for the "plight" of the American bourgeoisie, we would do well to examine its profits position. For, despite the huge overhead cost of the capitalist state, the bourgeoisie has never been so well off financially as it is today.

Naturally, when state expenditures exceed state receipts, i.e., income derived from current production, the difference must be covered by state borrowing, representing essentially income derived from past production. The periodic rapid increase in the government debt becomes a potent source of inflationary pressure on the economy. In fact, state income and expenditures, or fiscal policy, are by far the most powerful single factor in determining the level at which the economy operates. Besides exerting great influence on the size of the national product, the nature of state fiscal policies in large measure ordains the composition of the national product among the various classes. To a significant extent, therefore, the personnel of the state bureaucracy becomes, as it were, an arena for the conduct of the class struggle. This is obviously the case where class pressures are exerted on Congress and State and local legislatures. It is equally true and, in certain cases, more so, when policy can be influenced or modified by

Increasing State Intervention

administrative action, within the Executive branch of government. The recent attack of the United Labor Policy Committee on "big business domination of the Defense Program," and particularly on Defense Mobilizer Charles E. Wilson is a perfect illustration of the corroding impact of the Permanent War Economy on the functioning of capitalism, as well as inordinate power that is concentrated in the hands of a single individual who is merely an appointee.

Controlling supply and prices, to mention only the obvious, requires a far larger state bureaucracy than the relatively simple function of buttressing effective demand, which was the chief role of the state during the depression. The war economy also demands a permanent increase in the military bureaucracy, aside from the periodic need to assure an adequate supply of cannon fodder. As a consequence, omitting from consideration the period of World War II itself, the state's claim on the employable labor force has increased markedly, as can be seen from Table II on the following page.

The total employed labor force, including the armed forces, has increased from 46,120,000 in 1939 to 61,457,000 in 1950, an increase exceeding fifteen million, or approximately one-third. This is without reference to fact that the total employed labor force reached a peak of 65,220,000 in 1944 at the height of the war. In part, this was accomplished by a sharp reduction in the amount of unemployment and, in even larger part, by absorbing new entrants into the labor force arising from the growth in population.

Again, the highly significant fact is that there is no return to the pre war relationship, even in the case of the government employment ratio. Instead of one out of ten belonging to one or another segment of the state bureaucracy, as was the case in 1939, we now have one out of every eight employed persons in this category. We have already exceeded the government ratio that prevailed in 1941 and are moving rapidly toward the relationship that existed in 1942. For the government employment ratio to increase beyond this level, approaching the fantastic heights of 1943-1945, would undoubtedly require participation by American imperialism in an all-out war effort. Nevertheless, the warnings are apparent on every hand that manpower, even more than strategic materials, will be the limiting factor in the current effort of American imperialism to contain and then to destroy Stalinist imperialism.

The Permanent War Economy

TABLE II: RELATIONSHIP OF GOVERNMENT EMPLOYMENT TO TOTAL EMPLOYED LABOR FORCE, 1939-1950 (In Thousands)						
Year	Total Labor Force, incl. Armed Forces (1)*	Annual Average Unemployment (2)**	Total Employed Labor Force (Col.1- Col.2) (3)	Total Federal Govt. Employment (4) †	Total State and Local Govt. Employment (5) ‡	Total Govt. Employment Col.4+ Col.5) (6)	Govt. Employment Ratio (Col.4 - Col.5) (7)
1939	55600	9480	46120	1286	3287	4573	9.9%
1940	56030	8120	47910	1587	3306	4893	10.2
1941	57380	5560	51820	3032	3299	6331	12.2
1942	60230	2660	57570	6326	3235	9561	16.6
1943	64410	1070	63340	12020	3126	15146	23.9
1944	65890	670	65220	14395	3092	17487	26.8
1945	65140	1040	64100	14254	3124	17378	27.1
1946	60820	2270	58550	5841	3339	9180	15.7
1947	61608	2142	69466	3616	3564	7180	12.1
1948	62748	2064	60684	3442	3752	7194	11.9
1949	63571	3395	60176	3655	3895	7550	12.6
1950	64599	3142	61457	3370	4000	7730	12.6

* From Table D of The Permanent War Economy, Jan.-Feb. 1951 issue of *The New International*, (chapter II of this book) with actual 1950 substituted for estimate of 64,900,000.

** From Table C of The Permanent War Economy, Jan.-Feb. 1951 issue of The New International, with actual 1950 substituted for estimate of 3,100,000.

† Breakdown shown in Table II-A ; excludes Federal work relief employment totaling 3,216,000 in 1939, 2,792,000 in 1940, 2,192,000 in 1941, 909,000 in 1942, and 85,000 in 1943.

‡ Breakdown shown in Table II-A; excludes State and Local work relief employment totaling 29,000 in 1939, 38,000 in 1940, 17,000 in 1941, and 5,000 in 194 2.

Increasing State Intervention

Parenthetically, this is the decisive reason why American imperialism must seek and maintain allies, and why 'the MacArthur policy', to the extent that it would jeopardize this fundamental strategic aim, is suicidal.

The composition of government employment, as shown in Table II-A on the following page, reveals the crucial importance of manpower and demonstrates that not even American imperialism can maintain an economy of "guns and butter, too" if we assume that all-out war is in the offing.

Let us suppose, for example, that an all-out war effort against Stalinist imperialism will compel about the same manpower utilization by the military and Federal civilian bureaucracies as took place in 1944, and that it is desired at the same time to sustain the civilian economy at current high levels. An increase of almost eleven million in Federal employment over 1950 would be needed. Even allowing for full absorption of the unemployed, and the normal increase of several hundred thousand a year in those seeking work for the first time, there would still be a shortage of between seven and eight million. Even reducing State and local government employment to the 1944 level would save less than 900,000. Thus, private civilian employment would have to be reduced by six to seven million, or an equivalent amount of married women, retired workers and others not presently considered part of the labor force would have to be induced to seek and to accept employment. In either case, the impact on civilian output, aside from any shortages in materials or productive capacity, would be substantial.

Abstracting from the war situation itself, however, there has been approximately a tripling in the size of the Federal civilian bureaucracy, which rose from 571,000 in 1939 to an estimated 1,568,000 in 1950.

Even more dramatic has been the increase in the military bureaucracy, which increased from 342,000 in 1939 to an estimated 1,500,000 in 1950 – a growth of well over 300 per cent. As a permanent feature, the size of the military forces (without regard for the current build-up in connection with the Korean war) exceeds the number employed in public education. What a sad and fitting commentary on the moral bankruptcy of capitalism! Of at least passing interest is the sizable increase in the number of State and local government non-school employees, which declined from 1,877,000 in 1939 to

The Permanent War Economy

1,700,000 in 1944 and then rose to an estimated 2,342,000 in 1950 – representing a growth of more than 25 per cent from 1939 to 1950. Even the cost of local police and bureaucratic functions increases!

	TABLE II-A: COMPOSITION OF GOVERNMENT EMPLOYMENT, 1939-1950* (In Thousands)					
	FEDERAL			STATE AND LOCAL		
Year	Civilian, except work relief	Military	Government Enterprises	Public Education	Non-school except work relief	Government Enterprises
1939	571	342	373	1267	1877	143
1940	653	549	385	1273	1872	161
1941	957	1676	399	1281	1846	172
1942	1719	4154	453	1270	1794	171
1943	2519	9029	472	1244	1709	173
1944	2545	11365	485	1226	1700	166
1945	2444	11302	508	1224	1734	166
1946	1864	3434	543	1277	1883	179
1947	1462	1599	555	1334	2042	188
1948	1408	1468	566	1369	2187	196
1949	1443	1604	608	1422	2277	196
1960**	1568	1500	662	1457	2342	201

* These breakdowns of columns four and five of Table II represent full-time and part-time employees.
** Estimated.

More than eleven per cent of government employment is currently to be found in nationalized enterprises. The process of erosion has begun, even in America, the

Increasing State Intervention

stronghold of capitalist private property. While some of the more class-conscious capitalists are prone to question where it will all end, they are all consoled by the actuality of profits exceeding anyone's imagination. Although the figures are still relatively small, the increase in employment in government enterprises, from a combined total of 516,000 in 1939 to an estimated 863,000 in 1950, is noteworthy – not only because this is an increase of almost 70 per cent, and nearly 80 per cent for Federal government enterprises alone, but because of the steadily rising trend. The sphere of nationalized production is gradually being enlarged, and this is not just a question of the post office, but rather of public utilities and atomic energy and, to some extent, transportation. It is no longer solely a question of nationalizing those industries that are incapable of operating at a profit. A new element has been injected and it has arisen only because of the dual aims of the war economy. Private capitalists either lack the resources or cannot be entrusted with such vital war tasks as development of synthetic rubber and atomic energy. Profitability is not the decisive consideration, but survival. The state, as the executive committee of the bourgeoisie, can do what no single capitalist or group of capitalists can do. Unlimited sums can be poured into any project which is deemed essential, whether it is profitable or not.

HAND IN HAND WITH THE INCREASE in taxes and the permanent growth in the state bureaucracy go an enormous increase in business and a fantastic increase in profits. This can readily be seen from an examination of the data for corporate sales, profits and taxes, shown in Table III on the following page.

We have shown the data for corporate sales, profits and taxes from 1929 to 1950, in order to demonstrate conclusively how the Permanent War Economy, with all its increasing state intervention, has paid off handsomely for the bourgeoisie. Although corporate tax liability for the decade 1929-1938 was negligible, totaling $9.2 billion for the entire ten years, corporate profits could not reach 1929 levels by a very sizable amount. Even corporate sales remained below 1929 despite state intervention during the depression. For the first ten years of the Permanent War Economy, however, corporate sales went up by leaps and bounds, reaching a level of $381.3 billion in 1948 and by 1950 were almost three times the level of 1929! Even when allowance is made for the depreciation of the dollar, the absolute increase in physical sales is fairly

The Permanent War Economy

TABLE III

CORPORATE SALES, PROFITS AND TAXES, 1929-1950

(Billions of Dollars)

Year	Corporate Sales (1)	Corporate Profits Before Taxes (2)	Corporate Tax Liability (3)	Corporate Profits After Taxes (2-3) (4)	Corporate Sales minus Gross Profits (2-1) (5)	Corporate Sales minus Net Profits (2-4) (6)
1929	$138.6	$9.8	$1.4	$8.4	$128.8	$130.2
1930	118.3	3.3	0.8	2.5	115	115.8
1931	92.4	-0.8	0.5	-1.3	93.2	93.7
1932	69.2	-3.0	0.4	-3.4	72.2	72.6
1933	73	0.1	0.5	-0.4	72.9	73.4
1934	89.6	1.7	0.7	1	87.9	88.6
1935	102	3.2	1	2.2	98.8	99.8
1936	119.5	5.7	1.4	4.3	113.8	115.2
1937	128.9	6.2	1.5	4.7	122.7	124.2
1938	108.6	3.3	1	2.3	105.3	106.3
1939	120.8	6.5	1.5	5	114.3	115.8
1940	135.2	9.3	2.9	6.4	125.9	128.8
1941	176.2	17.2	7.8	9.4	159	166.8
1942	202.8	21.1	11.7	9.4	181.7	193.4
1943	233.4	25	14.4	10.6	208.4	222.8
1944	246.7	24.3	13.5	10.8	222.4	235.9
1945	239.5	19.7	11.2	8.5	219.8	231
1946	270.9	23.5	9.6	13.9	247.4	257
1947	347.8	30.5	11.9	18.6	317.3	329.2
1948	381.3	33.9	13	20.9	347.4	360.4
1949	359.7	27.6	10.6	17	332.1	342.7
1950*	409	39.8	17.7	22.1	369.2	386.9

*Estimated, with corporate sales based on the same proportionate increase over 1949 as total business sales; corporate profits and taxes estimated by Council of Economic Advisers based on actual for first three quarters of 1950.

Increasing State Intervention

impressive. At the same time, corporate taxes totaled $97.5 billion for the first decade of the Permanent War Economy – a burden ten times that of the previous decade. Nevertheless, corporate profits after taxes increased from $20.3 billion in the decade 1929-1938 to $113.5 billion in the decade 1939-1948, an increase in the mass of net profit amounting to 459 per cent!

We have shown the data for corporate sales, profits and taxes from 1929 to 1950, in order to demonstrate conclusively how the Permanent War Economy, with all its increasing state intervention, has paid off handsomely for the bourgeoisie. Although corporate tax liability for the decade 1929-1938 was negligible, totaling $9.2 billion for the entire ten years, corporate profits could not reach 1929 levels by a very sizable amount. Even corporate sales remained below 1929 despite state intervention during the depression. For the first ten years of the Permanent War Economy, however, corporate sales went up by leaps and bounds, reaching a level of $381.3 billion in 1948 and by 1950 were almost three times the level of 1929! Even when allowance is made for the depreciation of the dollar, the absolute increase in physical sales is fairly impressive. At the same time, corporate taxes totaled $97.5 billion for the first decade of the Permanent War Economy – a burden ten times that of the previous decade. Nevertheless, corporate profits after taxes increased from $20.3 billion in the decade 1929-1938 to $113.5 billion in the decade 1939-1948, an increase in the mass of net profit amounting to 459 per cent!

The superiority of war and war economy over the New Deal and public works, so far as the capitalist class is concerned, is unmistakably clear. As a matter of fact, the inclusion of 1929 profits distorts our comparison of the depression era with the Permanent War Economy. Proper procedure would begin the comparison with the year 1930. For the nine-year period, 1930-1938, corporate profits after taxes equaled $11.9 billion, while corporate sales minus gross profits totaled $881.8 billion, yielding a rate of profit of 1.3 per cent. Take any nine years of the first twelve years of the Permanent War Economy, and what a difference! From 1939 to 1917, for example, corporate profits after taxes equaled $92.6 billion, while corporate sales minus gross profits totaled $1,762.3 billion, yielding a rate of profit of 5.3 per cent.

79

The Permanent War Economy

The pump primer of increasing war outlays produced a doubling of sales and, even with the gigantic increase in taxes, a 678 per cent increase in the mass of net profits and a 308 per cent increase in the rate of profit! Increasing state intervention does, after all, have some good points. The Permanent War Economy has yielded a profit bonanza that is without precedent in a highly developed capitalist nation and is almost embarrassing to the bourgeoisie. And, in complete confirmation of the trends previously developed in the rate of surplus value and relative class standards of living, the picture improves from the point of view of the bourgeoisie. A new peak of $33.9 billion before taxes and $20.9 billion after taxes was reached by American corporations in 1948. Even the slight decline of 1949 left profits above the already swollen wartime levels. It remained, however, for 1950, aided in no small measure by the outbreak of the Korean war, to reach new historic profits and sales peaks. For the first time in history, corporate sales exceeded $400 billion. Corporate profits before taxes are estimated at $39.8 billion, with corporate profits after taxes likewise reaching a new high of $22.1 billion. Compare these figures with the increase in wages, even after allowance for rising personal income taxes, and it is clear that state intervention under the Permanent War Economy has restored both the mass and rate of profit. Capitalism has revived, at least so far as the bourgeoisie are concerned. If only it can be sustained indefinitely, ponder the theoreticians of the bourgeoisie!

Despite the "inventory recession" of the first half of 1951, heavy industries, the "war babies," are not worried. "Current profits in some industries continue to be terrific," states Carlton A. Shivery, stock market commentator of the New York *World-Telegram and Sun*, in his column of May 1, 1951.

> That is true of oil, copper, steel, motor, rubber and the chemical industries. Many units in those industries are reporting for first quarter far higher net profits as compared with the same quarter of last year, and *the net profits as compared with fourth quarter, even after excess profits taxes, show little or no decline. Without the excess profits taxes the net profits for many corporations would be so large they would cause anxiety on many counts.* (Italics mine, T.N.V.)

Increasing State Intervention

There can be no doubt that the wasting of resources, both human and natural, in war and preparation for war is a profitable business (so far) for the American bourgeoisie. The manner in which the war economy is run, with negotiated contracts (between big business and its own representatives in the government) and huge tax concessions through rapid amortization, means that profits are, in effect, guaranteed by the state. How the bourgeoisie and their apologists have the effrontery to complain about those unions that have cost-of-living escalator clauses in their contracts is virtually beyond comprehension. Yet, it is only when we examine what has happened to the rate of corporate profit that the real skullduggery of the bourgeoisie and the immense profitability of the Permanent War Economy become apparent.

RATES ARE FAR MORE SUSCEPTIBLE OF juggling than absolute figures, although we can be reasonably certain that the mass of corporate profit has not been overstated. What this mass of profit is divided by determines the rate of profit. Four different methods of computing the "rate of corporate profit" are shown in Table IV on the following page.

There is first the concept of the National Association of Manufacturers, the super trade association of certain segments of the big bourgeoisie. Not content with computing the rate of profit on sales, the N.A.M. adjusts net profits after taxes for changes in inventory valuation, on the theory that increases in inventory due to price changes are fortuitous and really not part of the profits of the bourgeoisie, especially when prices are going up. This approach is rationalized by emphasizing that low-cost inventory must be replaced at current high costs. Which is well and good, but the corporation that stocked inventory at relatively low costs still obtains a windfall profit, on which it has to pay income taxes, whether a compensating future loss is anticipated or not. And in an inflationary period, inventory losses due to price declines are not very likely.

A more important fallacy in the N.A.M. method of computing the rate of profit is that when the mass of profit is divided by sales, the effect is to count profit itself as a cost of production. This is necessarily so since the sales price includes the profit. Despite widespread profiteering and cries that the Office of Price Stabilization is attempting to control prices through control of profits, profits are a result and not a cost of production. To treat profits as a cost of production is equivalent of demanding a perpetual

The Permanent War Economy

TABLE IV
RATES OF CORPORATE PROFIT. 1929-1950*

Year	Profit Margin on Sales†	Rate of Corporate Profit After Taxes (Col.4 ÷ Col.6 of Table III)	Alternative Rate of Corporate Profit After Taxes (Col.4 ÷ Col.5 of Table III)	Rate of Corporate Profit Before Taxes (Col.2 ÷ Col.5 of Table III)
1929	6.4%	6.5%	6.5%	7.6%
1930	4.9	2.2	2.2	2.9
1931	1.2	-1.4	-1.4	-0.9
1932	-3.5	-4.6	-4.7	-4.2
1933	-3.4	-0.5	-0.5	0.1
1934	0.4	1.1	1.1	1.9
1935	2.1	2.2	2.2	3.2
1936	3.0	3.7	3.8	5
1937	3.7	3.8	3.8	5.1
1938	3	2.2	2.2	3.1
1939	3.6	4.3	4.4	5.7
1940	4.7	5	5.1	7.4
1941	3.9	5.6	5.9	10.8
1942	4	4.9	5.2	11.6
1943	4.2	4.8	5.1	12
1944	4.3	4.6	4.9	10.9
1945	3.3	3.7	3.9	9
1946	3.2	5.4	5.6	9.6
1947	3.7	5.7	5.9	9.6
1948	5	5.8	6	9.8
1949	5.3	5	5.1	8.3
1950‡	4.4	5.7	6	10.8

* Derived from Table III, with the exception of the NAM concept of the rate of profit.
† From Profits and Prices, Economic Policy Division Series No. 31, October 1950, published by Research Department of N.A.M. Net profits after taxes are adjusted for changes in inventory valuation, as estimated by Department of Commerce as due to changes in price level.
‡ Estimated.

pyramiding of profits, for the larger the profit the larger the increase in profit that is required to maintain the former rate of profit. Nevertheless, even the N.A.M. figures cannot conceal the fact that the Permanent War Economy has done a pretty good job of restoring the rate of profit. Still, a rate of four or five per cent is less than the 6.4 per cent of 1929 and sounds sufficiently small to be inconsequential in its effect. The prevalence of figures, especially in press releases, calculating the rate of profit on sales is a tribute to the propaganda of the bourgeoisie and to its ability to promote its own self-interests, but is hardly conducive to scientific accuracy.

The mass of profit must therefore be divided by sales minus profit in order to begin to arrive at the rate of profit. This is done, without any changes for inventory valuation, in both the middle columns of Table IV. In both cases, the mass of profit is measured as the net profit after taxes. In the first case, however, corporate sales minus net profits are used as the denominator; in the second case, corporate sales minus gross profits are taken as the proper base on which to calculate the rate of profit. A rate of profit of six per cent is almost equal to the performance of 1929, and considerably better than the five per cent or less shown by the N.A.M.. The difference, percentage-wise, is substantial, especially if we take the figures for 1950, which we have already shown is the peak profit year in the history of American capitalism. The N.A.M. approach yields a rate of profit of but 4.4 per cent. Under our first method, we obtain a rate of corporate profit of 5.7 per cent, which is almost 30 per cent higher than the N.A.M. would show. Under our alternative method, the rate of profit becomes six per cent, which is more than 36 per cent higher than the N.A.M.'s figure!

The difference between our two methods, of course, is that in the former taxes are, in effect, treated as a cost of production, while in the latter the base on which profits are calculated is without reference to taxes. A moment's reflection will show that it is no more proper to consider taxes as a cost of production than profits. It is true that one of the great weaknesses of the present corporate tax structure is that most corporations are able to pass on higher taxes in the form of higher prices, thereby contributing to the inflation and maintaining the same mass of profit and, in some cases, the same rate of profit as existed before any given increase in corporation taxes. This, again, is hardly

The Permanent War Economy

a justification for treating a result of production, for taxes (on corporations) are merely taking a portion of profit or surplus value, as a cost of production.

Arriving at a true official rate of corporate profit therefore requires subtraction of both profits and taxes from sales before the rate of profit is computed. The rate of profit, in terms of obtaining a true picture of what is actually happening in the economy, therefore ought to be calculated before taxes, both with reference to the mass of profit and to volume of capital employed to obtain a given profit. This is done in the last column of Table IV. The picture that emerges is considerably different from any previously discussed. Since 1941 the rate of corporate profit has exceeded 1929! For war years and for 1950, the rate of profit runs in the neighborhood of eleven to twelve per cent – a level about 50 per cent higher than in 1929. The rate of profit in actuality is thus two and almost three times the modest picture shown by the N.A.M. That the bourgeoisie have had to disgorge half or almost half of their profits to their own state for the conduct of their war and preparations for their future war has precisely nothing to do with the degree to which the working classes are exploited in the process of production.

IT IS ONLY THE RATE OF PROFIT before taxes that gives us an inkling of what a life-saver the Permanent War Economy has been to the bourgeoisie. Even this is far from the whole picture, for the simple reason that profits are only one form of surplus value. The capitalist who makes profits must share his cut of surplus values created by the workers with the capitalist who obtains interest, with those who obtain rent and royalties, with those whom he pays huge salaries to manage his wealth, and with the state which demands taxes to protect him and his system. The true rate of profit for all industry can thus be obtained only by dividing the mass of surplus value by the total amount of capital, both constant and variable, employed in production.

To arrive at meaningful figures for the Marxian formula for the rate of profit, (s divided by c plus v), is not easy, but it can be approximated through the following technique. Having already derived the mass of surplus value in the last article, together with the mass of variable capital, it is only necessary to obtain the magnitude of constant capital. We know of no method whereby this can be done directly, as there would be far too many gaps in building up the total mass of constant capital on an industry-by-industry basis. Even if reliable and comprehensive capital investment figures could be obtained, we would still lack information on the turnover of capital – a factor of critical importance in developing the rate of profit.

Accordingly, it is necessary to start with sales data, and to try to build up total sales or receipts for all industry. Inasmuch as the market price of a commodity represents its value, the proceeds from sales necessarily embody the values transferred by the employment of constant capital in production and the values created by the employment of variable capital or labor power in production. This approach conceptually yields a true gross national product for all industry. It may be objected that in many industries the market price of a commodity deviates from both its production price and value. This is of no consequence for we are seeking the rate of profit for all industry. The deviations of market price from value must cancel out; otherwise, there would be no profit or surplus value for the capitalist class as a whole. This, incidentally, is the pitfall on which all non-Marxian theories of profit collapse, for on top of their faulty theoretical approach they are immersed in the analysis of the single entrepreneur or firm. While marginal utility, scarcity, speculation, or risk-taking may on occasion explain the fortuitous profits of an individual firm, such theories cannot begin to explain how it is possible for the entire capitalist class to start with a given quantity of capital and to emerge from the process of production and circulation with an amount of capital exceeding the starting sum by a definite and measurable increment.

The data on corporate sales are readily available and were presented in Table III. Our problem therefore resolves itself into one of estimating the sales or receipts of unincorporated enterprises. Here we can begin with a Commerce series on "Total Business Sales," which covers only retail and wholesale trade and manufacturing. These data, with a breakdown shown between corporate and noncorporate sales, are presented in Table V on the following page.

The data themselves are of more than passing interest. As one would expect, unincorporated enterprises play only a negligible role in the volume of manufacturing sales, but are fairly significant in wholesale trade, accounting for thirty per cent of volume. In retail trade, however, noncorporate sales are as important as corporate sales, actually accounting for more than half of total retail sales in every year under consideration except 1950. In other words, it is primarily in retail trade that the bulk of

The Permanent War Economy

the middle classes exists, a testimonial to the survival qualities of the corner grocery store and gasoline station.

	TABLE V CORPORATE AND NONCORPORATE RETAIL, WHOLESALE, AND MANUFACTURING SALES. 1939-1950*. (Billions of Dollars)								
	RETAIL TRADE			WHOLESALE TRADE			MANUFACTURING		
Year	Total	Corporate †	Non-corporate	Total	Corporate	Non-corporate	Total	Corporate	Non-corporate
1939	$42.0	$20.9	$21.1	$30.1	$21.3	$8.8	$61.2	$57.2	$4.0
1940	46.4	23.1	23.3	33.6	23.5	10.1	70.2	65.8	4.4
1941	55.5	27.4	28.1	43.4	29.7	13.7	98	92	6
1942	57.6	26.2	31.4	48.1	29	19.1	125.1	116.3	8.8
1943	63.3	27.3	36	51.3	30.3	21	153.9	141.9	12
1944	68.8	28.7	40.1	54.7	32.3	22.4	165.4	151	14.4
1945	75.8	31.2	44.6	59.8	34.7	25.1	154.6	138.7	15.9
1946	100	44.3	56	79.2	51.4	27.8	151.4	136.9	14.5
1947	119	56.9	62	93.1	65.2	27.9	191	177.8	13.2
1948	130	62.7	67.3	100.3	68.9	31.4	213.7	195.3	18.4
1949	128	62.3	65.9	90	61.3	28.7	200	182.4	17.6
1950‡	140	70.8	69.4	100.1	69.7	30.4	235	207.4	27.6

* Represents what Commerce terms "Total Business Sales" – "the sum of data for manufacturing and wholesale and retail trade. These figures are smaller than the non-farm business statistics used in gross national product computations by the amount of sales . . . for construction, utilities and other nonindustrial sectors."

† Includes automobile services.

‡ Corporate retail, wholesale and manufacturing sales estimated on the assumption that they increased by the same proportion over 1949 as total corporate sales, with non- corporate sales derived as a residual.

Increasing State Intervention

The most interesting fact about these figures is the tendency for the importance of manufacturing to increase as war outlays (and controls) increase. Thus, while total manufacturing sales were less than the combined total of retail and wholesale trade sales in 1939, accounting for 46 per cent of total business sales, they increased steadily as war outlays and controls gathered momentum, reaching a peak of 57 per cent of total business sales in 1943 and 1944. Then, there was a rapid decline until in 1946 the prewar rate of 46 per cent prevailed again. The basic tendency for wasteful distribution to diminish in importance, and for manufacturers to sell directly to the government as well as to exert a squeeze on middlemen, reasserted itself following 1946, with the result that in 1950 manufacturing: sales were 49 per cent of total business sales.

In a small way, these trends are corroborative evidence of the loss of effectiveness of the capitalist market as an allocator of resources. Looked at another way, while total wholesale trade sales increased 232 per cent from 1939 to 1950, and total retail trade sales augmented by 234 per cent during the same period, total manufacturing sales grew by 284 per cent. This is merely another way of saying that under the Permanent War Economy, aside from periods of all-out war, when the increase is even more striking, manufacturing has grown at a rate 20 per cent faster than distribution. The propensity of capitalism to dig its own grave through increasing industrialization and greater proletarianization of the labor force is thus strengthened under the Permanent War Economy.

To noncorporate sales for manufacturing, retail and wholesale trade, it was necessary to add sales or receipts for the remainder of unincorporated business activity, such as gross farm income, unincorporated construction activity, and the like. While there may be some duplication in the figures, and even some omissions, the gross figure for unincorporated business shown in column two of Table VI appears to be reasonable both as to level and trend.

THE SUMMATION OF CORPORATE AND noncorporate sales or receipts yields the gross value of production, or c plus v plus s. This magnitude, together with its components, and the average rate of profit for all industry from 1939 to 1950 are shown in Table VI on the following page

The Permanent War Economy

TABLE VI

AVERAGE RATE OF PROFIT FOR ALL INDUSTRY.

1939-1950 (Dollar Figures in Billions)

Year	Corporate Sales* (1)	Non-corporate Sales or Receipts (2)†	c+v+s Gross Sales or Receipts (Col.1+ Col.2) (3)	c Constant Capital (4)**	v Variable Capital (5)‡	c+v Total Capital (Col.4+Col.5) (6)	s Surplus Value (7)‡	s/(c+v) Average Rate of Profit (Col.7 ÷ Col.6) (8)
1939	$120.8	$74.7	$195.5	$112.3	$43.3	$155.6	$39.9	25.6%
1940	135.2	80.5	215.7	122.7	46.7	169.4	46.3	27.3
1941	176.2	99.8	276	158.9	56.6	215.5	60.5	28.1
1942	202.8	126.9	329.7	178.1	72.3	250.4	79.3	31.7
1943	233.4	148.7	382.1	198.4	89.7	288.1	94	32.6
1944	246.7	164.7	411.4	209.6	98.8	308.4	103	33.4
1945	239.5	180	419.5	216.7	98.1	314.8	104.7	33.3
1946	270.9	202.5	473.4	274.5	92.6	367.1	106.3	29
1947	347.8	203.7	551.5	333.1	98.8	431.9	119.6	27.7
1948	381.3	226.5	607.8	366.1	105.4	471.5	136.3	28.9
1949	359.7	223.1	582.8	346	105.6	451.6	131.2	29.1
1950	409	244.8	653.8	396.8	115	511.8	142	27.7

* From Table III, column one.

† To non-corporate retail, wholesale and manufacturing sales, shown in Table V, were added gross farm income, non-corporate and government construction activity; national income originating in finance, insurance and real estate, services, and government and government enterprises, and a miscellaneous factor based on the number of active proprietors in agricultural services, forestry and fisheries, mining, transportation, and communications and public utilities.

** Derived by subtracting net national product, shown in column six of Table I, from column three.

‡ From Table VIII of Part II.

Increasing State Intervention

Constant capital was derived, as explained in the footnote to column four, by subtracting net national product (which represents the sum of variable capital and surplus value) from the gross value of production. An alternative method, since the magnitude of variable capital and surplus value were previously derived, would have been to subtract surplus value from the gross value of production, thereby obtaining total capital, i.e., the summation of constant and variable capital. Then, from this last figure, variable capital could have been subtracted in order to obtain constant capital. The results would naturally be identical. Three facts of considerable importance emerge from this analysis of the average rate of profit:

1) The level of the average rate of profit is almost three times that shown in Table IV, confirming the easily observed fact that the capitalist who obtains profit must pay substantial tribute to the more parasitic members of the capitalist class who collect interest, rent, royalties, and absurdly large salaries (of course, in many cases, the division among capitalists as to the form and method of appropriating surplus value is not nearly as clear-cut as herein suggested).

2) The Permanent War Economy not only succeeded in restoring the profitability of American capitalism, but actually managed to increase the average rate of profit until 1944, i.e., there is a definite correlation between the ratio of war outlays to total output and the average rate of profit. An increase of 30 per cent in the average rate of profit, as occurred between 1939 and 1944-1945 is, in some ways, even more significant than the fact that the true average rate of profit for all industry reached a peak of one-third, for it is conclusive evidence that state intervention has as its major objective guaranteeing the profits of the bourgeoisie.

3) The Marxian law of the falling average rate of profit reasserts itself following the end of World War II, although it is significant that the maintenance of a ten per cent ratio of war outlays to total output is sufficient, in the short run at any rate, to maintain the average rate of profit at a higher level than existed in 1939 or even in 1940.

The data contained in Table VI represent the "guts" of the economic performance of American capitalism under the Permanent War Economy. From 1939 to 1950, the mass of surplus value rose from almost $40 billion to an estimated $142 billion, a rise

The Permanent War Economy

of 256 per cent, the largest increase of any of the components of economic performance. Virtually keeping pace was the increase in the magnitude of constant capital, which rose from $112.3 billion in 1939 to an estimated $3 96.8 billion in 1950, a rise of 253 per cent. The gross value of total output, as measured by gross sales or receipts, naturally comes next in rate of growth, increasing from $195.5 billion in 1939 to an estimated $653.8 billion in 1950, a rise of 234 per cent. Then follows total capital, which rose from $155.6 billion in 1939 to an estimated $511.8 billion in 1950, a rise of 229 per cent. In last place is the increase in the magnitude of variable capital, which rose from $43.3 billion in 1939 to an estimated $115 billion in 1950, a rise of but 166 per cent. All of these changes combine to yield an increase over the first twelve years of the Permanent War Economy of eight per cent in the rate of profit.

In the process of capital accumulation, it is, however, as Marx observes , "the composition of the total social capital of a country" that is crucial in understanding the economic laws of motion that prevail. The organic composition of capital relates the growth in constant capital to total capital, and it is the increasingly high organic composition of capital, as constant capital increases relative to variable capital, that threatens capitalists with self-destruction through concentration and centralization of the social means of production in fewer and fewer private hands and all the social consequences that then unfold. The trend in the organic composition of capital under the Permanent War Economy can easily be calculated from the data in Table VI, and we present below the rates for the years of significant change:

Year	1939	1941	1944	1946	1948	1949	1950
Composition of Capital	72.2%	73.7	68	74.8	77.6	76.6	77.5

The mass of the means of production were thus 72.2 per cent of the total capital, including labor power, employed in production in 1939. The percentage rose slightly, in conformity with the generally observed tendency toward an increasingly high organic composition of capital, to 73.7 per cent in 1941. There then followed a perceptible decrease, during American participation in World War II, to a nadir of 68 per cent in 1944. A slight increase in 1945 was followed by a substantial increase in the composition of capital in 1946, as peacetime output resumed, with the upward trend continuing until a new peak of 77.6 per cent was attained in 1948. A slight slump during the recession of 1949 was only preliminary to virtual restoration of the 1948 peak in 1950. The organic composition of capital has thus increased by more than seven percent between 1939 and 1950, and by 14 per cent from 1944 to 1950.

The decline in the organic composition of capital during the war years is not surprising in view of the huge increase in the ratio of war outlays to total output, for it can be directly traced to the decline in the productivity of labor that takes place in war-time, to the physical necessity of increasing output through abnormal reliance on manpower, to the drastic decline in net private capital formation, and to the vicissitudes of the class struggle that placed the proletariat in a position to accomplish a slight reduction in the rate of surplus value. As a matter of fact, all these factors operated in the United States from 1942-1945; the only wonder is that the decline in the organic composition of capital during World War II was not greater.

Since, at an 80 per cent composition of capital, four dollars of means of production are needed to yield a wage of one dollar to the average worker, the relative diminution in the variable constituent of capital as capital accumulates makes it increasingly difficult under capitalism to employ the entire available labor force. This pressure continues to exert itself even though the Permanent War Economy has, in its own way, as previously explained, "solved" the problem of unemployment. Precisely where the breaking point is likely to be, no one can say, but it is clear that the composition of capital is already dangerously high and constitutes a sword of Damocles, hanging over the unsuspecting head of such a highly-geared capitalist economy that in a few years it is possible to produce all the automobiles, television sets, etc., that can be sold under capitalist conditions of production. If, therefore, only a very high ratio of war outlays to total output can reduce the composition of capital or, at least, arrest the tendency toward a constantly increasing composition of capital, then the economic motives for American imperialism to engage in such activities in foreign policy as warrant an

The Permanent War Economy

increase in war outlays, even if the ultimate consequence is all-out war, are laid bare for all those with eyes to see who wish to see.

IT IS NOT NECESSARY TO RELY ON OUR calculations and derived figures to conclude that the Permanent War Economy has yielded an unprecedented profit bonanza for the bourgeoisie, restoring both the mass and rate of profit to record-breaking levels. We can first look at the results of a study by the Securities and Exchange Commission for manufacturing corporations listed on the stock exchange. This study, covering the years 1938 to 1947, is indicative of what has happened to the largest aggregates of capital. Its results are embodied in Table VII on the following page

It will be seen that the rate of profit on sales is consistent with the ratios that we developed earlier in this article. Net profit before income taxes for these leading manufacturing corporations was only $1.6 billion in 1938, with net profit after taxes $1.3 billion. A spectacular rise until 1944 then took place, followed by a decline in 1945 and in 1946, and then a reaching of new heights in net profits before taxes in 1947. At more than $10 billion in 1945, these 1,306 manufacturing corporations averaged a net profit before income taxes in excess of $7.7 million, which was about four times the level of 1939.

Even after income taxes, these, principal manufacturing corporations earned $6.4 billion in 1947, or almost five million dollars on the average. Despite the rise in corporation income taxes, this was three times the level of 1939! The return on net worth, which represents invested and reinvested capital, is by far the most interesting set of figures in the table as, without reference to the turnover of capital, the return on net worth indicates the expansive qualities of capital. On a before-income-tax basis, the rate of return on net worth rose from 6.4 per cent in 1938 and 10.2 per cent in 1939 to a wartime peak of 27.9 per cent in 1943 and then declined to 17.6 per cent in 1946, but immediately rose again to 27.4 per cent in 1947. The confirmation of our earlier conclusions is readily apparent.

The rate of return of net profits *after* income taxes on net worth is the final proof that our contentions are completely accurate with respect to the impact of the Permanent War Economy on profits. From a rate of 5.1 per cent in 1938 and 8.3 per cent in 1939, the return on investments in major manufacturing corporations rose to 12 per cent in 1941, then leveled off during the war at a rate between 9.6 and 10.1 per cent, rose to 11.9 per cent in 1946 and

Increasing State Intervention

jumped to 17.2 per cent in 1947! At the 1947 rate of return, assuming maintenance of the tax rates in existence at that time, a capitalist would receive back his entire investment in a manufacturing enterprise in less than six years. To match a performance of this kind one must return to the earlier days of capitalism when it was in its ascendancy. Such a rate of return, almost twenty years after American capitalism entered the permanent crisis of world capitalism, is a tribute not only to the effectiveness of the Permanent War Economy in preserving capitalism, but also to the enormous inner strength and productive capacity of American capitalism.

	TABLE VII MASS AND RATE OF PROFIT OF LISTED MANUFACTURING CORPORATIONS. ACCORDING TO SEC SURVEY, 1938-1947*					
	NET PROFIT AFTER INCOME TAXES			NET PROFIT BEFORE INCOME TAXES		
Year	Amount (Billions of Dollars)	As a % of Sales	As a % of Net Worth†	Amount (Billions of Dollars)	As a % of Sales	As a % of Net Worth†
1938	$1.6	6.6%	6.4%	$1.3	5.3%	5.1%
1939	2.5	9.5	10.2	2.1	7.7	8.3
1940	3.7	12.2	14.7	2.6	8.4	10.1
1941	6.4	15	24.7	3.1	7.3	12
1942	7	12.7	25.7	2.6	4.8	9.6
1943	7.9	11.1	27.9	2.8	3.9	9.7
1944	8.2	10.4	27.4	3	3.8	10.1
1945	6.4	8.6	19.9	3.1	4.2	9.6
1946	6	9.6	17.6	4.1	6.5	11.9
1947	10.1	11.7	27.4	6.4	7.4	17.2

* Securities and Exchange Commission Survey Series Release No.151, published April 27, 1949, covers manufacturing corporations listed on the stock exchange, with the number of companies varying from 1,013 in 1938 to 1,306 in 1947.

† Net worth is calculated as of the beginning of the year.

The Permanent War Economy

Unfortunately, the SEC study does not go beyond 1947. We can, however, turn to the annual study of National City Bank of New York to obtain a reliable picture of current profits of leading corporations. To facilitate examination, we have divided the data contained in the National City Bank's *Monthly Letter* of April 1951 into two tables. In Table VII I-A on the following page, we present the data comparing profits after taxes and book net assets (net worth) in 1950 with 1949.

AS MEMORANDA ITEMS, WE HAVE selected the four manufacturing industries that show the greatest net profit after taxes. These are the pillars of heavy industry. Their performance in 1949 is clearly comparable to 1947 (and 1948 was even a better profits year than 1947 or 1949), but in 1950 it is breathtaking. Forty-five petroleum companies increased their net profits after taxes from $1,413,000,000 in 1949 to $1,730,000,000 in 1950, an increase of 22 per cent. Fifty-five iron and steel corporations increased their net profits after taxes from $555,000,000 in 1949 to $786,000,000 in 1950, an increase of 41 per cent. Sixty-five chemical concerns increased their net profits after taxes from $543,000,000 in 1949 to $743,000,000 in 1950, an increase of 37 per cent. Twenty-six automobile companies increased their net profits after taxes from $857,000,000 in 1949 to $1,054,000,000 in 1950, an increase of 23 per cent.

For 1,693 leading manufacturing corporations, net profits after taxes increased from $7,046,000,000 in 1949 to $9,288,000,000 in 1952, an increase of 32 per cent. No wonder, then, that a special joint study of the SEC and Federal Trade Commission (summarized in *The New York Times* of April 27, 1951) reports that:

> Profits of manufacturing corporations touched the highest point in history during 1950 . . . The report disclosed that the 1950 net income of the corporations before payment of Federal taxes was 61 per cent higher than in 1949, or $23,200,000,000, compared with 1949's total of $14,400,000,000. Net income after taxes of manufacturing corporations in 1950 was estimated at about $12,00,000,000, or 43 per cent more than in 1949.

Increasing State Intervention

The study shows that this phenomenal profit performance occurred despite an increase of almost 100 per cent in provision for Federal taxes.

TABLE VIII-A

MASS OF PROFIT OF LEADING CORPORATIONS

IN 1950 COMPARED WITH 1949,

ACCORDING TO NATIONAL CITY BANK OF NY*

Number of Companies	Industrial Groups	REPORTED NET INCOME AFTER TAXES		Increase % 1949 to 1950	BOOK NET ASSETS AS OF JAN. 1 †	
		1949	1950		1949	1950
		(Millions of Dollars)			(Billions of Dollars)	
(45)	Petroleum products	$1,413	$1,730	22%	$10.7	$11.6
(55)	Iron and steel	555	786	41	4.8	6.1
(65)	Chemical Products	543	743	37	3.2	3.6
(26)	Autos and trucks	857	1054	23	2.8	3.3
1693	Total manufacturing	7046	9288	32	60.7	64.4
98	Total mining, quarrying	219	282	29	1.8	1.9
178	Total trade (retail and wholesale)	577	679	18	4.3	4.6
248	Total transportation	503	873	73	15	15.2
293	Total public utilities	1066	1300	22	12	13.3
99	Total amusements, services, etc.	93	102	10	0.9	1
695	Total finances	964	1040	8	10.6	11.6
3304	GRAND TOTAL	10468	13563	30	96.4	101.9

* National City Bank of New York, Monthly Letter, April 19 61.

† Net assets at beginning of each year are based upon the excess of total balance sheet assets over liabilities; the amounts at which assets are carried on the books are far below present-day values, thereby implying an abnormally high return on net worth.

The Permanent War Economy

The joint study also shows that the larger the assets, the smaller the rate of increase in net profits after taxes, again confirming the Marxian analysis of the results of capital accumulation. Those companies "with assets of $750,000 or less allowed an average profit increase in 1950 over 1949 of 106 per cent." At the other end of the scale, "those of $100,000,000 and over averaged 32 per cent increase in net profits after taxes in 1950 compared with 1949." The previous record year of 1948 was exceeded by 11 per cent.

Returning to the National City Bank study, the percentage increase in net income after taxes in 1950 over 1949 for leading corporations ranges all the way from eight per cent for 695 finance companies to 73 per cent for 248 firms engaged in transportation. Thus, for the grand total of 3,304 companies included in the study, net profits after taxes rose from $10,468,000,000 in 1949 to $13,563,000,000 in 1950, an increase of 30 per cent. The book net assets of these same corporations rose from $95.4 billion in 1949 to $101.9 billion in 1950, with manufacturing representing about half the number of companies and an equivalent portion of total capital investment.

The rate of profit for these same companies in the National City Bank study is shown in Table VIII-B on the following page.

Impressive as is the percentage margin on sales, even more spectacular is the return on net assets. While the performance for leading manufacturing corporations as a whole confirms the results of the SEC study previously cited in Table VII, with an increase in return on net assets from 13.9 per cent in 1949 to 17.1 per cent in 1950, it is interesting to note that the 65 chemical companies increased their return on net assets from 17.1 to 21.3 per cent, and the 26 auto and truck companies went from 30.2 to 32.3 per cent. Thus, for a corporation like General Motors, the most terrific profit-maker in the history of American capitalism, invested capital is paid for every three years!

In every category except finance the return on net assets rose from 1949 to 1950, with the grand total for the entire 3,304 leading corporations rising from 11.0 per cent to 13.3 per cent, which is an increase of over 20 per cent in the rate of return, despite an increase of $6.5 billion in net assets

On the assumption that all capital invested and reinvested is employed in production, the comparison between the return on sales with the return on net assets

Increasing State Intervention

indicates the turnover of capital and its different rates among major industries. "The shorter the period of turnover," says Marx (*Capital* Vol. III, Kerr ed., p.85), "the smaller is the fallow portion of capital as compared with the whole, and the larger will be the appropriated surplus value, other conditions remaining the same." Although it would be preferable to obtain the rate of turnover on capital by dividing total sales by total invested capital, the same result can be obtained by dividing the percentage return on net assets by percentage margin on sales. Inasmuch as the difference between capital turnover in 1950 and in 1949 is negligible, we present below merely the turnover times for major industrial categories, based on Table VIII-B, on the following page, in 1950:

Industrial Group	Manu-facturing	Mining, Quar-rying	Trade (retail and wholesale)	Transfor-mation	Public Util-ities	Amuse-meats, Services, etc.	Total all Groups
Turnover in 1950	2.2	1.2	3.9	0.7	0.7	1.9	1.7

In other words, for the companies contained in the National City Bank study as a whole, capital was turned over 1.7 times in 1950, or about every seven months. The variation among industrial groups is extreme, ranging all the way from the slow turnover time of 0.7 in such heavy fixed capital industries as transportation and public utilities to the very rapid turnover of 3.9 in retail and wholesale trade, where a tremendous volume of business can be done with a relatively small capital investment as capital turns over once in almost every three months. This, of course, is another reason why calculating the rate of profit solely with reference to sales is completely misleading. For total manufacturing, the turnover is 2.2, but for autos and trucks the turn over time is 3.6, indicating why the automobile industry is so profitable.

The Permanent War Economy

TABLE VIII-B
RATE OF PROFIT OF LEADING CORPORATIONS IN 1950 COMPARED WITH 1949. ACCORDING TO NATIONAL CITY BANK OF NY*

Number of Companies	Industrial Groups	% RETURN ON NET ASSETS †		% MARGIN ON SALES	
		1949	1950	1949	1950
(45)	Petroleum Products	13.2%	14.9%	9.9%	10.8%
(55)	Iron and Steel	11.6	15.3	7.2	8.1
(65)	Chemical Products	17.1	21.3	10.3	11.7
(26)	Autos and Trucks	30.2	32.3	8.9	8.9
1693	Total Manufacturing	13.9	17.1	6.8	7.7
98	Total Mining, Quarrying	12	15	12.3	12.6
178	Total Trade (Retail and Wholesale)	13.4	14.8	3.3	3.8
248	Total Transportation	3.4	5.7	4.8	7.7
293	Total Public Utilities	8.8	9.8	11.9	13.1
99	Total Amusements Services, etc.	9.9	10.5	4.8	6.7
695	Total Finance	9.1	9	-	-
3304	GRAND TOTAL	11	13.3	6.6	7.7

*National City Bank of New York, *Monthly Letter*, April 1951.

† "Net assets at beginning of each year are based upon the excess of total balance sheet assets over liabilities; the amounts at which assets are carried on the books are far below present-day values," thereby implying an abnormally high return on net worth.

Increasing State Intervention

THE BOURGEOISIE AS A CLASS recognizes, although with considerable reluctance, that government planning and state intervention and compulsory controls are necessary as a matter of survival if the aims of the Permanent War Economy are to be fulfilled. As Truman stated in the President's Economic Message to Congress of January 12, 1951:

> A defense emergency requires far more planning than is customary or desirable in normal peacetime. The military build-up is a planned effort. The mobilization of industrial support for this military build-up is a planned effort. The industrial cutbacks and civilian restraints, necessary to achieve military and economic mobilization, are planned efforts ... In these critical times, it is recognized that Government must assume leadership in this planning. It has the prime responsibility for national security. It has access to the basic information. The most important operation toward this end is broad programming of various major requirements; the balancing of these requirements against supply; and the development of policies to satisfy needs according to priority of purpose.

These are the functions that under capitalist theory are normally reserved for prices and the market economy. That the market increasingly atrophies as a regulator of production or allocator of resources compelling increasing state intervention is the most distinctive change in the *modus operandi* of capitalism as the war economy develops. The question logically arises: why cannot voluntary controls work? Charles E. Wilson, defense mobilization director, gave a brief and direct answer to this question in a speech reported in *The New York Times* of January 18, 1951:

> What about our economy in the face of such expansion, such expenditures, such use of materials? How do we keep it from running away? There is only one answer – controls. I hate the word – so do you. But

there is no other way. *Voluntary methods will not work. That has been proven.* (Italics mine, T.N.V.)

In other words, experience has shown that appeals to loyalty, patriotism, etc., are no substitute for the state power of coercion. Practical experience has thus gone a long way toward reconciling the bourgeoisie to increasing state intervention, especially when the ratio of war outlays to total production exceeds ten per cent. As that arch exponent of laissez-faire capitalism, Ludwig von Mises, expresses the alternative (*Economic Planning*, 1945, p.13): "If the market is not allowed to steer the whole economic apparatus, the government must do it." To be sure, von Mises argues that even in wartime, if the "right methods" are used, controls are unnecessary (*Bureaucracy*, 1944, pp.30-31):

> It has been objected that the market system is at any rate quite inappropriate under the conditions brought about by a great war. If the market mechanism were to be left alone, it would be impossible for the government to get all the equipment needed. The scarce factors of production required for the production of armaments would be wasted for civilian uses which, in a war, are to be considered as less important, even as luxury and waste. Thus it was imperative to resort to the system of government-established priorities and to create the necessary bureaucratic apparatus.
>
> The error of this reasoning is that it does not realize that the necessity for giving the government full power to determine for what kinds of production the various raw materials should be used is not an outcome of the war but of the methods applied in financing the war expenditure.
>
> If the whole amount of money needed for the conduct of the war had been collected by taxes and by borrowing from the public, everybody would have been forced to restrict his consumption drastically. With a money income (after taxes) much lower than before, the consumers

Increasing State Intervention

would have stopped buying many goods they used to buy before the war. The manufacturers, precisely because they are driven by the profit motive, would have discontinued producing such civilian goods and would have shifted to the production of those goods which the government, now by virtue of the inflow of taxes the biggest buyer on the market, would be ready to buy.

However, a great part of the war expenditure is financed by an increase of currency in circulation and by borrowing from the commercial banks. On the other hand, under price control, it is illegal to raise commodity prices. With higher money incomes and with unchanged commodity prices people would not only not have restricted but have increased their buying of goods for their own consumption. To avoid this, it was necessary to take recourse to rationing and to government-imposed priorities. These measures were needed because previous government interference that paralyzed the operation of the market resulted in paradoxical and highly unsatisfactory conditions. Not the insufficiency of the market mechanism but the inadequacy of previous government meddling with market phenomena made the priority system unavoidable. In this as in many other instances the bureaucrats see in the failure of their preceding measures a proof that further inroads into the market system are necessary.

We may not be pardoned for reproducing at length the views of one of the last living theoreticians of nineteenth century capitalism, but his views are unique and the subject is important. Among the factors that von Mises conveniently overlooks are the political impossibility of curtailing consumption so drastically by reliance on fiscal policy alone, the fact that government competition with private industry for scarce materials would accelerate the inflation that is inevitable once a sizable portion of production is devoted to war purposes, that confiscatory taxation (probably including a capital levy) undermining the very foundations of capitalism would be required, that Draconian fiscal controls are themselves inconsistent with the "automatic" theory of the

The Permanent War Economy

market and would undoubtedly require implementation through forced savings and direct exercise of the police power of the state to ensure compliance, and that even if it were prudent for the bourgeoisie to ignore the lessons of history and accept the advice of von Mises, the time required to enable the state to direct production through indirect controls would unquestionably be fatal.

THE TIME ELEMENT, ESPECIALLY IS recognized by the authors of the only comprehensive analysis of production controls in the war economy (*Wartime Production Controls* by David Novice, Melvin Anshan and W.C. Trapper, Columbia University Press, 1949, p.16):

> In peace the major influence upon economic activity is profit. The ultimate measure of the desirability of undertaking certain industrial activities or carrying them out in certain ways is the anticipated effect of the final result on the individual enterprise's profit and loss statement. Since the peacetime economy is made up of a multitude of individual enterprises, it is important to each one, *but not to the nation*, whether its particular choice of policy or method is profitable or not. The classic justification for non-interference by government in business is that the accidents of individual choice result in greatest possible production from the national resources. *In time of war, however, the nation cannot wait for each of these individual experiments to produce the desired result. An over-all control of economic activity must be substituted for individual planning under the profit motive.* And not only must the control agency make the industrial decisions; it must do its job without either the profit and loss test of the wisdom of its policies and efficiency of its methods, or the time required to apply any other test. (Italics mine – T.N.V.)

In other words, when it is a question of *survival*, neither price nor profit can guide the allocation of resources. Nor, for that matter, can the state as a general rule be expected to operate in response to such motives. After flirting with the reasons for this

Increasing State Intervention

fact for three pages, the authors finally come sufficiently close to hitting the nail on the head (p.18): "Because the effect of price is *random and non-selective*, in time of war price manipulation cannot be used as the major tool for directing the use of the nation's resources." (Italics mine – T.N.V.) It therefore follows that: "*As the volume of military requirements increases, the area of control must grow. Ultimately, in the total war economy there must be total industrial control.*" (Italics mine – T.N.V.)

Not only is controlling production for specific objectives through the price mechanism like scattering seeds to the four winds to plant a kernel of wheat in a particular spot, but it places the various sections of the capitalist class in an untenable position with respect to their fellow capitalist competitors. As Novice et al. put it, citing the experience of 1942, pp.67-68:

> Caught in the competitive forces of the free market, no single producer of refrigerators or passenger automobiles could contemplate closing his doors in the face of eager crowds of customers (and endangering the continuance of his carefully nurtured distributor organization) in order to prepare his production lines to make machine guns, tanks, guns, and airplane subassemblies. *Such decisions could be made only on an industry-wide basis, and this could be brought about swiftly only through government direction.* (Italics mine – T.N.V.)

Moreover, in many cases, as previously mentioned, it would be impossible to induce the desired capital investment solely by appealing to the profit instincts of individual capitalists. As a matter of record, the Federal government financed in the neighborhood of $35 billion of industrial, military and housing facilities during World War II. Almost half of this total was for the creation of new manufacturing facilities, the vast majority of which private capital could not have undertaken even if it possessed the necessary accumulations of capital for the simple reason that, without substantial state aid, the prospects of profits would be far too remote. To be sure, many of these facilities were subsequently sold to private capital at a fraction of their cost, so that those whose products had peacetime uses

The Permanent War Economy

could be operated by private industry at a profit. Nevertheless, the fact remains that exclusive reliance on the immediate profit motive to direct investment into desired channels during a major war (and even during a minor war as at present) would markedly reduce the military effectiveness of any industrialized nation.

The preeminent role played by state capital accumulations during World War II occurred, it must be emphasized, despite the huge aggregations of private capital that existed and which received the overwhelming portion of war contracts.

> Analysis . . . indicated that in the third quarter of 1942 the 100 largest company consumers of each basic metal used the following percentages of the metal consumed by all manufacturing companies: carbon steel, 49 per cent; alloy steel, 70 per cent; copper, 79 per cent; copper-base alloy, 66 per cent; and aluminum, 81 per cent. A combined listing (eliminating duplications) yielded a total of 391 different companies (approximately 2,000 plants). In the third quarter of 1942 these 391 companies used 56 per cent of the carbon steel consumed by all manufacturing companies; 75 per cent of the alloy steel, 82 per cent of copper; 71 per cent of copper-base alloy; and 85 per cent of aluminum . . . The same 391 companies shipped more than three-fourths of the total dollar value of all direct military-type products. (*Wartime Production Controls*, p.346.)

ASIDE FROM THE PROBLEMS OF PRODUCTION, which requires direct state controls, such as priorities, allocations and the over-riding directive power of the state, the state, representing the interests of the bourgeoisie as a whole, must try to keep the inflation within tolerable limits. Naturally, inflation is so managed as to place the main burden on the backs of the working classes and many individual capitalists amass huge and quick profits. Still, an unbridled inflation can interfere with production and disrupt the plans of the military and civilian state bureaucracies. Accordingly, state intervention is extended wherever necessary, without any objections from contemporary American financiers, further circumscribing the area within which private capital is permitted by its own state to function. An excellent example is the recent decision to make the government the sole importer of rubber and tin. As Wilson's first quarterly report states (*The New York Times*, April 2, 1951):

> By designating Government agencies to act as exclusive importers of commodities, such as rubber and tin, and by working in international commodity committees to allocate scarce materials among free countries, we are helping to end the current scramble for these materials which has forced their prices unnecessarily high.

The *international* aspects of the Permanent War Economy are yet another reason why increasing state intervention is mandatory for American bourgeoisie as a matter of self-preservation, but we must leave to another article treatment of its implications.

We shall also leave for subsequent analysis consideration of the implications of the various techniques used to try to "freeze" the class struggle and of the increasingly obvious Bonapartist tendencies that may be discerned as a result of what amounts to an "interlocking directorate" between the military bureaucracy and big business.

The virtual guarantee of profits by the state is the *sine qua non* of increasing state intervention under the Permanent War Economy. The scandals in the letting of war contracts never seem to deter repetition of the most unsavory performances of the past, even when the cast of characters is changed. "By far the most important lesson," state the authors of *Wartime Production Controls* (p.382), "is that the power to contract is the power to control."

While the very mechanism of price control, based on perpetuating a rate of profit representing an all-time modern historical peak, is balm for the wounds of the more individualistically-minded members of the bourgeoisie, at least the larger ones, the forces that constantly work toward a transformation of traditional capitalism proceed with a logic of their own. The Office of Price Stabilization issues various types of "mark-up" regulations that result in the fixing of price ceilings at levels guaranteed to

The Permanent War Economy

maintain super-profits, but along comes its boss, Eric Johnston, Economic Stabilization Administrator, to announce (April 21, 1945) that "no industry will be permitted to raise prices if its dollar profits amount to 85 per cent of the average of its three best years during the 1946-49 period, inclusive."

Whether this policy will be implemented remains to be seen. And, as we have demonstrated, profits in 1946 to 1949 were so high that 85 per cent of this level hardly represents impoverishment. The significant point, however, is that it is difficult to foresee the limits of state intervention, assuming that the Permanent War Economy continues for an indefinite number of years. The promulgation of a profit-limiting policy, even if strictly confined to paper as was the case with OPA during World War II, would horrify the rugged individualists of the pre-1941 era but today is a necessary genuflection to the exigencies of the class struggle.

The all-pervading character of state intervention, with its *modifications* of the nature and laws of capitalism, should not come as a surprise to any Marxist, for more than 70 years ago Engels wrote (*Origin of Family*, p.207):

> But it (the state power of coercion) increases in same ratio in which the class antagonisms become more pronounced, and in which neighboring states become larger and more populous. A conspicuous example is modern Europe, where the class struggles and wars of conquest have nursed the public power to such a size that it threatens to swallow the whole society and the state itself.

The New International May 1951 — T.N. VANCE

Part IV — Military-Economic Imperialism

It is precisely in its international aspects that the new stage of capitalism, which we have termed the Permanent War Economy, reveals most clearly its true character as well as its inability to solve any of the fundamental problems of mankind. This is not due to any failure on the part of the American state to recognize the decisive importance of foreign economic policy, as witness both the Gray and Rockefeller reports within the past year, but rather to the historical impasse in which capitalism finds itself.

The capitalist world is not what it was in 1919 or in 1929. Even the depression-shrunk capitalist market of 1939 was relatively larger, and offered greater opportunities for profitable investment of American surplus capital, than the crisis-ridden world of today, confronted as it is with the unrelenting pressure exerted by Stalinist imperialism. Just as the domestic economy is increasingly dominated by the impact of war outlays, both direct and indirect, even more so is foreign policy in every ramification subordinated to military (euphoniously termed "security") considerations.

The tragedy of the situation, from the point of view of American imperialism, as we have previously pointed out (see especially *After Korea – What?* in the November-December 1950 issue of *The New International*) and as the more far-sighted representatives of the bourgeoisie perceive, is that American imperialism cannot hope to defeat Stalinist imperialism by other than military means; and yet a military victory, even if it be achieved, threatens to destroy the very foundations upon which capitalism now rests. Not only would the military defeat of Stalinist imperialism remove the entire political base upon which the Permanent War Economy depends for justification of huge war outlays, without which the economy would collapse, but the very process of achieving a military solution of the mortal threat posed by the existence of an aggressive Stalinist imperialism is guaranteed to complete the political isolation of American imperialism, undermine its economic foundations, and unleash socialist revolution on a world scale.

THE ARENA OF STRUGGLE between American and Stalinist imperialism is truly global, but it necessarily centers on Europe and Asia. There are sound economic reasons for increasing American preoccupation with these areas; aside from their obvious political importance as actual or potential foci of Third Campism. As Defense Mobilizer

The Permanent War Economy

Charles E. Wilson* graphically points out in his second quarterly report (*New York Times*, July 5, 1951):

> Potentially, the United States is the most powerful country in the world but we cannot undertake to resist world communism without our allies. Neither we nor any other free nation can stand alone long without, inviting encirclement and subjugation.
>
> If either of the two critical areas on the border of the communist world – Western Europe or Asia – were to be overrun by communism, the rest of the free world would be immensely weakened, not only in the morale that grows out of the solidarity of free countries but also in the economic and military strength that would be required to resist further aggression. Western Europe, for instance, has the greatest industrial concentration in the world outside of the United States. Its strategic location and military potential are key factors in the free world's defense against Soviet aggression.
>
> If Western Europe fell, the Soviet Union would gain control of almost 300 million people, including the largest pool of skilled manpower in the world. Its steel production would be increased by 55 million tons a year to 94 million tons, a total almost equal to our own production. Its coal production would jump to 950 million tons, compared to our 550 million. Electric energy in areas of Soviet domination would be increased from 130 to 350 billion kilowatt-hours, or almost up to our 400 billion.
>
> Raw materials from other areas of the free world are the lifeblood of industry in the United States and Western Europe. If the Kremlin overran Asia, it would boost its share of the world's oil reserves from 6 per cent to over half ... and it would control virtually all of the world's

---

* This is "Electric Charlie". (EH)

Military-Economic Imperialism

natural rubber supply and vast quantities of other materials vital to rearmament.

And in manpower, in the long run apt to be the final arbiter, should Stalinism conquer Europe and Asia, American imperialism would be outnumbered by a ratio of at least four to one!

In the words of the Gray *Report to the President on Foreign Economic Policies* (*New York Times*, Nov. 13, 1950):

> We have now entered a new phase of foreign economic relations. The necessity for rapidly building defensive strength now confronts this nation and other free nations as well. This requires a shift in the use of our economic resources. It imposes new burdens on the gradually reviving economies of other nations. Our foreign economic policies must be adjusted to these new burdens... Our own rearmament program will require us to import strategic raw materials in greater quantities than before.

Wilson, in his report previously cited, hints at the dependence of the American war economy on the minerals and raw materials of the "underdeveloped" areas:

> For most of these metals [cobalt, columbium, molybdenum, nickel and tungsten and other alloying metals] we are dependent primarily on foreign sources, and defense requirements of other nations are also increasing.

It remains, however, for the Rockefeller report (*Advisory Board on International Development,* summarized in *The New York Times,* March 12, 1951) to place the problem

The Permanent War Economy

of raw materials in proper perspective, and at the same time to reveal the weaknesses that have accumulated in the structure of American imperialism. The section is worth quoting in full:

> With raw material shortages developing rapidly, an immediate step-up in the production of key minerals is vital if we are to be able to meet the growing military demands without harsh civilian curtailments.
>
> *Two billion dollars energetically and strategically invested over the next few years could swell the outflow of vital materials from the underdeveloped regions by $1,000,000,000 a year.*
>
> This increased production can best be carried out under *private* auspices and wherever possible *local capital* within the country *should be encouraged to enter into partnership with United States investors in these projects.*
>
> Both immediate and longer-range peace needs warn of grave consequences unless such a development program is undertaken *promptly*. Although the United States accounts for more than *half* of the world's heavy industry production, it mines only about a *third* of the world's annual output of the *fifteen basic minerals*.
>
> Soviet shipments to the United States of chrome and manganese, so essential for steel-making, have already been choked back. The advisory board hopes that the people in the Soviet-controlled areas will be able to regain their freedom. However, today their trade is tightly controlled.
>
> *In the manganese and tungsten deposits of Latin America, Africa and Asia, the chrome production of Turkey and the Philippines, the timber stands of Brazil and Chile, the pulpwood of Labrador lie resources for developing substitute sources for materials which come from areas now dominated by the Soviets or most vulnerable to aggression.*

Military-Economic Imperialism

> Continued dependence of the free nations upon *imports and markets* of Soviet controlled areas weakens them in enforcing measures of economic defense.
>
> Peace, free institutions and human well-being can be assured only within the framework of an *expanding* world economy.
>
> With an expanding productive base it will become possible to increase individual productivity, raise living levels, increase international trade, meet the needs of the growing populations in the underdeveloped areas and perhaps even resettle peoples from the industrial areas under growing population pressure.
>
> Our objective should not be to *"mine and get out"* but to strive for a balanced economic development which will lay an enduring base for continued economic progress. *Workers should receive a full share in the benefits as quickly as possible.*
>
> *Improving the standard of living of the people of the underdeveloped areas is a definite strategic objective of the United States foreign policy.*
>
> The advisory board recommends the continued encouragement of the free labor unions in the underdeveloped areas.
>
> And that the International Labor Organization's recommendations as to fair labor standards be used as a guide for minimum labor standards in the underdeveloped areas. (Italics mine – T.N.V.)

Actually, coincident with the outbreak of the Korean war, American imperialism was aware of its vulnerability in strategic materials in the event of continuing "hot" and "cold" war with Stalinist imperialism and sought to remedy the situation. As Paul P. Kennedy puts it in *The New York Times* of August 5, 1951:

> The shift in emphasis from purely economic to economic-military aid within the foreign assistance program began to take vague shape as

early as July 1950. At that time Mr. Foster,* in something of a surprise move, advocated the diversion, in some countries, of ECA** matching funds toward military production facilities.

The Administration has requested $8.5 billion for fiscal 1952, of which $6.3 billion would be in military aid and $2.2 billion for continued economic aid. Economic assistance is now defined as "providing resources necessary for the support of adequate defense efforts and for the maintenance, during defense mobilization, of the country's general economic stability." In view of the strong outburst by that staunch defender of democracy and the Democratic Party, Senator Connally of Texas, that "the United States can't support the whole free world and remain solvent," it may be wondered why there should be any bourgeois opposition to a program geared exclusively to serving the military-economic needs of American imperialism. The answer lies in two facets of the program that have not been as well publicized as the immediate request for $8.5 billion.

It now appears that the $8.5 billion is intended as only part of a three-year $25 billion program. Mr. Kennedy, in the same article previously cited, states:

> Both Secretary of State Dean Acheson and Secretary of Defense George C. Marshall have estimated that there is little possibility of building up the free world's fighting force on less than the $8.5 billion the first year, *which would be the first installment of $25 billion over a three-year spread.* (Italics mine – T.N.V.)

---

* William C. Foster, administrator of the ECA. (EH)

** The Economic Cooperation Administration popularly referred to as the Marshall Plan. (EH)

Military-Economic Imperialism

This is approximately twice as large as forecasts made earlier in the year by Administration spokesmen. Admittedly a large portion of Military Assistance funds will go to Asia and the Pacific area.

Again quoting Mr. Kennedy:

> The ECA answer to Senator Connally's charge that the United States is spreading itself too thin by going into Asia and the Pacific area is that; *production of materials is the greatest present problem. To get the materials available in Asia, the United States must give in exchange technical and economic assistance,* the agency contends. (Italics mine – T.N.V.)

THE INCREASING DEPENDENCE of American imperialism on foreign sources, chiefly present or former colonial areas, of key raw materials is attributable to many causes. Rapid exhaustion of natural resources, particularly iron ore and petroleum, within the United States, in response to the almost insatiable appetite of the Permanent War Economy for means of destruction and the ability to transport and operate them, is clearly a factor of considerable importance. Along with this has gone the sizable increase in production, coupled with tremendous accumulations of capital, analyzed in previous articles in this series. Historically, however, the decisive factor has been the utter failure of American imperialism to operate in the traditional finance capital manner.

This failure has not been due to any lack of desire on the part of American imperialism to export a sizable portion of its accumulations of private capital, thereby acquiring both markets and sources of primary materials in sufficient quantities to maintain the domestic level of profit and simultaneously to assure a steady flow of those raw materials essential to industry in war or peace. In part, this development has been due to the fateful consequences of the Permanent War Economy. The state, as demonstrated in the May-June 1951 issue of *The New International* (Chapter III), guarantees profits for all practical purposes. The market incentives to export 10 per cent or more of both production and accumulated capital, traditional in the first three

The Permanent War Economy

decades of the twentieth century, in order to maintain the profitability of industry as a whole, have atrophied to a surprising extent. The state now consumes the largest portion of accumulated capital. The state likewise undertakes by far the major responsibility for capital exports in the form of government loans and grants. The nature of state capital exports is such, with political considerations predominant, that markets and raw materials tend to be reduced in importance.

In largest part, however, the failure of American imperialism to perform according to the early textbooks is traceable to steady dwindling of the world capitalist market. How can American capitalists invest in Chinese tungsten mines, when China has come within the orbit of Stalinism and American capital has been forcefully driven out of China? Such examples of forcible exclusions of American imperialism from important sources of strategic materials could be multiplied many times since the advance of Stalinist imperialism in the post-World War II period.

Even more significant, however, is the fact that in the non-Stalinist world the climate for American investments has not been exactly favorable. Nationalization, confiscation, the threat of expropriation, and a host of other factors have combined to make private American capitalists extremely cautious about investing surplus capital in any foreign enterprise. This was not the case in the 1920's, when American net foreign investments increased about 100 per cent during the decade ending in 1931, at which time they reached a peak variously estimated at between $15 billion and $18 billion.

Considering the increases that have occurred in production, accumulation of capital, and the price level, a comparable figure for today would be in the neighborhood of $50 billion! Yet, despite the absence of data, it is clear that *American net foreign investments today are lower than they were in 1931*. What the precise figure is we cannot say, as recently the first such census since before the war was undertaken by the Department of Commerce and the results will not be available for another year. Nevertheless, according to *The New York Times* of May 31, 1951, which reported the news of the new census, "Sample data collected by the Department of Commerce in recent years indicate that the new census will show a value of more than $13,000,000,000." This figure represents direct investments as distinct from portfolio

Military-Economic Imperialism

investments, but it is most unlikely that portfolio investments will be more than a few billion dollars, as bonds of foreign governments have not proved very attractive to American investors after the sad experiences of widespread defaults in the 1920's and 1930's.

The fact of the matter is that, from the point of view of American imperialism, American net foreign investments should be at least three times their present level. But this is a manifest impossibility, both politically and economically. Neither the capital nor the market is available, even if all the necessary incentives were present, which is obviously not the case.

It may be easier to grasp the magnitude of the problem that confronts American imperialism today if we first look at the figures representing the heyday of American imperialism and then compare them with the present situation. The tabulation below portrays the movement of American foreign investments, both gross and net, from 1924 to 1930.

UNITED STATES PRIVATE LONG-TERM FOREIGN INVESTMENTS 1924-1930 (Millions of Dollars)		
Year	Total of Net New Foreign Investment*	New Long-Term Capital Outflow †
1924	$1,005	$ 680
1925	1,092	550
1926	1,272	821
1927	1,465	987
1928	1,577	1,310
1929	1,017	636
1930	1,069	364
Average	1,214	764
* Includes new foreign loans plus new net direct foreign investment. † Total foreign investment minus amortization receipts and net sales of outstanding foreign securities.		

The Permanent War Economy

The data are based on *The United Slates in the World Economy* (US Department of Commerce, 1943) and taken from a paper, *Foreign Investment and American Employment*, delivered by Randall Hinshaw of the Board of Governors of the Federal Reserve System before the 1946 annual meeting of the American Economics Association. During this seven-year period, gross foreign investment was never less than $1 billion in any one year, and averaged over $1.2 billion annually. The large proportion of portfolio investments that existed resulted in heavy amortization payments which, together with net sales by American investors of outstanding foreign securities, reduced the net foreign investment during this period to an average of $764 million. The sizable difference between gross and net foreign investment in 1930 is due to the onset of the world crisis and the large-scale liquidation by Americans of foreign investments which, in turn, aggravated the world crisis.

During the 1930's, the world-wide depression, plus the acts and threats of Nazi imperialism, caused a shrinkage of American foreign investments of about $4 billion. The Department of Commerce thus estimates total American foreign investments at the end of 1939 at $11,365,000,000. It is apparent that there was a further decline during the war and, beginning in 1946, a relatively modest increase. While the estimates of American foreign investments in the postwar period are undoubtedly quite crude, we summarize below the movement of United States private long-term capital (from the June 1951 issue of *Survey of Current Business*) as indicative of the pitifully low levels to which traditional American imperialism has sunk:

OUTFLOW OF UNITED STATES PRIVATE LONG-TERM CAPITAL, 1948-1950 (Millions of Dollars)		
Year	Total Outflow of Private Long-Term Capital*	Net Outflow of Private Long-Term Capital†
1948	$1,557	$ 748
1949	1,566	796
1950	2,184	1,168
Average	1,769	904

*Includes total of direct foreign investments plus other investments, as loans, and is not comparable to the similar column in the previous table for 1924-1930, which is net of direct investments.
† This column is conceptually comparable to the similar column in the previous table.

Military-Economic Imperialism

While an average net foreign investment of $904 million appears to be significantly higher than the $764 million shown for the period 1924-1930, such a conclusion would be totally misleading. In the first place, the higher figure for 1950 is due entirely to a sharp bulge in the third quarter, amounting to $698 million, which is mostly in the form of portfolio investments, obviously a result of a sharp flight of capital from the dollar following the outbreak of the Korean war. That this was a temporary phenomenon, not possibly to be confused with any resurgence of traditional American imperialism, is shown by the sharp drop in the fourth quarter of 1950 to a mere $60 million of net foreign investment. Moreover, the preliminary figure for the first quarter of 1951 is only $212 million.

In other words, in dollar terms, net foreign investments of American capital are currently at the same level as twenty years ago. While this amount was consistent with the requirements of an expanding American imperialism at that time, today it is nothing but a source of frustration to the policy-makers among the bourgeoisie. For, these exports of private capital are taking place today when gross private domestic investment is averaging about $40 billion annually or more, and when net private capital formation runs from $25-30 billion a year. Net foreign investments at present should actually be at least four times their current level in order merely to match the performance of two decades ago. Another way of expressing the same thought is to equate the present volume of net foreign investments to about $200 million annually to permit direct comparison with the pre-depression period. It is therefore hardly surprising that American imperialism is having difficulties in obtaining adequate supplies of the key raw materials required to keep the economy operating at capacity.

Without doubt, exact information on the changing character and composition of American foreign investments, particularly direct investments, would throw even more light on the raw materials shortage. Unfortunately, it is not even possible to guess at the profound changes that must have taken place during and since the war. We would expect the trend that manifested itself prior to the war, when between 1929 and 1939 American investments in the Western Hemisphere increased from 59 per cent of the total to 70 per cent, to have continued. To be sure, the Western Hemisphere is not exactly barren of raw materials, but aside from a relatively few projects, in such countries as Venezuela and Bolivia, the emphasis has not been on the mining of

The Permanent War Economy

strategic minerals. Thus, the disparity between the needs of the Permanent War Economy and the ability of American imperialists to deliver the necessary raw materials may be even greater than the dollar figures on foreign investments would indicate.

THE VACUUM CAUSED BY the paucity of private exports of capital has had to be filled by the state. That is the primary significance of the Marshall Plan and all other state foreign aid programs. The amounts have been quite sizable, averaging about $5 billion annually since the end of World War II, even according to the admittedly conservative figures of the Department of Commerce (as reported in the March, 1951, *Survey of Current Business*). The data, by country, are shown in the tabulation on the following page.

Gross foreign aid by the American government during this period totaled about $30.2 billion, but reverse grants and returns on grants plus principal collected on credits equaled $2.4 billion, bringing the net total to $27.8 billion. How much of the $9.2 billion of credits will be returned and how, much will ultimately assume the status of outright gifts remains to be seen. It is interesting to note, however, that as of December 31, 1950, according to the Department of Commerce,

> World War I indebtedness [owing to the United States government] amounted to $16,276 million, of which $4,842 million represented interest which was due and unpaid.

It is also pertinent to observe that preliminary figures for the first quarter of 1951 indicate that net foreign aid exceeded $1.1 billion, amounting at an annual rate to about $4.5 billion for the year. The probability is that the actual figure will exceed $5 billion, as the transition from economic to military aid is well under way.

With two-thirds of net grants and almost 90 per cent of net credits having gone to Marshall Plan countries, the result has been that these major allies being sought by American imperialism have received almost three-fourths of total net foreign aid

Military-Economic Imperialism

	FOREIGN AID BY COUNTRY		
	July 1, 1945 Through December 31, 1950		
	(Millions of Dollars)		
Country	*Net Grants**	*Net Credits†*	*Net Foreign Aid*
Belgium-Luxembourg	$ 509	$ 174	$ 683
Britain	1,523	4,487	6,010
France	1,873	2,037	3,910
Germany	3,026	67	3,093
Greece	1,100	98	1,198
Italy	1,689	357	2,046
Netherlands	549	381	930
Turkey	166	82	248
Other ERP Countries	1,837	327	2,164
ERP SUB-TOTAL	12,272	8,010	20,282
Other Europe	1,088	451	1,539
American Republics	135	219	354
China-Formosa	1,567	116	1,683
Japan	1,706	14	1,720
Korea	333	21	354
Philippines	655	100	755
All Other Countries	851	265	1,116
GRAND TOTAL	$18,607	$9,196	$27,803

* Assistance that takes the form of an outright gift for which no payment is expected, or which at most involves an obligation on the part of the receiver to extend reciprocal aid to the US or other countries.
† Assistance under an agreement that calls for ultimate repayment.

The Permanent War Economy

extended since the end of World War II. Clearly, there is room for expansion of aid in many directions to hoped-for and deserving allies, actual or potential. Nor will the fact that almost one-half of total net foreign aid has been awarded to Britain, France and Germany escape the attention of those who appreciate the full significance of American military-economic strategy.

The policy of purchasing allies with government grants and credits in order better to contain expanding Stalinist imperialism did not originate with the Marshall Plan, which began operations in April 1948. As a matter of record, more than one-half of total net foreign aid ($14.5 billion out of the $27.8 billion total) was disbursed prior to the launching of the Marshall Plan. The Marshall Plan merely continued an already established policy by changing somewhat the form of aid and creating a new agency to administer it.

Some of the major categories that received forcing aid (on a gross basis) prior to April 1948 are:

Category	(Millions of Dollars)
Special British loan	$ 3,760
UNRRA, post-UNRRA, and interim aid	3,172
Civilian supplies	2,360
Export-Import Bank loans	2,087
Lend-Lease	1,968
Surplus property (incl. merchant ships)	1,234
TOTAL	$14,571

Military-Economic Imperialism

Thus, these six categories accounted for the overwhelming bulk of foreign aid prior to the ECA program. They reveal quite clearly the unique rôle of "relief and rehabilitation" under the Permanent War Economy. It will be recalled that from 1946-1950 (see Basic Characteristics of the Permanent War Economy in January-February, 1951, issue of *The New International*, Chapter I in this book) indirect war outlays played a crucial role in maintaining the ratio of war outlays to total output at the 10 per cent level. Virtually equal in magnitude to direct war outlays, indirect war outlays were indispensable in maintaining the Permanent War Economy at a successful rate. And expenditures for relief and rehabilitation averaged about one-third of total indirect war outlays during this period. As a matter of fact, there is good evidence to believe that if proper valuation were given to Army-administered supplies, especially in Germany, and Japan, the role of relief and rehabilitation would be even greater than the figures indicate.

Naturally, a large portion of the billions of dollars spent for relief and rehabilitation fulfilled humanitarian purposes. Nor is it possible or necessary to assess the motives that animated Washington at this time. The decisive fact is that relief and rehabilitation expenditures, accomplished what private export of capital could not. The state began to acquire a major interest in foreign economic programs, as well as to relieve any pressure that might develop due to the rapid accumulation of capital. If, in the process, recipients of state foreign aid were "persuaded" to grant American imperialism military bases and to pursue various political and economic policies desired by Washington, so much the better. The *quid pro quo* generally present in American foreign aid programs became even more obvious with the launching of the Marshall Plan. Objectively, therefore, state foreign aid has served to fill the void left by the failure of private capital to function in a traditional imperialist manner and has served to bolster the political program of American imperialism.

ADMITTED MILITARY AID is now rapidly supplanting economic aid. In reality, of course, the entire foreign aid program directly or indirectly contributes to the grand strategy of American military policy. In this respect, state intervention in the foreign economic field parallels, and even leads, state intervention in the domestic economy, as increasingly a higher proportion of state expenditures are for "defense" purposes.

The Permanent War Economy

While it is true that the program officially labeled "Mutual Defense Assistance Program," apparently to be called by Congress "Mutual Security Program," spent the $516 million included in the total foreign aid analyzed above in the year 1950, it would be a mistake to conclude that admitted military aid occurred only during the past year. For example, there is the so-called Greek-Turkish aid program, which by the end of 1950 had disbursed some $656 million. Of this amount, $165 million was spent prior to the launching of the Marshall Plan, $258 million during the last nine months of 1948, $172 million in 1949, and $61 million in 1950. That this program has been overwhelmingly military in character can hardly be denied. Other programs, such as China, smaller in monetary cost, could be mentioned. As the chart below shows, even on the official definition, there has always been some military aid since the end of World War II. Through the first quarter of 1951, military foreign aid has admittedly reached $2 billion. In reality, of course, the figure has been much higher, and now openly exceeds so-called foreign economic aid.

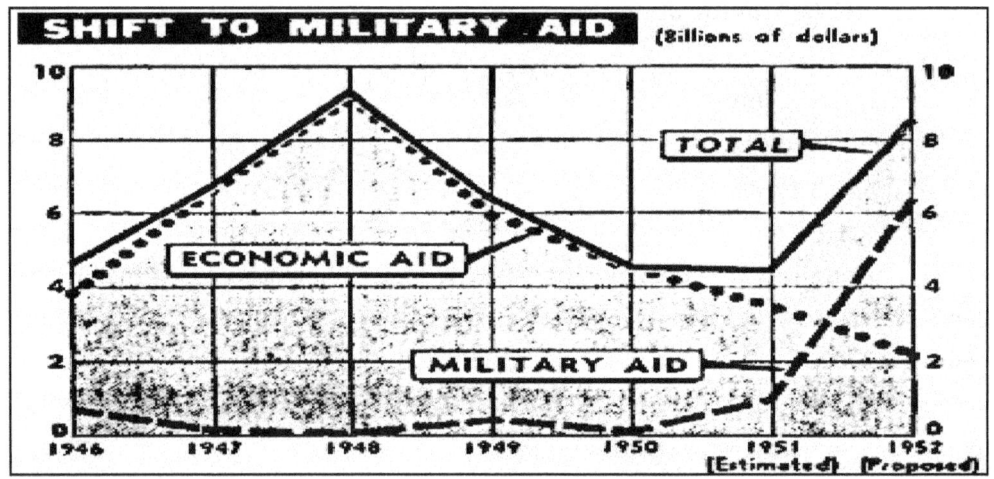

Figure 6 From the *New York Times*, Aug. 5, 1951

By 1952, admitted military foreign aid is expected to account for three-fourths of total foreign aid. This is without half a billion dollars which overseas bases, included

Military-Economic Imperialism

in the military construction program. Officially labeled economic foreign aid, which reached a peak exceeding $8 billion in 1948, and has been averaging about $5 billion annually, will decline to an estimated $2 billion. On this basis, even a recalcitrant Congress may be expected to continue to vote for these sizable outlays without too much difficulty. The possibilities of further increasing state foreign aid through pouring dollars into the bottomless pit of "mutual security" are clearly almost without limit. Increasing war outlays have no lack of justifications from the apologists for, and representatives of, the bourgeoisie. For sheer brazenness, however, we doubt that the reasons attributed to ECA administrator Foster as justifying the shift from economic to military aid can be equaled.

> The arguments forwarded by the administrator at that time [July 1950, as reported by Mr. Kennedy in the aforementioned dispatch to the *New York Times*] have become more elaborate in proportion to increasing international tension, but *basically they are the same arguments now being posed*. These are:
>
> *(1) Most of the Marshall Plan participating countries are now far enough advanced economically to direct their attention from internal problems to those of possible aggression.*
>
> *(2) An economy that has been restored must progress in the assurance of protective strength.* (Italics mine – T.N.V.)

While comment would be entirely superfluous, under this line of reasoning economic aid would necessarily have to be a prelude to military aid. American imperialism has no choice, nor does it grant any choice to its satellites. The slogan, publicly and privately, becomes: "Join our military camp, or no aid." While Washington is unduly sensitive to the term, here is a classic expression of imperialist coercion, albeit with new motives and new methods, but with the same tragic results of war, misery and starvation for the masses of humanity.

The Permanent War Economy

As we have previously observed, the Permanent War Economy becomes increasingly international in scope, bringing within the orbit of American imperialism every industry and population as yet outside of the orbit of Stalinist imperialism. A detailed analysis of the increase in the ratio of war outlays to total production in England, France and the rest of the non-Stalinist world is unnecessary, nor does space permit. It suffices to point out the rapid *rate* of increase in the "defense" budgets of the North Atlantic Treaty powers in 1951 as compared with 1950. These increases, according to the *New York Times* of May 27, 1951, are: Norway, 117 per cent; Denmark, 67 per cent; United Kingdom, 53 per cent; Italy, 53 per cent; France, 45 per cent; and the Benelux countries, 39 per cent. Nor are the bases from which these increasing military expenditures start entirely negligible in terms of the proportion of total output already devoted to means of destruction. The Wilson report, for example, states:

> Our European allies have increased their planned rate of defense expenditures from approximately $4.5 billion a year prior to the Korean conflict to almost $8 billion in 1951. Higher spending rates are projected for subsequent periods.

It is no wonder, therefore, that Western European capitalism, operating on such an unstable foundation compared with the United States, has already experienced an inflation exceeding the American during the past year. The social consequences in every country, particularly Britain, are profound, but outside the scope of our analysis. Moreover, because of the dominant position of America in the world's markets, especially in the present scramble for critical raw materials, the economies of every non-Stalinist country, even those with considerable nationalization and far-reaching state controls, are at the mercy of every whim and vagary of Washington, planned, or capricious. Under the circumstances, the low state of American popularity throughout the non-Stalinist world should not be a surprise to the American bourgeoisie.

THE IMPACT OF THIS NEW PHASE OF American imperialism is far broader in its foreign implications than would appear merely from an analysis of the increase in armaments budgets throughout the world, or from the changes in national economies resulting from inflation and steadily increasing state intervention. Precisely because the new method of sustaining American imperialism is geared to the needs of American military strategy, the

Military-Economic Imperialism

ultimate consequences may be so far-reaching as to destroy the remaining foundations of capitalism. To combat a Stalinist imperialism operating from the base of bureaucratic collectivism, with its ability to subordinate all its satellite economies to the demands of Moscow and to standardize military equipment, procurement and transportation, requires a more or less comparable "internationalization of war preparations" on the part of American imperialism and its more indispensable allies in Western Europe.

It may still be possible in some circles to question the relative superiority of a nationalized economy over competitive capitalism in ordinary matters of production and distribution, but in the conduct of modern war, and therefore of war preparations, even a bureaucratic, brutal and horribly inefficient Stalinism is incomparably more successful in achieving the necessary coordination and integration of its war-making potential, due to its collectivist base, than the most highly developed capitalist nations could ever hope to achieve without vast structural changes. Under the impact of common financing, centralized administration cutting across national boundaries, standardization of armaments, and pooling of production resources – all of which are indispensable if American imperialism has any hopes of defending Western Europe against Stalinism – national sovereignty must be subordinated to the superior power, economic and military, and wisdom emanating from Washington and its representatives, especially Eisenhower.

A remarkable article on this entire problem, by its chief European economic reporter, Michael L. Hoffman, appeared in the *New York Times* of Aug. 5, 1951. Its analytical portion is worth reproducing in full:

> Nobody can foresee with anything like exactness just how this [a common military budget and a common military procurement administration] would affect the economy of Europe. But European and United States economists have considered the matter fairly carefully already, and the following are some of the consequences that can now be predicted with some degree of confidence.

The Permanent War Economy

For practical purposes, *national parliaments would lose control of from one-third to nearly half of their own national budgets.* They could complain, or refuse to vote taxes, or make all kinds of other trouble, but *once in the European army a government would pretty much have to accept its defense burden as given.*

It would be quite inconceivable that this degree of rigidity could be introduced into national government budgets without bringing in its train a *far greater degree of coordination in budgeting generally than exists now.*

Every participating country would acquire suddenly an *entirely new kind of interest in its neighbors' prosperity.* It is true now, but not very deeply burned into the consciousness of most people, that Germany cannot thrive without France, France without Italy, and so on. This would become obvious if the taxpayers saw their burdens mounting because some other country could not support a larger share.

Discussions of trade and monetary policy would take place in an entirely new atmosphere, in which everybody would be forced to keep an eye on Europe as a whole.

It could be expected, at the very least, that the duplication and misdirection of investment caused by uncoordinated national armament programs would be reduced greatly. The range of industry affected by military procurement under modern conditions is so great that a unified procurement service for a European army would become the outstanding market for a large number of European industries.

It has been Europe's experience for ages that the growth of armed forces under the control of governments with sovereignty over larger and larger territorial units generally has been followed by the establishment of currencies, commercial law and other social institutions on a larger and larger territorial basis. There is nothing inevitable about this progression, but those European and United States leaders and officials who have been convinced of the necessity for getting rid of

Military-Economic Imperialism

national barriers to economic expansion in Western Europe like to believe that the "law" will work once again. (Italics mine – *T.N.V.*)

In reality, of course, such integration and coordination as may be achieved in Western Europe can only occur under the stimulus, organization and direction of American imperialism. European capitalism is long since incapable of saving itself. Were it not for the aid and support received from the American bourgeoisie, the European bourgeoisie would have abdicated or been overthrown. Farfetched and alarming as it may seem, the Kautskyian theory of "ultra-imperialism" may yet see its realization, in the event the Third Camp fails to intervene actively in the course of history before it is too late, in the form of world hegemony being achieved by either American or Stalinist imperialism.

The role of military aid in the new phase of American imperialist development will be even more pervasive and all-embracing than the role of relief and rehabilitation. With overriding priority over materials, production facilities and manpower, military aid appears to be the vehicle that will permit American imperialism to complete its task of subjugating the economies of the lesser capitalist imperialist powers, of controlling their basic international policies, of influencing their domestic policies, and, above all, of dominating their colonial markets and trade. Naturally, there will be struggles, intense social conflicts, in many countries where the ability and will to resist subordination of legitimate class and national interests to Washington remains. Stalinism will naturally seek to exploit these contradictions wherever they appear. What the outcome of these complex stresses and strains will be may well determine the course of history for decades. Of one thing, however, we may be absolutely certain: the restoration of traditional American finance capital imperialism to sound health is excluded.

THE NEW POLICY OF AMERICAN imperialism, judging by its most eminent official and private spokesmen, is heartily in favor of the bloodless conquest of Europe and its empires, yet it seeks to accomplish this strategic aim by emphasizing the old, traditional methods, while paying lip-service to the new methods imposed by the exigencies of the times. The objective of European political union, with implied American control, has been voiced by innumerable leaders of the American bourgeoisie. Notable among these has been Mr. R. C.

The Permanent War Economy

Leffingwell, head of the House of Morgan, who in an article in *Foreign Affairs* for January 1950, entitled *Devaluation and European Recovery*, states:

> Monetary union without political union is impossible. There cannot be a common currency without common sovereignty and a common parliament and common taxes and common expenditures.

Or, in the more oblique language of the Gray report (recommendation 21):

> The United States should help to strengthen appropriate international and regional organizations and to increase the scope of their activities. It should be prepared, in so far as practicable, to support their activities as the best method of achieving the economic and security objectives which it shares with other free nations.

In the area of investment policy, the key to imperialist activity and perspectives, the language of publicly enunciated foreign economic policy more clearly parallels that of private sources. Leffingwell, for example, in the article cited above, comments on the fundamental contradiction of American imperialism as a creditor nation with a large favorable balance of trade, as follows:

> As a creditor nation, our tariffs should be for revenue only, except where needed to protect industries essential for the national defense . . . What we need to do is to increase our imports more than we increase our exports . . . Private American foreign investment would help. Indeed, the fundamental trade disequilibrium is so great that the international accounts can scarcely be balanced without great American investment overseas, both public and private . . . If American foreign investment is to be encouraged, our government and foreign governments must reverse their policies and give

Military-Economic Imperialism

firm assurance to American investors that their investments will be respected and protected, and that they may hope to profit by them, and collect their profits.

Almost as forthright is the Gray report:

> Private investment should be considered as the most desirable means of providing' capital and its scope should be widened as far as possible . . . Further study should be given to the desirability and possibility of promoting private investment through tax incentives, in areas where economic development will promote mutual interests, but where political uncertainty now handicaps United States private investment.

Two specific steps are advocated for immediate action to stimulate private investment:

> (a) The negotiations of investment treaties to encourage private investment should be expedited;
>
> (b) The bill to authorize government guaranties of private investment against the risks of non-convertibility and expropriation should be enacted as a worthwhile experiment.

Since all this encouragement of private investment may be expected to remain confined to paper, the Gray report also places "heavy reliance" on public lending, and seeks to "make sure that our own house is in order – that we have eliminated unnecessary barriers to imports, and that our policies in such fields as agriculture and shipping are so adjusted that they do not impose undue burdens on world trade."

The Permanent War Economy

Here, again, the public spokesman must be more circumspect than the private. Says the Gray report:

> With respect to our own agricultural policies we should, over the long-run, attempt to modify our price support system, and our methods of surplus disposal and accumulation of stocks, in ways which, while consistent with domestic objectives, will be helpful to our foreign relations.

Such double talk, together with the limitation proposed for shipping subsidies, is, of course, aimed at achieving the same objective as Leffingwell: abandonment of the American farmer so that industry may resume its customary exports of commodities and private capital.

EVER SINCE 1917, WHEN THE UNITED States became a creditor nation, the basic contradiction inherent in a finance capital imperialist nation exporting private capital while simultaneously maintaining a substantial export surplus in commodities and services has become more acute. The essence of the problem is clearly the necessity to make it possible for recipients of American private capital to pay the carrying charges, to remit the profits, and ultimately to repay the loans and investments. In the 1920s the problem was solved through large-scale remittances abroad of recent immigrants to the United States, coupled with ultimate repudiation of a substantial portion of American-held foreign securities. In the long run, however, *if American imperialism is to function in the traditional manner*, the United States must import more than it exports; i.e., it must acquire an unfavorable balance of trade sufficient to cover the tribute exacted by American capital. To be sure, remittances of gold temporarily help to achieve the necessary balance, but the United States has long since acquired the overwhelming portion of the world's gold supply. Foreign countries, fundamentally, can only earn the dollars they need by carrying the majority of trade in their own ships, by inducing American tourists to spend a sizable amount of dollars abroad, and by exporting more commodities to the United States than they import from the United States. Since, with relatively few exceptions, foreign countries cannot compete with American manufactur-

Military-Economic Imperialism

ers, they are reduced to exporting to the United States raw materials, minerals and farm products.

When England was confronted with a similar problem in 1847, she repealed the "Corn Laws," permitting foreign wheat and other agricultural commodities to be imported into England without tariffs. The result was the abandonment of British agriculture, accompanied by a gigantic increase in industrial output. Perhaps, if the Farm Bloc were not so strong, American imperialism might have been able to achieve a classic solution of its crucial imperialist contradiction. It is, however, politically impossible and historically too late to solve the problem in this manner. The experience of the last few years indicates the only way in which American imperialism ran hope to continue to maintain an export level between five and ten per cent of total output, as the data on the following page (from the June, 1951, *Survey of Current Business*) show.

American exports of almost $17 billion in 1948, almost $10 billion in 1949, and more than $14.4 billion in 1950 amounted to 7 per cent, 6.8 per cent, and 5.6 per cent, respectively, of net national product. This is relatively less than the ratio that "normally" prevails with the exception of years of deep depression. Its importance cannot be measured simply by reference to the absolute amounts involved. For many industries and, by and large, for the economy as a whole, the profitability of the remaining 90-95 per cent of output that is sold on the domestic market depends on maintenance of these exports. It is not only that exports make possible indispensable imports, but that surplus value is created at every stage in the process of production. Elimination of all exports, aside from certain obviously serious political and economic consequences, would not merely reduce profits of certain industries, possibly sending them into bankruptcy, but would immediately lower drastically the rate and mass of profit for all industry, and with cumulative effects.

The Permanent War Economy

AMERICAN EXPORTS AND MEANS OF FINANCING, 1948-1950 (Millions of Dollars)			
Item	*1948*	*1949*	*1950*
Exports of goods and services	$16,967	$15,974	$14,425
Means of Financing			
Foreign sources:			
United States imports of goods and services	10,268	9,603	12,128
Liquidation of gold and dollar assets	780	−60	−3,645
Dollar disbursements (net) by:			
International Monetary Fund	203	99	−20
International Bank	176	38	37
United States Government:			
Grants and other unilateral transfers (net)	4,157	5,321	4,120
Long and short-term loans (net)	886	647	164
United States private sources:			
Remittances (net)	678	522	481
Long and short-term capital (net)	856	589	1,316
Errors and omissions	−1,037	−785	−156

Even though imports have been at the $10 billion level, the visible surplus in the balance of payments for commodities and services was $6.7 billion in 1948, almost $6.4 billion in 1949, and $2.3 billion in 1950. The narrowing of the gap in 1950 is due more to the rise in imports as the scramble for raw materials developed after the outbreak of the Korean war than to the fall in exports. It was more than offset, however, by the flight of gold and dollars from America as "hot" money sought the greater safety of haven in Uruguay and other places.

It is clear that American government funds have been decisive in maintaining exports. Obviously, without state foreign aid, exports would have been some four or five billion dollars less, which in turn would have had a severely depressing effect on both the American and world economies. It is equally evident that if you give the purchaser the means with which to buy what you have to sell, you can continue to do business as long as you are able to maintain your customer's purchasing power. This is equivalent to a perpetual subsidy in the present case by the American state on the order of $5 billion annually. How long American imperialism can maintain foreign subsidies of this magnitude, now to be increased to a level of $8 billion as foreign aid shifts from predominantly economic to military commodities, is uncertain, but there is a limit and there will be a day of reckoning.

An increase of American foreign investments "from the present $1,000,000,000 a year to a minimum of $2,000,000,000 a year," as called for by the Rockefeller report would not begin to solve the problem of the dollar gap. Moreover, as American foreign investments accumulated over the years, assuming that any such recrudescence of traditional American imperialism was possible, the interest and dividend bill would likewise increase, and foreign countries would eventually be even shorter of dollars than at present. Let us not forget that the returns of capital invested abroad historically are much greater than the domestic rate of profit. That is one of the chief attractions of finance capital imperialism. An example of current profitability is provided by the report "that the Prince of the Kuwait Sheikdom has rejected a new offer of the Anglo-American-owned Kuwait Oil Co. to boost his oil royalties ... The offer of the company was to up the royalties from four and a half shillings to 25 shillings (63 cents to $3.50 a ton)." (*World Telegram and Sun*, Aug. 6, 1951.) In other words, to forestall any desire to emulate the nationalization action of Iran, the Kuwait Oil Co. is able to offer an increase of 450 per cent in the royalty paid. The Prince of Kuwait is said to have rejected this offer and to be holding out for a 50-50 split of profits!

The Permanent War Economy

Barring a sharp rise in privately-financed imports, which is virtually impossible, American imperialism is forced to place its main reliance in achieving practically every objective of foreign economic policy on continued state aid. Private foreign trade and investments, as in the case of domestic profits, are in effect guaranteed by the state, and the state itself must make good the failure of private investment through permanent gifts and loans.

IN PROMULGATING THE POINT FOUR program on Sept. 8, 1950, Truman declared:

> Communist propaganda holds that the free nations are incapable of providing a decent standard of living for the millions of people in the underdeveloped areas of the earth. The Point Four program will be one of our principal ways of demonstrating the complete falsity of that charge.

The mountain has labored and brought forth a mouse. Thirty-four and a half million dollars were appropriated for the first year. The appropriation for the second year will be considerably less than the $500,000,000 recommended by the Gray and Rockefeller reports. Inasmuch as the Gray report was devoted to foreign economic policy as a whole, while the Rockefeller report concentrates on development, it is to the Rockefeller report that we must turn for an authoritative statement of American hopes and policies in this field.

"The people who live in what have been termed the underdeveloped areas of Latin America, Africa, the Middle East, Asia and Oceania need our help and we need theirs," states the Rockefeller report. Point Four is thus not entirely a one-sided and exclusively humanitarian venture.

> Considered from the point of view of the strategic dependence of the United States on these regions, *it must be emphasized that we get from them 73 per cent of the strategic and critical materials we import – tin, tungsten,*

Military-Economic Imperialism

chrome, manganese, lead, zinc, copper – without which many of our most vital industries could not operate. (Italics mine – T.N.V.)

The major recommendation is, consequently, an expansion of Point Four:

A balanced program of economic development calls for simultaneous progress in three broad fields of economic endeavor. Along with the production of goods – which is a job for private enterprise – must go public works, such as roads, railways, harbors and irrigation works; also improvement in the basic services, like public health and sanitation, and training people in basic skills. *The financing of both the public works and these basic services are largely governmental functions.*

The Gray Report on United States foreign economic policy, submitted to the president last year, recommended that United States economic assistance to the underdeveloped areas be increased "up to about 500 million dollars a year for several years, apart from emergency requirements arising from military action." The advisory board believes that the expenditure of $500,000,000 in these areas is justified. (Italics mine – T.N.V.)

How an expenditure of 50 cents per person annually can have any material effect in raising living standards in the colonial areas is carefully avoided, as there is opposition within the bourgeoisie even to this pathetically small amount. Consider the following from the August 1951 *Monthly Letter of the National City Bank:*

The difficulty with development is not lack of money, but such factors as lack of skills to use modern machinery, political instability, prejudice against foreigners, onerous taxation and arbitrary limits on business profits. It is doubtful if the American taxpayer should venture, through the Export-

The Permanent War Economy

Import Bank, where neither the private capitalist nor the World Bank has dared to tread.

Earlier, we pointed out that the Rockefeller report, like the Gray report, places its main reliance on stimulating private investment. While "a full kit of financial tools" is recommended, as usual it is the matter of tax incentives that is most revealing:

> Adoption of the principle that income from business establishments located abroad be taxed only in the country where the income is earned and should therefore be wholly free of United States tax.
>
> To avoid any drop in tax revenue during the emergency we recommend that only new investment abroad be freed of United States tax during the present emergency. As soon as the emergency is lifted the exemption should be extended to future income from investment abroad regardless of when the investment was made.
>
> This would apply to corporations. Individuals would receive only partial exemption.

It may be anticipated that such tax concessions will not be very popular. Together, however, with the guaranties offered in the Gray report, it is clear that the bourgeoisie is desperately seeking every expedient to restore its former position. The sentiments underlying the humanitarian side of Point Four should not be minimized. They correspond to a vast yearning by the majority of the human race for emancipation from misery, starvation and exploitation. A socialist America could make real strides in helping the underdeveloped areas rapidly to overcome the backwardness imposed by centuries of feudal and imperialist exploitation. But a capitalist America can do little more than produce reports and a pittance of genuine aid.

The New International **August 1951** — T.N. VANCE

Part V – Some Significant Trends

Sacred to the operation of traditional capitalism is the ability of the individual capitalist to decide what and how much to produce, as well as the prices at which he will sell his commodities. Under the Permanent War Economy, however, the state assumes *directive* powers, through various types of controls, that largely supersede the power of the individual capitalist. The bourgeois is no longer undisputed master of his own house. He continues to produce commodities and to accumulate surplus values, in greater volume than ever before as we have previously shown, but only as a result of large-scale state intervention. The ability of the state to direct the economy is basic to the successful operation of the Permanent War Economy. As was shown in Part III, *Increasing State Intervention*, May-June, 1951, issue of *The New International*, the entry of American capitalism into the permanent crisis of world capitalism with the Great Depression of the 1930's marked the beginning of the shift of power from the individual capitalist to the state apparatus, representing the interests of the bourgeoisie as a class. While the *character* of state intervention in depression differs from state intervention under the Permanent War Economy, both periods require large-scale state bureaucracies. To this extent, as well as the psychological preparation for increasing state intervention of both the bourgeoisie and the public at large, depression may be considered a necessary prerequisite to the war economy.

The New Deal served as a school for the development of numerous technical experts in the art of managing state monopoly capitalism and in the equally important area of planning the increase in state revenues required to sustain the expanding state bureaucracy. In 1929, for example, the number of Federal civilian employees was 227,000. In 1933, the figure was only 306,000. It almost doubled by 1939, reaching 571,000. This provided a solid foundation for the expansion that took place under the Permanent War Economy, described in Part III. Some of the key personnel were trained and, more importantly, the practice was begun of borrowing industrial and financial leaders from private industry to administer the various state programs. The New Deal, in short, was an essential framework for the development of the Permanent War Economy.

That a very significant shift has occurred in the role of the state in the economy is officially recognized in the 1951 edition of the National Income Supplement to the *Survey of Current Business*, published by the Department of Commerce.

The Permanent War Economy

The most notable change since 1929 in the use of the Nation's output is a shift from private to government use. In terms of the current dollar estimates of gross national product, government purchases of goods and services, which absorbed 8 per cent of the gross national product in 1929, took 15 per cent in 1950. Personal consumption expenditures, on the other hand, dropped from 76 per cent of the total in 1929 to 68¼ per cent last year.

This profound shift can be seen from the summary tabulation boxed below.

PERCENTAGE DISTRIBUTION OF GROSS NATIONAL PRODUCT			1929	1950
In billions of current dollars:				
	Personal consumption expenditures		75.9%	68.5%
	Gross private domestic investment		15.2	17.3
	Net foreign investment		0.7	−0.8
	Government purchases of goods and services		8.2	15.0
	TOTAL		100.0	100.0
In billions of 1939 dollars :				
	Personal consumption expenditures		72.5	70.4
	Gross private domestic investment		17.4	16.1
	Net foreign investment		0.9	0.0
	Government purchases of goods and services		9.2	13.5
	TOTAL		100.0	100.0

Some Significant Trends

It will be seen that the changes in the composition of gross national product were due in considerable measure to differential price movements. Nevertheless, on a constant dollar basis, the role of the state increased almost 50 per cent and occurred at the expense of both consumer outlay and capital accumulation. Actually, a better picture would emerge if the distribution were in terms of net national product, as has been our previous practice. The role of the state in 1950, according to these figures, is somewhat less than we estimated, primarily because our 1950 estimates understated the degree of inflation and the real increase in production that actually took place. We estimated gross national product at $278 billion, while the official figure is now revealed as $283 billion. None of these minor discrepancies in any way invalidates our analysis.

THE REAL SIGNIFICANCE OF THE CHANGE that has occurred is carefully overlooked by the Commerce experts' desire to relate "comparable" years. The history of the last 22 years, despite serious inadequacies in the underlying data, is graphically portrayed by the changing relationship of government purchases of goods and services to total gross national product. (See table on the following page.)

It can be seen that the depression of the 1930's was accompanied by the first great advance in state intervention in the economy. While the proportion of total output, as measured by gross national product, that went to government purchases of goods and services reached in depression years the level that exists in the postwar period, the significant change that has occurred is the fantastic growth in the proportion going to the Federal government, i.e., the state. From an insignificant level of 1.3 per cent in 1929, it quadrupled during the New Deal, reaching a peak of 6.2 per cent in 1938, undoubtedly sparked by the realization that the "recession" of 1938 was largely due to the decline in state expenditures in the latter half of 1937. We are already familiar with the gigantic rise in war outlays that resulted from World War II, accompanied by a relative decline in the role of state and local government expenditures. The decisive change that has taken place is reflected in the fact that the ratio of Federal government purchases to total output in the postwar period markedly exceeds the prewar period. A ratio of 8 or 9 per cent, virtually all of which is accounted for by direct and indirect war outlays, in its own way signals the advent of a new epoch in the history of capitalism.

The Permanent War Economy

	RATIO OF GOVERNMENT PURCHASES OF GOODS AND SERVICES TO GROSS NATIONAL PRODUCT, 1929-1950		
Year	Total*	Federal	State and Local
1929	8.2%	1.3%	6.9%
1930	10.1	1.6	8.5
1931	12.1	2.0	10.1
1932	13.8	2.5	11.3
1933	14.3	3.6	10.7
1934	15.0	4.6	10.4
1935	13.7	4.1	9.6
1936	14.2	5.8	8.4
1937	12.8	5.0	7.8
1938	15.1	6.2	8.8
1939	14.3	5.6	8.7
1940	13.7	6.1	7.7
1941	19.5	13.4	6.2
1942	37.0	32.2	4.8
1943	45.6	41.8	3.8
1944	45.2	41.7	3.5
1945	38.5	34.8	3.7
1946	14.6	9.9	4.7
1947	12.3	6.8	5.6
1948	14.1	8.1	6.0
1949	16.9	9.9	7.0
1950	15.0	8.1	7.0
* Breakdown does not necessarily add to total due to individual rounding.			

Some Significant Trends

Without continuing war outlays and state foreign aid, and in the long run these must be on an ever-increasing scale, the vaunted economy of American imperialism would grind to an abrupt halt. Roosevelt and Truman are absolutely correct when they reply to their bourgeois critics with the statement that they have saved capitalism. That capitalism is more "prosperous" than it has ever been, as Truman is fond of boasting, requires a very important qualification. It is true, as we have demonstrated, that profits reached an all-time high in 1950 and that the Permanent War Economy operates so as virtually to guarantee the profits of the bourgeoisie as a class.

The "prosperity" of the Permanent War Economy, however, is rather precarious. The state decides not only how many airplanes, tanks and munitions in general shall be produced, but of necessity determines how many automobiles, refrigerators, tractors, *etc.*, shall be produced and, within limits, the prices at which they shall be sold. From a capitalist point of view, the economic development under the Permanent War Economy must be viewed as unhealthy. The patient achieves a form of recovery from what may be likened to shock therapy. But the treatment is far from painless and even the doctors cannot say whether the cure will be lasting.

The official hope is that "another two years or so" of controls will see American military output achieving sufficient magnitude so that the economy can sustain both the necessary level of war outlays together with a high level of civilian outlays *without continued controls*. This is clearly a consummation devoutly to be wished, but impossible of realization. An economy devoting 20 per cent or thereabouts of total output to war outlays cannot function without large-scale state intervention, requiring direct and indirect controls.

So powerful has been the development of the productive forces under American capitalism that, just as there is periodically an overproduction of the means of production and an overproduction of the means of consumption, it is not excluded that there can be an overproduction of the means of destruction under the Permanent War Economy. Normally, this does not happen in a war economy precisely because war consumes means of production, consumption and destruction more rapidly than they can be produced. Yet, prior to V-E Day, with a few exceptions, there had been

The Permanent War Economy

accumulated a sufficient stockpile of many types of munitions to permit cutbacks and to enable the armed forces to fight for many months without additional production.

It was not only the dismantling of the war machine in large measure that produced the notable American inferiority in weapons *vis-a-vis* Stalinist imperialism at the outbreak of the Korean war. It was also, and perhaps more importantly, the high rate of obsolescence that obtains in the means of destruction. This gap is clearly in process of being overcome at a fairly rapid rate. Assuming, therefore, that large-scale warfare or another "Korea" does not break out, or that an armistice is concluded in Korea, the question arises whether American imperialism will not reach a point in the next few years where the warehouses will be bulging with all types of means of destruction and there will be no place to use them.

Such a development is a possibility. Present evidence, however, indicates that the high rate of military obsolescence, together with the talked-about expansion in the production of "fantastic" weapons, should offset for several years the tendency to accumulate an oversupply of munitions in the absence of total war.

A sharp reduction in war outlays in the near future is therefore unlikely and would in a remarkably short time cause a collapse of the economy. Moreover, it would certainly invite the very aggression of Stalinist imperialism that the military build-up is presumably designed to prevent. It may therefore be expected that American imperialism will continue on the only course open to it until the vast collision with Stalinist imperialism (World War III) takes place.

A STATE MONOPOLY CAPITALIST régime in the true sense of the term has developed under the impact of depression and war. It bears a certain resemblance to Bonapartism, but Bonapartism has been traditionally applied by Marxists to a temporary régime of crisis, which poses the issue of revolution or counter-revolution and which marks the end of parliamentarism. As Trotsky puts it in *Whither France?*, "The essence of Bonapartism consists in this: basing itself on the struggle of two camps, it 'saves' the 'nation' with the help of a bureaucratic-military dictatorship." There is, of course, as yet no bureaucratic-military dictatorship in Washington, although there are possible tendencies in that direction. Nor can the present régime, given the tempo at which

Some Significant Trends

world history moves, be classified as temporary. There are, however, numerous features of state monopoly capitalism that possess all the earmarks of clearly discernible trends, and which warrant brief mention in this penultimate article in our series on the Permanent War Economy.

In his excellent analysis of the relationship between Bonapartism and fascism in *The Only Road for Germany*, Trotsky observes that:

> As soon as the struggle of the two social strata – the haves and the have-nots, the exploiter and the exploited – reaches its highest tension, the conditions are given for the domination of bureaucracy, police, soldiery. The government becomes 'independent' of society. Let us once more recall: if two forks are stuck symmetrically into a cork, the latter can stand even on the head of a pin. That is precisely the schema of Bonapartism. *To be sure, such a government does not cease being the clerk of the property-owners. Yet the clerk sits on the back of the boss, rubs his neck raw and does not hesitate at times to dig his boots into his face.* (Italics mine – T.N.V.)

For the time being the fascist threat is absent, nor are the "soldiery" in a position of domination. Yet the domination of bureaucracy and the growing power of the police (the FBI) are increasingly evident. As we have remarked earlier, the inter-marriage between the big bourgeoisie and the upper echelons of the military bureaucracy is a basic characteristic of the Permanent War Economy. An important research project is available to someone ambitious enough to document this relationship in every detail. It suffices, however, to point out that innumerable officers were commissioned from the ranks of big business, such as "Generals" Knudsen and Sarnoff, and that many military leaders have become "captains of industry," as, for example, Generals Somervell and

The Permanent War Economy

Clay.* Of decisive importance is the network of standing committees and organizations relating to ordnance and military procurement needs. These exist in every industry whose output is important to the war machine and is basic to the military planning of all parts of the armed services. Meetings are held periodically, information on latest military techniques and their impact on production requirements is exchanged, and pilot contracts are continually being let to facilitate research and development. Above all, industry is constantly being geared to achieve rapid and complete mobilization in the event of a supreme crisis.

In the event that American imperialism is constrained to maintain more or less indefinitely an armed force of 3,500,000 or more, the power of the military in its daily impact must grow and the alliance between the military caste and the big capitalists will solidify until the day may come when we can truly speak of a "Europeanization" of American politics. This entire development alone is ample reason for describing the present regime as state monopoly capitalist. There are, however, other and perhaps even more significant reasons for stressing this aspect of the Permanent War Economy.

In passing, it should be noted that much of the right-wing criticism of state monopoly capitalist trends is garbed in the raiments of liberalism. Consider, for example, General MacArthur's Cleveland speech of September 6, 1951, in the course of which he stated that there has been "a steady drift toward totalitarian rule . . . a persistent . . . centralization of power in the Federal government . . . ravenous effort to further centralize the political power . . . a determination to suppress individual voice and opinion which can only be regarded as symptomatic of the beginning of a general trend toward mass thought control." At an another point in the political spectrum comes the charge of Sidney Hook (*New York Times*, September 30, 1951) that we are experiencing a species of "cultural vigilantism" that threatens the foundations of our

---

* The references are to Morris Knudsen, cofounder of Morrison-Knudsen involved, among other projects, airfields and ships; David Sarnoff, founder of NBC, named Reserve Brigadier General of the Signal Corps in 1945; Brehon B. Somervell, commanding General of Army Services in WWII; and Lucius D. Clay, Jr. Joint Strategic Plans Group in the Organization of the Joint Chiefs of Staff. (EH)

Some Significant Trends

democratic structure. Such criticism, regardless of source, possess general validity. Their widespread character is symptomatic of the inroads already made in the body politic by the growing power of the state.

IT IS ABOVE ALL IN THE HANDLING of strikes and labor disputes that the monopoly capital character of the state becomes clear. Especially noteworthy has been the role of the state in the various rail strikes, with the Army actually assigned responsibility for running the railroads. There was a time not so long ago when the mere presence of armed forces in a strike, when the soldiers were so to speak performing a picketing function, evoked widespread criticism of threats of fascism and charges of military dictatorship. We have indeed traveled far along the road away from traditional bourgeois democracy when military force can be substituted for the normal process of the class struggle without even raising an outcry of "strikebreaker" in more than the radical press.

With production plans vital to the operations of the war economy, a strike in almost any basic industry immediately threatens to disrupt the war machine or vital war preparations. Hence, the appeals to national patriotism, the resort to fact-finding devices and, where necessary, the mobilizing of public opinion to support intervention by the police power of the state, whether it be coal, transport, airplanes, copper or other crucial industry.

The very technique used to control the class struggle, the widespread establishment of tri-partite wage boards, is in essence a device of monopoly capital. The state, represented by the "public" representative, attempts to resolve each dispute through the technique of arbitration, with the state posing as disinterested and above classes. In those cases where this classless approach fails to work, the power of another arm of the bourgeois state is invoked – the courts, through the use of the injunction. Finally, when no other card is left to play, the state shows that it is still the "clerk of the property-owners" by using its military-police power. Roosevelt was a past master in the use of this technique. But regardless of personalities it is the underlying trend that is significant. The erection of the tri-partite labor-board approach to solving specific class struggles into an entire system, with philosophic justification and techniques for handling every variety of dispute, is more than ample justification for planning the label

The Permanent War Economy

"state monopoly capitalist" on the political regime under which the Permanent War Economy functions.

The labor bureaucracy willingly accepts its role as junior partner in the regime. It balks only when it either feels that it is being "unfairly" discriminated against in the handing out of administrative positions of power and prestige, or when the pressure from the ranks, under the lash of inflation, compels it temporarily to assert a position of independence. Despite these truths, the abortive history of the United Labor Policy Committee is not without interest.

THE UNITED LABOR POLICY COMMITTEE was organized in December, 1950, representing all segments of organized labor except Lewis' United Mine Workers. Its first statement of December 20, 1950, spoke eloquently of "justice and workability" in stabilization measures, but the heart of its concern was its basic objective of equal representation in the organs of the state bureaucracy:

> We are fully aware [state the representatives of the AF of L, the CIO, the Railway Labor Executives Association, and the IAM] of the grave emergency confronting our nation. We dedicate ourselves to help make our country strong and to use that strength to bring: peace and abundance to mankind.
>
> *It is imperative that labor be granted active participation and real leadership in every important agency in our mobilization effort. We regret that to date labor has not enjoyed opportunity for full participation in the mobilization effort. Free labor can make its fullest contribution only if it is permitted to serve at* all *levels of defense mobilization both with respect to* policy *and* administration.
>
> No one group has a monopoly of ideas in the mobilization of our resources. Each group has much to offer and cooperatively we can defeat the world-wide challenge of dictatorship. (Italics mine – *T.N.V.*)

Some Significant Trends

This bid for changing the role of junior partnership into one of equal partnership for labor fell on deaf ears, as how could the bourgeoisie be expected to take seriously the position of a labor bureaucracy that appeared to be quite satisfied with its rôle of junior partner in World War II. The Administration, of course, should have had the political savvy to recognize that this bid for increased status stemmed not only from the hurt feelings of the labor bureaucracy, but also reflected dissatisfaction by the vast majority of trade-union workers with the increasing burden that inflation was casting on them. No one, however, has accused the Truman administration of genuine political sagacity. It was therefore quite appropriate for the Wage Stabilization Board to issue Regulation No. 6 on February 16, 1951, establishing a 10 per cent formula that jeopardized both escalator clauses and productivity formulae in union contracts.

The promulgation of Regulation No.6 immediately prompted the United Labor Policy Committee to declare that a crisis existed and to withdraw from the Wage Board. We assume that our readers are generally familiar with the document issued by the ULPC on this occasion and therefore only reproduce the more interesting passages:

> The price-stabilization program is a cynical hoax on the American people . . .
>
> *Profit margins are being guaranteed.* Every consideration possible is being given by government price agencies to enhance the position of business and *to protect fat profits* . . .
>
> The Congress is now considering a program to raise all taxes in such a manner that *people in the lower income brackets will be forced to bear a still heavier share of the tax burden* . . .
>
> So far, *virtually the entire defense mobilization program, has been entrusted to the hands of a few men recruited from big business* who believe they have a monopoly on experience, good ideas and patriotism . . .

The Permanent War Economy

This was fairly strong language from a junior partner. Consequently, when Eric Johnston, Economic Stabilization Administrator, approved Regulation No. 6 on February 27, even though it was followed on March 1st with Regulation No. 8, designed to achieve a compromise on the escalator clause question, the United Labor Policy Committee had no choice but to make good its threat. All its representatives from all phases of the administration of the war economy were withdrawn and a policy of boycott established.

The United Labor Policy Committee statement of February 28th, announcing withdrawal of all labor representatives from the war program, carries out the theme of the February 16th statement; the language is even stronger:

> On Feb. 16 we announced that we had become thoroughly disillusioned with the conduct of the defense mobilization program. *We made the deliberate charge that big business was dominating the program, that the interests of the plain people of this country were being ignored and that the basic principle of equality of sacrifice in the national effort to protect freedom against Communist aggression had been abandoned* . . . After full and complete exchanges of information, our original convictions have been more than confirmed.
>
> *We are today confronted with a price order which amounts to legalized robbery of every American consumer, together with a wage order which denies justice and fair play to every American who works for wages.* The door has been slammed in our faces on the vital problem of manpower, which directly affects the workers we represent . . .
>
> *We have also arrived at the inescapable conclusion that such representation which already has been accorded to labor in defense agencies and such further representation as is now offered are merely for the purpose of window dressing.* (Italics mine – T.N.V.)

Some Significant Trends

The gauntlet had been thrown down by the labor bureaucracy. Moreover, Wilson was an extremely vulnerable target. A way had to be found to preserve one of the cornerstones of the state monopoly capitalist régime. In less than two weeks the formula emerged for a tri-partite 18-man board, which would have jurisdiction over all labor disputes, not only wages. Labor was willing. Gone was its indignation over "big-business domination," the "hoax" of price control, the "guarantees of profits," the iniquitous tax program, *etc.*

But industry, as represented by the Business Advisory Council, the NAM, and the Chamber of Commerce, did not like the deal its representatives were cooking up for it. Accordingly, it issued a statement on March 13, 1951, aimed at reasserting its senior partnership. Advocating a clearly defined wage stabilization policy, the representatives of industry declared:

> **This may result in a number of strikes.** *It is obvious that strikes under such circumstances are not ordinary labor disputes between employers and employees; they are strikes against the government itself,* designed to coerce or induce it into making concessions.
>
> *A firm policy in dealing with such strikes is essential to the maintenance of a sound stabilization policy and to preservation of a proper respect for government itself. Such strikes should not be met with appeasement or concession. They should be handled in accordance with existing law, including, where appropriate, the national emergency provisions of the Labor-Management Relations Act.* (Italics mine – *T.N.V.*)

It sounded like industry was ready for a showdown. Wiser heads prevailed, however, and after a month of dickering, industry announced that it would accept the 18-man wage stabilization and disputes board "under presidential request, but protesting the wisdom of the entire set-up." A compromise formula was put forward limiting the powers of the new board to recommendations in dispute cases, and another

The Permanent War Economy

compromise was worked out with respect to manpower control. But, in so far as anti-inflation controls are concerned, labor achieved not one iota of its demands.

We have cited at some length the history of the United Labor Policy Committee, which then shortly fell apart as it had outlived its immediate usefulness in the eyes of the AF of L, because it is illustrative of a basic trend of state monopoly capitalism. It is also quite revealing of the role of the labor bureaucracy, whose indictment of big-business domination and economic inequality of the war economy remains entirely accurate, despite the victory on the question of the escalator clause.

A Marginal Note

A FRIENDLY CRITIC HAS QUESTIONED our conclusion regarding the standard of living on the ground that "empirical" evidence appears to indicate that workers are better off today than they were, say, in 1939. The statistical evidence presented, or the analysis flowing from the data, are not questioned. But there seems to be some feeling that our case has been overdrawn. After all, more workers have automobiles now than ever before. Many have television sets, which didn't exist. We admit that unemployment is at extremely low levels, etc. "How, then, is it possible," asks our critic, "for the workers to have experienced a decline in their living standards?"

In the first place, we have shown that the *average* per capita standard of living did rise – 17 per cent in 1950 over 1939. We did, however, calculate a slight decline in the per capita standard of living of the working classes – to be exact, a decline of 1.3 per cent from 1939 to 1950. Of course, at the same time, there was a marked improvement in the standards of living of the farming classes, the middle classes and the bourgeoisie. Moreover, it is obvious that with such a slight decline in the standard of living of the working classes, it is quite possible to find this or that worker whose living standards have increased.

We are, of course, not aware of the "empirical" evidence referred to in apparent refutation of one of the fundamental laws of motion of the Permanent War Economy: that an increase in capital, instead of causing an increase in unemployment, is accompanied by

Some Significant Trends

relatively full employment and declining standards of living. We suggest, however, that the "empirical" evidence be examined a little more closely. It will be found that the increase in employment far exceeds the increase in the number of families. In other words, the average working class family currently contains a much larger number of wage earners than in 1939. This is primarily due to the inability today of most workers to survive on the basis of one income per family, which was generally typical of the pre-Permanent War Economy period.

Two and three incomes per working-class family are far from being atypical in 1951. Naturally, in many such cases, it is quite possible for the *family* income, on a real basis, to exceed that of 12 years ago. This does not in any way upset our conclusion that the rate of surplus value has increased, or any other basic conclusion. Even the possible improvement on a family basis must be tempered by consideration of the profound change in income tax laws, not so much with regard to rates as to the decrease in exemptions for dependents. The result has been that the working classes now bear the major brunt of the income tax, whereas previously they were almost totally unaffected.

Seekers after empirical evidence should also interview workers, such as teachers and other civil servants, whose incomes are relatively fixed. They are part of our data on the working classes and they have suffered a catastrophic decline in their standards of living. It should also be remembered that for every working-class family that is able to have two, three or more separate incomes, there is almost an equal number who are not in this position and who, in order to make ends meet, find the one and only income earner forced to take on a second job. This abnormal increase in labor power, solely a product of the inflation, is also encompassed in our figures. All empirical evidence that we have seen supports our general conclusions. The consumer "buying strike" of the spring and summer of this year is additional evidence that the inflation has reached a critical point and that living standards are declining. The fact that redemptions of E bonds exceed purchases, and that liquid savings in general are at extremely low levels, are genuine empirical evidence that our fundamental thesis is eminently correct.

We have digressed at this point not so much to answer our empirical critic, but to observe that the relative stability of the price level during the past six months has eased somewhat the pressure on the labor bureaucracy, but everything, they said about the fraudulent price control program and the unfair tax program, *etc.*, remains true to this very

The Permanent War Economy

day. As the ratio of war outlays to total output continues to increase, there must be a renewed upsurge of the inflationary pressure. As Wilson's third quarterly report of September 30, 1951, correctly puts it:

> Despite the present relative stability a critical period in our battle against inflation lies ahead. We must anticipate and prepare for the strong inflationary pressure that will be again encountered as defense spending grows and personal and business incomes mount.

At that point, which should be reached early in 1952, the attempts to "freeze" the class struggle through tripartite labor boards may run into serious difficulties. If we base ourselves on Marxism, we should be concerned with such fundamentals as what is happening to real wages and real profits, with the basic trends in the class struggle, and not with episodic and invalid "empirical" evidence that dissolves into thin air at the first touch of reality.

CONTROL OF THE PURSE STRINGS has always been viewed by Marxists, and correctly so, as a crucial element in the power of any régime. Inasmuch as the American state must go through a tortuous process of Congressional hearings and committees before funds are appropriated, it may be objected that in this vital point there is no possible resemblance to monopoly capitalism. Such a view would be entirely superficial. In fact, one of the really distinguishing characteristics of the present state monopoly capitalist régime is the inability of the legislature to deny in general any requests of the armed forces for funds. This is obviously true in time of actual warfare. It is no less true today, when the need for haste is not as great. Aside from carping criticism against the number of oyster forks ordered by the Navy or a picayune reduction in state foreign aid, there is very little that the Congress can do in the face of a certified statement from the military that they need $60 billion worth of munitions in the next year or $100 billion in two years, or whatever the precise military requirements may be.

Even if all the details were made available, which they are not on grounds of military security in the case of atomic weapons, *etc.*, and even if a Congressman felt himself qualified to question specific military requests, it is politically hazardous for a Congressman to

Some Significant Trends

advocate a reduction in this or that *military* item in the face of the customary statement by a representative of the armed forces that "this is the minimum required to assure the military security of the country; we will not be responsible for military safety if less than this amount is appropriated." For all practical purposes, therefore, direct war outlays and most indirect war outlays are sacrosanct. The legislature can do little better than rubber stamp the military requests. *De facto* control of the government purse strings has passed into the hands of the state executive bureaucracy. Even in the present situation, with the Truman administration on the whole confronted with a divided and hostile Congress, the state power to obtain funds is effectively independent of any control by the elected representatives of the people.

It is thus a comparatively simple matter for the state monopoly capitalist regime to manipulate the national debt in a manner best calculated to advance its own political fortunes as well as the class interests of the bourgeoisie. The spectacular rise in the national debt has been one of the chief methods whereby inflation has been promoted and an excellent indicator of increasing state intervention in the economy. The total gross debt of the United States government for selected fiscal years (ending on June 30th) of historical significance is shown in the following tabulation:

NATIONAL DEBT FOR SELECTED YEARS(Billions of Dollars)	
Year	*Amount*
1915	$ 1.2
1919	25.5
1930	16.2
1933	22.5
1939	40.4
1945	259.1
1946	269.9
1950	257.4
1951	255.3

The Permanent War Economy

World War I increased the national debt by some $24 billion, with the total reaching a peak of $25.5 billion in 1919. Under the influence of the last period of genuine capitalist prosperity, the national debt then declined to $16.2 billion in 1930, the beginning of the Great Depression. Under the New Deal, the national debt rose from $22.5 billion in 1933 to $40.4 billion in 1939, as state intervention in the economy commenced in a significant way. It remained, however, for World War II to cause an unbelievable increase of $219 billion by 1945 and $229 billion by 1946, when the national debt reached a peak of $269.9 billion – the increase in the debt exceeding one year's total output at that time.

The national debt has become so large that any thought of ever paying it off has long been abandoned. The interest charges alone run to about $6 billion annually at the present time. Inasmuch as the national wealth exceeds the national debt by at least a 2:1 ratio, it may be thought that there is no danger in the existence of such a huge debt. In fact, some bourgeois economists of the Keynesian school have projected figures intended to "prove" that the United States can support a total debt, public and private, running into trillions of dollars. From an abstract point of view, it is possible to contend that the only economic limit to the size of the national debt is the ability to meet the annual interest bill. With interest rates considerably lower than what they used to be, under this approach the national debt could easily be doubled or tripled without any serious danger being encountered.

The government, however, does not borrow money merely through the device of printing bonds. If this were the case, it could simply print money – and there would be a galloping inflation of the printing press variety, where the value of the dollar would literally sink to virtually zero. Needless to say, an inflation of this type, of which there are many examples in history (Germany in 1923 being a classic case), places the question of social revolution on the order of the day. The government must sell its bonds. Approximately one-third of the national debt is held by the banks, so controlled under the Federal Reserve System that for all practical purposes they are forced to buy government bonds at the dictate of the Treasury. Under the banking system, these government bonds in the hands of the banks become the base for a tremendous expansion of bank credit, thereby feeding the fires of inflation. Moreover, in a very real

Some Significant Trends

sense, that portion of the national debt held by insurance companies, corporations and some individuals, represents prior accumulations of capital for which there is no profitable outlet. Of course, tax-exempt securities should be excluded from any such analysis.

While the national debt has actually declined during the first year of the Korean war, it reached a low of $254.7 billion in April, 1951. At the end of August, 1951, it was $256.7, an increase of $2 billion in four months. Further increases in the national debt may be expected as expenditures for war purposes continue to increase. With redemptions of E bonds (of which there is a total of less than $35 billion outstanding, with more than $19 billion falling due in the next four years) currently running about twice as high as new purchases, it remains to be seen whether the new savings bond drive will be sufficiently successful to prevent additional large-scale government borrowing from the banks. In the absence of a pay-as-you-go tax program, the state will naturally have no choice but to borrow the sums needed to finance war outlays.

This type of "creeping" inflation, it should be emphasized, has already reduced the purchasing power of the dollar by about 50 per cent since 1939. Until it gets out of hand, it may prove to be good politics for the incumbent administration, in so far as it generates a pseudo-prosperity conducive to corralling votes. In the long run, however, as maintenance of the Permanent War Economy becomes more and more expensive, and a greater and greater portion of the burden is thrown onto the backs of the working and middle classes, the inflation must continue, bringing with it the threat of a complete capitalist breakdown in general bankruptcy, *i.e.*, unless war does not intervene first. Of course, long before general bankruptcy is imminent, the class struggle will erupt in a new and violent form as the impoverished segments of the population led by the proletariat attempt to throw off their intolerable burdens.

THE NATURE OF THE WAR against Stalinism being waged by the American bourgeoisie is such that anti-bourgeois-democratic aspects continually receive encouragement and nourishment. The aim of the American capitalist class is peace, *but on a capitalist foundation*. This not only dictates the necessity of destroying Stalinism root and branch, but of guarding against socialist developments in England, France and Germany, as well as preventing the nationalist and colonial revolutions in Asia from

The Permanent War Economy

developing in an anti-capitalist direction. While the current political perspective is one of "neither peace nor war," American imperialism is fully aware that the only method on which it can rely is the use of overwhelming military might.

Wherein, it may be asked, does this differ from World War II and the American aim to destroy German Nazi and Japanese militarism and imperialism? With respect to the mobilization of military force, there is little difference, except perhaps in a quantitative sense. Long and bitter as was World War II, American imperialism will be faced with an even more formidable foe in Stalinist imperialism. We are fully aware of American superiority in steel production, oil production, transport, and presumably in atomic energy developments. Yet, barring internal political collapse, there can be little doubt that Stalinism will be capable of mobilizing greater military power than the Nazis could at their peak. Moreover, Stalinism does not fight solely with military methods; it also employs political methods on a scale that neither the Germans nor Japanese could begin to approach.

The American bourgeois struggle against Stalinism may therefore require a greater proportion of output devoted to war outlays over a much longer period than was the case in World War II. If such be the case, it can only strengthen all the tendencies that we have already observed to be at work under the Permanent War Economy.

There can be no question, however, about the contrast between World Wars II and III on the political front. Fundamentally, the internal problem in World War II was one of preventing military and industrial espionage in the normal sense of the term. To be sure, a few German Bundists had to be rounded up and either deported or jailed, and, under the influence of hysteria, the Japanese-American population on the West Coast was interned in concentration camps in the interior. But there was no political movement that could penetrate significant layers of American society as a whole, providing not only an excellent nucleus for a possible Fifth Column, but an inexhaustible reservoir of American agents bound by political loyalty to a hostile foreign imperialism. Such, however, is the case with Stalinism.

It is precisely in its handling of the internal menace posed by the existence of a native Stalinist movement that the anti-bourgeois-democratic development of the

Some Significant Trends

American bourgeoisie stands most clearly revealed. One has only to cite the nature and manner by which the "subversive" list has been promulgated and used or the recent secrecy order to see how far along the road to authoritarianism, in this respect, American imperialism has traveled. Of course, the primary motivation is fear. But it is not only fear of Stalinism, but fear of any possible anti-capitalist development. It would have been a relatively simple matter, especially in view of the boasts of the FBI that it has its finger on virtually every Stalinist, to have immobilized every Stalinist organization and leader as actual or potential agents of an enemy imperialism. Yet, this was not done. Instead, decree power was used to blanket the most militant anti-Stalinist organizations together with Stalinists as enemies of American imperialism.

American imperialism is first and foremost concerned with preservation of its capitalist and imperialist base. If, in the process, the Bill of Rights, the heart of bourgeois democracy, has to suffer, that is perhaps regrettable, but not as important to the bourgeoisie as maintenance of its property and its system of exploitation. Imagine what the leaders of the American bourgeoisie in its progressive period would say in face of a secrecy order that gives any clerk in any government department the right to classify material as secret or confidential, without any right of appeal, in what is still ostensibly peacetime! We do not say that bourgeois democracy no longer exists in the United States. On the contrary, it does and we shall fight for the preservation of the democratic rights it affords against all its enemies, including the bourgeoisie. But it is important to note the political trends that are unfolding as the Permanent War Economy becomes more and more entrenched. The *trend* is away from bourgeois democracy. All that is needed is the emergence of a real threat of a militant working class movement, on the one hand, and on the other a fascist threat, and then the question of Bonapartism will become an actual one.

WIDESPREAD CORRUPTION IN OFFICIAL and private life has historically been an infallible sign of decadence. The disintegration of the moral fabric of civilization has its roots in a social system that fetters the productive forces and is no longer capable of playing a progressive role. Capitalism has never been particularly distinguished for the honor and integrity of its ruling class. One has only to recall the various methods employed by the "robber barons" in the eighteenth and nineteenth centuries during the

The Permanent War Economy

stage of primitive accumulation of capital to understand why graft and corruption are an integral part of the capitalist method of production. Yet, it is difficult to find a parallel in modern history for the vast corruption disclosed by the Kefauver Committee and various grand juries. The honest public official becomes the rare exception, an occasion for editorial praise.

Bribery takes many forms and is not restricted to public officials tempted by inadequate incomes. On the contrary, American business has erected bribery into a symbol of aggressiveness and an accepted, if not quite legitimate, method of doing business. "Anyone and anything can be bought for a price" is the underlying philosophy. This prevails from a Jay Gould who boasted that he could hire one-half of the working class to shoot the other half to the modern buyer or purchasing executive in a large corporation who expects to be "smeared" if someone wants to sell him something and who expects to "smear" the supplier of something that is difficult to buy if he wants to buy it. It is therefore hardly surprising that virtually every political machine, Democratic or Republican, in any city of size is clearly linked with organized crime.

Every now and then a reform movement temporarily ousts the corrupt machine and, on occasion, a juicy scandal, such as the Teapot Dome affair, is revealed at the level of the Federal government. The present degree of corruption, however, is far more extensive and all-pervading than ever before, and necessarily so because of the development of state monopoly capitalism. This is the era of the "mink coat," the "deep freeze" and other "gifts" that are generally accepted as the normal method of doing business in Washington. "After all," says the typical bourgeois, "it is *our* government; it is there to be cheated and who cares if we cheat ourselves." An exaggeration? We do not believe so. The American mores tend to condone successful bribery and corruption. It is only those who get caught who are looked upon with a degree of scorn.

With such a background, it is no wonder that as the state intervened more and more actively in all phases of the economy, bribery and corruption have mushroomed to the point where they have become a central political issue. If a businessman cannot do business without a piece of government paper, a priority for raw materials, an allocation, an export license, (a gas coupon), *etc.*, his instinctive thought is to "buy" one.

Some Significant Trends

The larger the business, the more prone he is to think of this approach and the greater the possibility of his having the means to carry it out successfully. After all, if congressmen can be "bought," in the interests of favorable legislation, why not "purchase" a piece of paper that is essential for doing business?

Official recognition of the importance of corruption was given by Truman in his special message to Congress of September 27, 1951, calling for disclosure of incomes of United States officers and employees. While the immediate motive was undoubtedly political, to protect the Democrats from the epidemic of public charges of corruption, the message confirms our analysis and reveals another important trend to which state monopoly capitalism under the Permanent War Economy has given rise. States the President:

> As the burdens of the government increase during this defense period, and more and more citizens enter into business or financial dealings with the government, it is particularly necessary to tighten up on our regulatory procedures, and to be sure that uniformly high legal and moral standards apply to all phases of the relationship between the citizen and his government. (sic!)

Why is this necessary? Perhaps, because officials in the RFC and other agencies, including the Bureau of Internal Revenue, not to mention the war procurement agencies, are lining their pockets at the expense of the taxpayer and then obtaining highly remunerative positions with the same companies they have helped to circumvent Federal regulations? Hardly this, although the President is "disturbed" because

> I am told that people all around the country are getting a mistaken and distorted impression that the government is full of evildoers, full of men and women with low standards of morality, full of people who are lining their own pockets and disregarding the public interest.

The Permanent War Economy

On the one hand, it is apparently a deliberate plot to discredit the government service:

> Attempts have been made through implication and innuendo, and by exaggeration and distortion of the facts in a few cases, to create the impression that graft and corruption are running rampant through the whole government.

On the other hand, there *is* pressure, and there *are* those who succumb:

> In operations as large as those of our government today, with so much depending on official action in the Congress and in the executive agencies, there are bound to be attempts by private citizens or special interest groups to gain their ends by illegal or improper means.
>
> Unfortunately, there are sometimes cases where members of the executive and legislative branches yield to the temptation to let their public acts be swayed by private interest. We must therefore be constantly on the alert to prevent illegal or improper conduct, and to discover and punish any instances of it that may occur.

Truman therefore proposes that all elected and appointed officials receiving salaries of $10,000 or more, plus flag and general officers of the armed services, together with the principal officials and employees of the major political parties, as well as those government employees receiving more than $1,000 annually from outside sources, should be required by law to disclose their entire incomes from all sources, public and private. "The disclosure of current outside income," states Truman, "will strike at the danger of gifts or other inducements made for the purpose of influencing official action, and at the danger of outside interests affecting public decisions." Such information would also "be of obvious help in tracking down any case of wrongdoing."

Some Significant Trends

We doubt that such a law would be particularly effective in eliminating the prevailing widespread corruption, for its roots are much deeper than the President indicates. The "black market" mentality will simply discover new techniques to achieve its objectives. Nevertheless, in spite of the fact that there is little possibility of such a law being passed, we heartily support Truman's proposal. As he says, "people who accept the privilege of holding office in the government must of necessity expect that their entire conduct should be open to inspection by the people they are serving." We think that the people would like to obtain a few facts and figures on the extent of corruption that exists, and that they are entitled to such information.

It is undoubtedly sheer coincidence that on the very same day that Truman proposed his anti-corruption legislation, Senator Williams of Delaware, a kept lackey of the DuPonts, succeeded in having the Senate vote to eliminate tax-exempt expense allowances of the president, vice-president and members of Congress, and is quoted in the press as being motivated by the thought that:

> *Our country was founded upon the principle that the ruling class would be subject to the same laws as other citizens.*

This is a very touching thought, and we are happy to learn that there is a ruling class in these United States. As to how equitable the tax laws are, we must leave this very important subject to the next and concluding article in this series, when we shall also indicate our concept of a socialist political program to cope with the problems confronting the working class as a result of the development of the Permanent War Economy.

The New International September 1951   — T.N. VANCE

Part VI – Taxation and the Class Struggle

Preliminary figures for 1951 indicate that 25 per cent of current production went to government in the form of taxes, as measured by the ratio of total government receipts (Federal plus state and local) minus total government receipts of social insurance contributions to net national product. This represents an all-time high, exceeding the peak World War II year of 1943 when the ratio was 24.5 per cent. The relationship of government income to current production and surplus value was shown in Table I of Part III (see May-June, 1951 issue of The New International). For the estimated ratio of 22 per cent for 1950 presented there, we can now substitute the actual ratio of 24 per cent.

As was stated in Part III, "The increase in state functions, accompanied by a loss in the effectiveness of the capitalist market, has meant a colossal expansion in government expenditures, which, in turn, has necessitated a phenomenal increase in taxes." With the state (all branches) consuming one-fourth of current output and two-fifths of surplus value, it is no wonder that all segments of the American population have become tax conscious.

Taxes, their amount, character and incidence, are a reflection of the class struggle. This is necessarily so in any class society. It is particularly true under American capitalism where practical politics is keenly alert to group and class pressures, both crude and subtle. In the epoch of the Permanent War Economy, when the ratio of total taxes to current production has increased from 16 per cent in 1939 to an estimated 25 per cent in 1951 – a rise in impact on all classes of better than 50 per cent – taxation becomes a central political and economic question of the highest magnitude.

Who pays the taxes becomes another way of asking who pays for war and war preparations and who bears the major burden of inflation. While the state is periodically forced to resort to borrowing, as shown in the previous article, in the long run the power of the state and the state bureaucracy is dependent on the portion of output that can be siphoned off in the form of taxes of various kinds.

It was not until 1941 that Federal tax receipts exceeded those of state and local governments. And it was only beginning in 1943 that the Federal personal income tax reached magnitudes sizable enough to penetrate the consciousness of the average individual. With the passage of the Revenue Act of 1951, we have now reached a situation where every class resents its tax burden. The bourgeoisie complain that "taxes have destroyed individual initiative and are impairing the accumulation of capital." The workers

The Permanent War Economy

gripe and grumble that "they cannot make ends meet and that their take-home pay is inadequate to cope with the rising cost of living." In between, the various layers of the middle classes and farming classes bewail "the pressure exerted on entrepreneurial income and professional salaries by rising costs of production, especially taxes."

TOTAL TAX RECEIPTS have increased almost sixfold since 1939. With the major components of taxes accounting for 85-90 per cent of total tax receipts, the basic changes in the tax picture are shown in Table I on the following page.

The data are from the 1951 National Income Supplement to the *Survey of Current Business* of the Department of Commerce. Aside from the major tax components shown, other sources of Federal tax revenue are estate and gift taxes, which rose from $61 million in 1929 to $371 million in 1939 and to a peak of $900 million in 1948, declining to $658 million in 1950; and customs duties, which have not changed materially over the years, yielding $599 million in 1929, $344 million in 1939, and $550 million in 1950. Other sources of state and local government tax revenue are corporate profits tax accruals, which were $145 million in 1929, $156 million in 1939, and rose to a peak of $895 million in 1950; and motor vehicle licenses other than those classified as personal taxes, which were $153 million in 1929, $182 million in 1939, and rose to a peak of $469 million in 1950. In addition, both Federal and state and local governments receive a variety of miscellaneous taxes and fees. Other than Federal grants-in-aid to state and local governments, these miscellaneous revenues do not have a significant effect on the tax structure so far as quantitative impact is concerned.

It will be seen that in 1929 Federal tax revenues were less than one-half the amount collected by state and local governments, with property taxes of $4.5 billion amounting to almost one-half of the total tax yield. In spite of the Great Depression and increasing state intervention under the New Deal, the tax picture remained fundamentally the same in 1939, the only significant change being the more than threefold increase in excise and sales taxes. With the advent of the Permanent War Economy, there occurred a sharp rise in virtually all existing forms of taxation, the most noteworthy increases being in the Federal personal income tax, corporation income and excess profits taxes, and excise and sales taxes. Despite the fact that property taxes rose from $4.3 billion in 1939 to $7.3 billion in 1950, their share of revenue raised by major tax sources declined from 40 per cent to 12 per cent.

TABLE I
MAJOR TAX COMPONENTS, 1929 and 1939-1950
(Billions of Dollars)

Year	Federal Personal Income Taxes	Federal Corporate Profits Tax Accruals	Federal Excise Taxes	State & Local Personal Tax And Nontax Receipts	State & Local Sales Taxes	Property Taxes*	Total Major Tax Components
1929	$1.2	$1.3	$0.6	$1.4	$0.4	$4.5	$9.4
1939	0.9	1.3	1.8	1.2	1.6	4.3	11.0
1940	1.0	2.7	2.1	1.2	1.7	4.4	13.1
1941	1.6	7.6	2.8	1.3	1.9	4.4	19.6
1942	4.1	11.3	3.4	1.3	1.9	4.4	26.4
1943	15.9	13.9	4.1	1.3	1.8	4.6	41.5
1944	17.1	13.1	6.3	1.4	1.9	4.6	43.4
1946	19.8	10.8	6.2	1.6	2.1	4.6	46.0
1946	18.0	9.1	7.3	1.6	2.7	4.8	43.5
1947	20.4	11.3	7.3	1.9	3.2	5.3	49.4
1948	19.8	12.4	7.5	2.1	3.7	5.9	51.4
1949	17.7	10.4	7.6	2.5	3.9	6.6	48.7
1950	18.8	17.7	8.3	2.7	4.3	7.3	59.1

* Excludes personal property taxes.

The Permanent War Economy

Federal personal income taxes yielded less than $1 billion in 1939, but on a gross basis (prior to refunds) produced $15.9 billion in 1943 due to the drastic lowering of exemptions and the sharp rise in rates. Prior to 1943 the average worker was virtually unaffected by personal income taxes. After 1943, taxes become an important element in the cost of living, giving rise to the eminently reasonable demand by the trade unions that personal income taxes should be included in the BLS "cost-of-living" index. Naturally, the income tax yield fluctuates not only with respect to the effective tax rate, but also in relation to the size of the national income. From 1945 to 1950, the gross yield of the Federal personal income tax varied between a high of $20.4 billion in 1947 and a low of $17.7 billion in 1949. But during the same period, personal income rose from $172 billion to almost $225 billion – an increase of more than 30 per cent. The proportion of total tax receipts accounted for by the personal income tax – the one relatively progressive feature in the American tax structure – therefore declined steadily as both real output and total tax receipts increased.

Consequently, even though the Federal personal income tax yield is estimated to rise sharply in 1951 to about $25 billion, the progressive aspects of the American tax structure are still sharply outweighed by its regressive features. This conclusion is without reference to the specific nature of the income tax itself. It is based on the fact that corporation taxes, excise and sales taxes, and business property taxes are shifted entirely or almost entirely to the average consumer. Since these taxes account for the bulk of the total tax revenue, the concept that those who can afford to should pay the major part of the tax load is conspicuously absent in the American tax picture – despite the personal income tax.

THE ILLUSION THAT the bourgeoisie bears the real brunt of taxes is one of the biggest swindles ever perpetrated by capitalist propaganda. Capitalist apologists like to refer to the sharply rising rates on large individual incomes, which for the calendar year 1951 reach a maximum of 87.2 per cent of net income (possibly affecting those with individual incomes in excess of one million dollars), but the incidence of taxation can only be seen when the entire tax burden by classes of income is analyzed. It is just as impermissible to confine one's judgments on the American tax structure solely to the personal income tax as it is to draw conclusions on the average worker's standard of

Taxation and the Class Struggle

living without reference to salary deductions, rising prices or the increase in total output.

All taxes and their impact must be considered, as well as the differences in income levels and proportionate shares in total output. Rather than go back to our own estimates, presented in Part II on Declining Standards of Living, we prefer to rely on official sources wherever possible.

First, it is necessary to establish that there has been no fundamental change in the distribution of personal income by income levels, despite the vast growth in total output and personal incomes. This can be done by a percentage analysis of money income going to each fifth of the population, as shown in Table II below.

TABLE II
MONEY INCOME RECEIVED BY EACH FIFTH OF FAMILIES AND SINGLE PERSONS, 1935-36, 1941, 1948 AND 1949
(Percentage of Money Income)

Families and Single Persons Ranked from Lowest to Highest Income				
Year	1935-36*	1941*	1948*	1949†
Lowest fifth	4.0%	3.5%	4.2%	3%
Second fifth	8.7	9.1	10.5	9
Third fifth	13.6	15.3	16.1	17
Fourth fifth	20.5	22.6	22.3	24
Highest fifth	53.2	49.6	46.9	47

* Taken from Table 4 of Taxes and the Human Factor by Theodore J. Kreps, The Public Affairs Institute, 1951, sources: National Resources Planning Board (1935-36), Department of Labor (1941), and 1950 Survey of Consumer Finances of Federal Reserve Board (1948).
† From the 1950 Census as reported by the Census Bureau in The New York Times of December 2, 1951.

The Permanent War Economy

While much has been made of the slight improvement in the position of the middle income groups at the expense of the highest fifth, the changes are all well within the margin of error inherent in all such data. Moreover, there have been certain conceptual changes in this type of analysis over the years. In addition, comparisons between a depression year and a war economy year are apt to be misleading. Fundamentally, there has been no change. If the rich haven't gotten richer as the poor have become poorer, the relative disparities in income levels have not changed. The rich remain rich while the poor remain poor – despite the tremendous increase in output, both in real and monetary terms. The richest twenty per cent of the population receives almost half the income, in 1948 averaging $9,911, while the poorest 20 per cent receives 3-4 per cent of the income, in 1948 averaging $893.

The distribution of personal income by income levels is before taxes and provides a necessary background for consideration of the impact of all taxes. If the tax burden falls chiefly on the upper fifth, then it would be possible to speak of a relatively progressive tax structure. This is especially so since those in the lower 60 per cent received a maximum income of less than $4,000 in 1948 – the minimum required to maintain any type of "decent" standard of living by any set of criteria. Or, if the upper income groups are bearing a noticeably heavier proportion of the total tax burden as total tax receipts increase, there would at least be evidence that the tax structure is becoming less regressive.

The facts are, however, that the American tax structure was and remains regressive to an amazing degree. The wealthy pay only a slightly higher percentage of their income in taxes than do other groups, and the poorest pay a higher percentage of their income in taxes than the middle income groups. The reason, as has already been mentioned, is that the Federal personal income tax is overshadowed by other taxes whose burden is an inverse proportion to income. That this is indeed the situation and that it has not changed fundamentally under the Permanent War Economy, despite the enormous increase in taxes, can be seen from Tables III and IV below.

Thus, just prior to the advent of the Permanent War Economy, taxes took about one-fifth of total personal income, with state and local government taxes accounting for more than one-half of the total tax yield. The completely regressive nature of state and

Taxation and the Class Struggle

local taxes, together with the semi-regressive nature of Federal taxes, produced a situation where the lowest income groups paid a higher proportion of their income in taxes than did all income groups under $10,000. It is only when the top income class of $20,000 and over (consisting of 0.3 per cent of spending units who received 9.1 per cent of total personal income) is considered that a feeble approach to a progressive tax system is apparent. And, obviously, a member of the bourgeoisie who in 1938-39 received $20,000 cheerfully paid about one-third of his income in taxes, while the average worker who received less than $1,500 could ill afford to pay about one-fifth of his income in taxes.

TABLE III TOTAL TAXES IN 1938-39 AS PERCENTAGE OF PERSONAL INCOME. BY INCOME CLASSES*			
	TAXES AS PERCENTAGE OF INCOME		
	Federal	State & Local	Total
Under $500	7.9%	14.0%	21.9%
$500 to $1,000	6.6	11.4	18.0
$1,000 to $1,500	6.4	10.9	17.3
$1,500 to $2,000	6.6	11.2	17.8
$2,000 to $3,000	6.4	11.1	17.5
$3,000 to $5,000	7.0	10.6	17.6
$5,000 to $10,000	8.4	9.5	17.9
$10,000 to $15,000	14.9	10.6	25.5
$15,000 to $20,000	19.8	11.9	31.7
$20,000 and over	27.2	10.6	37.8
TOTAL	9.2	11.0	20.2
* Taken from Table I of T.N.E.C. Monograph No.3, Who Pays the Taxes?			

With personal income having tripled by 1948, the opportunity to recast the American tax structure in a progressive direction, despite the fivefold increase in total tax receipts, was present. Obviously, this could have been done without impoverishing the bourgeoisie who,

The Permanent War Economy

as demonstrated in Part III, had accumulated sufficient surplus values to permit considerable easing of the tax burden of the lower income groups. Equally obviously, as can be seen from Table IV, this was not done.

TABLE IV 1948 TAX PAYMENTS AS PER CENT OF INCOME BY INCOME BRACKETS*			
	TAXES AS PERCENTAGE OF INCOME		
Spending Unit Income Bracket	Federal	State & Local	Total
Under $1,000	13.9%	9.7%	23.6%
$1,000 - $1,999	13.5	6.8	20.3
$2,000 - $2,999	15.5	6.1	21.6
$3,000 - $3,999	15.8	6.0	21.8
$4,000 - $4,999	16.1	5.6	21.7
$6,000 - $7,499	17.7	5.4	23.1
$7,600 and over	26.3	5.5	31.7
TOTAL	18.8	5.8	24.7

* Taken from Table 5 of Kreps, op. cit., which, in turn, is based on The Distribution of Tax Payments by Income Groups in 1948, by R.A. Musgrave, J.J. Carroll, L.D. Cook, and L. Franc, published in The National Tax Journal, March 1951.

Thus, after a decade of the Permanent War Economy, taxes took about one-fourth of total personal income, with Federal taxes now accounting for more than three-fourths of the total tax yield. Nevertheless, the completely regressive nature of state and local taxes still combines with such regressive features of Federal taxes as excise taxes and corporation taxes to produce a situation where the lowest income group still pays a higher percentage of its income in taxes than all except the 5.3 per cent of the spending

Taxation and the Class Struggle

units in the $7,500 and over category. If there were a finer income breakdown in the higher income groups, the beginnings of a progressive tax structure would become apparent at a somewhat lower figure than in 1938-39, but there has been no fundamental change in the incidence of taxation nor in the character of the American tax structure.

The worker who received $1,000 in 1938-39 and paid approximately 18 per cent in total taxes may have had his income increased to $2,500 in 1948, with his tax payments rising to 21 per cent. His contribution to total government tax receipts would then have gone up from $180 to $525, leaving his net income after taxes at $1,957 against $820 – an increase in effective money income of 141 per cent. Meanwhile, the bourgeois whose income in 1938-39 was $10,000, on which he likewise paid 18 per cent in total taxes, may have had his income increased to $30,000 in 1948, with his tax payments rising to 40 per cent. The bourgeois' contribution to total government tax receipts would then have increased from $1,800 to $12,000, leaving his net income after taxes at $18,000 against $8,200 – an increase in effective money income of only 120 per cent. On the surface, therefore, the worker is better off and capitalist inequality has tended to be reduced as a result of rising taxes.

Such growing "equality" the bourgeoisie can well afford, for if our hypothetical worker and bourgeois are assumed to represent their respective classes, what has happened is that total effective money income of both classes has risen from $9,020 to $19,975 – an increase of $10,955, of which $9,800, or 89.5 per cent, has gone to the bourgeoisie. The bourgeois is now only nine times better off than the worker, whereas previously his effective money income was ten times greater, but again nothing fundamental has changed in the relative positions of the basic classes of modern capitalist society. The state, however, whose function is more and more to protect the rule and the wealth of the bourgeoisie, is being financed in steadily increasing measure by the workers and lower middle classes. Therein lies the secret of the role of taxation under the Permanent War Economy, while equality of incomes remains just as much a mirage on the horizon as it ever was.

The data in Table IV can be used to derive the relative class burdens of taxation, if certain arbitrary assumptions be made to relate income brackets to classes. The results are necessarily rough, but demonstrate conclusively that the bourgeoisie by no means bear the major share of financing their state. If we assume that those in the $7,500 and over group, comprising 5.3 per cent of the number of spending units, represent the bourgeoisie and their main supporters among the upper middle classes, we can calculate their class tax burden, since Kreps notes that the effective tax rates are computed on an estimated personal income in 1948 of $211.9 billion, which is close enough to the reported figure of $209.5 billion. With this upper income group receiving 28.8 per cent of personal income, it is apparent that they received $61 billion, on which they paid an over-all tax rate of 31.7 per cent, or a total tax bill of $19.3 billion. This is equivalent to slightly more than one-third of total tax payments. In other words, the working classes and lower middle classes contribute almost two-thirds of total tax payments.

THE KREPS PAMPHLET, previously cited, constitutes one of the most effective indictments yet published on the inequities of the present American tax structure. In addition, it effectively refutes the arguments advanced by the apologists of the bourgeoisie that the masses must necessarily bear the major burden of tax increases. Kreps states and proves that "the principal beneficiaries of inflation were (in terms of actual dollars and cents) not the lower-income-bracket wage-and-pension-receiving masses but the upper-bracket-income entrepreneurs and owners of properties and equities." Readers of earlier articles in this series are thoroughly familiar with the facts of income distribution, which thoroughly debunk the carefully cultivated notion that the working masses have been the beneficiary of inflation.

Another assiduously propagandized falsehood is that the low-income masses are under-taxed and should therefore bear the major burden of new taxes. The factual refutation of this argument has already been presented, but there is another side to this coin which is most interesting. Not only do the upper income groups pay a smaller proportion of taxes than they claim or than they should by any standard of justice or equity, but they pay much less than they legally and morally should. The tax laws are drafted and administered by the representatives of capital in the interests of the ruling class. As Kreps puts it, ". . . opportunities for tax avoidance and tax evasion are much larger in the high-income brackets than in those below $3,000."

Taxation and the Class Struggle

The gap between Treasury reports of adjusted gross personal income, based on income tax returns, and Commerce estimates of personal income is extremely large. In 1948, for example, the Commerce figure was $45 billion higher than the Treasury total. Today, it must run well over $60 billion. Only a portion of this income that somehow miraculously evaporated when income tax returns were filled out can be attributed to non-monetary aspects of personal income included by Commerce, or to legal tax avoidance by low-income groups such as the exemption of military pay below $1,500 and the right to postpone reporting of accrued interest on E-bonds. Kreps states:

> Tax avoidance, completely legal but nonetheless real favors those in the upper income groups; for example, those who own their own homes. In the $7,500 and over bracket two out of three own their own homes whereas in the brackets between $1,000 and $3,000 the figure is about half that percentage. Now homeowners are not required to report the constructive income which they receive from their investment in their home (which may keep them out of a higher tax bracket). In addition, they can actually deduct local taxes on their home, and interest on the mortgage if there be one, which deduction cuts down their Federal income taxes at the highest marginal rate applicable to their income. Renters (of whom there are proportionately more than twice as many in the lower income brackets) simply pay out rent each month from an income total on which they pay taxes in full.
>
> Moreover, the splitting of incomes of married persons, which means nothing on lower bracket incomes (below $4,000), involves progressively more and more dollars of tax savings to each couple in the upper brackets, another reason why the per cent of income taken by taxes in the upper income brackets is not as high as one might expect.
>
> Those receiving entrepreneurial incomes are given several additional loopholes . . . Those owning oil properties can take 27.5 per cent depletion allowances year after year. Capital gains are taxed only 25 per

cent [now 26 per cent – T.N.V.] after but a six months' waiting period. Businessmen can split the income from their business several ways simply by making their wives, infant children and relatives 'partners' – though they may be called upon to prove that they did not do so simply for tax avoidance purposes. Executives can receive compensation in the form of stock options subject only to the rate on capital gains rather than the full income tax rates. And so on.

In other words, there are very few opportunities for legal tax avoidance in the lower income brackets. The worker's tax is withheld at the source and unless he has incurred unusually heavy medical expenses or some similar permitted deduction he pays 100 per cent of his income tax obligation. The worker cannot carry back or forward his "losses" that may have arisen due to unemployment, but the owner of capital can. The worker cannot deduct "business expenses" which the average businessman does to the full limit of what he can get away with. In fact, deduction of business expenses for entertainment, travel, etc., has reached such scandalous proportions that virtually every businessman has established charge accounts with restaurants, night clubs, etc., to "prove" that he spent the sums deducted as business expenses. That he also feeds and entertains himself while actually or theoretically promoting business is apparently outside the administration of the tax law. There can be little doubt that the amount of tax avoidance that occurs through the one device of "business expenses" amounts to billions of dollars.

The upper income individual can pose as a public-spirited person, and incidentally on occasion promote his own business interests, by making his 15 per cent contribution to charity. The lower income person simply does not have the means, nor does he as a rule possess the economic, social or political motives for such contributions. Related to this eminently respectable tax-dodging device is the legal evasion granted to the creators of trust funds, which not only avoids current income taxes but permits fortunes to be passed on to heirs with a notoriously minimum amount paid in estate taxes. The adroit use of gifts and gift taxes, it should be noted, is an integral part of this type of tax avoidance. The low amount of gift and estate taxes, observed earlier, and their decline since 1948 would undoubtedly prove to be a more profitable source of Congressional inquiry, in terms of added income to the government, than even the corruption in the Bureau of Internal Revenue.

There are many other legal loopholes. The excess profits tax, in particular, is so full of loopholes that it is practically a joke. So overt is the loophole situation that when President Truman signed the Revenue Act of 1951 on October 20th, he was constrained to say:

> Furthermore, this legislation does little to close the loopholes in present tax laws, and in some respects provides additional means by which wealthy individuals can escape paying their proper share of the national tax load through such devices as excessively liberal 'capital gains' provisions, family partnerships and excessive depletion allowances on oil and gas and certain mineral properties.

It should be obvious that the function of legal loopholes is not primarily to provide additional business for accountants and tax lawyers. Legal avoidance of taxes is part of the system by which the ruling class perpetuates its wealth and power. The tax laws are admittedly rigged in the interests of business. Elimination merely of obvious legal loopholes would by itself raise sufficient revenue to have made unnecessary the increases in the income tax under the Revenue Acts of 1950 and 1951. It must be emphasized that legal tax avoidance amounts to billions upon billions of dollars and that the bourgeoisie is virtually the sole beneficiary of such largesse. Not the lower income groups but the upper income groups are under-taxed!

In addition to tax avoidance, there is tax evasion, which is presumably illegal. States Kreps:

> Opportunities for tax evasion are similarly much more abundant in the upper income brackets than in the lower. Evasion is next to impossible

The Permanent War Economy

> where employers or fiduciaries make reports and act as collecting agencies in withholding taxes at the source, i.e., for wage earners, pensioners, public employees, etc. These have no chance to under-report their income [but the *New York World-Telegram and Sun* of December 10, 1951, reports that the government had warrants out on October 31st for more than $96 million owed by employers as tax delinquency on workers' payroll deductions – T.N.V.].

But note [in Table V on the opposite page] the types of income on which under-reporting occurred in 1946.

If the data in Table V are indicative of what normally transpires, 14 per cent of income tax net income is evaded by failure to report the legally correct amount. Which income levels are guilty of such evasions? Obviously, the upper income groups, for only 71 per cent of entrepreneurial income, 37 per cent of interest payments, 76 per cent of actual dividends paid, and 45 per cent of rents received, appeared on income tax returns. Income from these sources goes overwhelmingly to the upper income groups. Even in the case of wages and salaries, where there is a five per cent under-reporting, amounting in 1946 to $5 billion, or 25 per cent, of the total of $20 billion unreported, much, if not most, of the under-reporting would undoubtedly be traceable to the upper income groups.

Whether income tax evasion due to bribery of tax officials would add significantly to the amount of revenue the government should be collecting, we do not know. Perhaps the present Congressional investigation will throw some quantitative light on the picture. One thing is certain, however, and that is that it is not the low-income groups that bribe and corrupt government officials. The best proof that under-reporting and evasion of taxes among the upper income group are costing the government billions of dollars annually in lost tax revenues is to be found in the reported decision of Secretary of the Treasury Snyder to require the individual auditing of each taxpayer's return in the $25,000 and over bracket rather than the sampling technique used for the mass of income tax returns.

Taxation and the Class Struggle

TABLE V TAX EVASION IN 1946* (Millions of Dollars)				
Source of Income	Personal Income (Derived from Commerce)	Adjusted so as to be Comparable with Totals Reported on Income Tax Returns	Amount Reported on Income Tax Returns	Ratio of Reported Income to Actual
Civilian wages and salaries	$101,549	$102,546	$97,409	.95
Nonfarm entrepreneurial income	21,813	20,816	23,146	.71
Farm entrepreneurial income	10,840	11,929		
Military income	11,556			
Interest	9,317	2,989	1,105	.37
Dividends		4,933	3,730	.76
Fiduciary income (of individuals)		1,120	1,108	.99
Rent	5,460	4,013	1,799	.45
Social Security, etc	3,506			
Other income	868			
TOTAL	$164,909	$148,346	$128,287	.86

* Taken from Kreps, op. cit., source: National Bureau of Economic Research, *Studies in Income and Wealth*, Vol. XIII, to be published.

DECEPTION IN TAX MATTERS now extends to the government's official press releases. All official Washington releases on the Revenue Act of 1951 stated, in effect, that: "The

The Permanent War Economy

bill increases the tax on most individual incomes by 11.75 per cent." Whereupon, the average citizen concluded that, if his income remained the same, he would pay only 11.75 per cent more in Federal income tax in 1951 than he did in 1950. He was also led to believe that his 1952 tax would, barring a further increase in tax rates, be about the same as in 1951. This particular fraud was exposed in an article in the *New York World-Telegram and Sun* of November 20, 1951, based on an analysis supplied by Fred S. Peabody, for 20 years a special agent in the Income Tax Bureau and now an accountant and tax expert. A selection of cases to portray the actual impact of the Revenue Act of 1951 on individual income taxes is shown in Table VI.

				TABLE VI IMPACT OF REVENUE ACT OF 1951 ON SELECTED INDIVIDUAL INCOME TAXES				
Net Income	Number of Exemp-tions	1950 Rates	1951 Rates	1951 INCREASE OVER 1950 TAX		1952 Rates	1952 INCREASE OVER 1950 TAX	
				Amount	Per Cent		Amount	Per Cent
$900	1	$ 38	$ 45	$ 7	18.42%	$ 49	$ 11	28.94%
$2,000	2	106	125	19	18.00	136	30	28.30
$3,000	3	161	188	27	16.77	206	44	27.32
$4,000	4	213	249	36	16.90	271	58	27.22
$4,950	5	257	301	44	17.11	328	71	27.62
$10,000	2	1,466	1,667	210	14.42	1,822	366	26.13
$50,000	1	23,997	26,753	2,761	11.51	28,466	4,469	18.63

Taxation and the Class Struggle

The article states:

> You'll notice that some really do pay only about 11 per cent. The fellow who has to struggle with a net $50,000 income gets off with that.
>
> 'But simple arithmetic,' said Mr. Peabody, 'shows that for 1951 the increase over 1950 is much greater than the 11.75 per cent announced in Washington. Most persons will pay between 16.75 and 18 per cent.'
>
> What Mr. Peabody emphasizes is that the percentage increase cited on passage of the new tax bill last October was 'apparently based on the increase in tax to be withheld from wages beginning Nov. 1, instead of on the increase in tax you will pay for the full 1951 year.'
>
> The gimmick was the sizable credit which everybody was allowed on the tax paid last spring on part of his 1950 income . . .
>
> 'The Revenue Act of 1951,' Mr. Peabody explained, 'eliminated the 13 per cent credit allowed on the first $400 of tax granted under the 1950 law. So it is obvious that the percentage increase over the 1950 rate is at least 13 per cent of the first $400 of tax.
>
> 'It is believed that the loss of this 13 per cent cut affects a large majority of taxpayers. The rest lost a reduction of 9 per cent under last year's law.
>
> 'As the increased rates . . . did not become effective until Nov. 1 their full effect won't be felt until next year. Then most persons will pay between 27.25 and 28.25 per cent more than they would have paid on the same income at 1950 rates.'

Thus, the real impact of the new tax increase is on the workers and lower middle classes and won't be felt until March 15. At that time, those who have regularly been receiving sizable refunds because too much has been withheld will find that they get little or no refund, while others will find that they have to pay substantial additional sums to the government. The impact on March 15, 1953 on 1952 incomes will be even greater, as indicated, without any further increase in the income tax.

179

The Permanent War Economy

There is no need to cite the increases in excise taxes on liquor, cigarettes, gasoline, etc., or other regressive features of the Revenue Act of 1951. The facts are there for all who wish to take an unbiased look at them. It is frequently argued, however, that regardless of justice, etc., it is necessary to increase taxes more heavily on the lower income groups because that is the only way to reduce consumption of consumer commodities that are draining materials away from war output, and that inflation cannot be prevented without mopping up the "excess income" of the low-income masses. Both arguments are basically false, as Kreps demonstrates.

TABLE VII ESTIMATED DISTRIBUTION OF CONSUMER EXPENDITURES FOR 1948* (In Per Cent of Total)						
Spending Unit Income Brackets	Total Retail Sales	Retail Food Sales†	Retail Sales Less Food†	Liquor Sales	Tobacco Sales †	Durable Sales
Under $1,000	3.9%	4.1%	3.9%	0.9%	3.9%	2.2%
$1,000–$1,999	9.3	11.4	8.2	8.9	11.4	5.6
$2,000–$2,999	18.1	20.5	16.7	17.2	21.1	18.2
$3,000–$3,999	20.7	21.8	20.1	22.5	22.9	20.0
$4,000–$4,999	14.4	14.2	14.5	12.7	14.3	15.8
$5,000–$7,499	16.1	14.6	16.9	16.4	14.1	17.0
$7,500 and over	17.5	13.3	19.8	21.4	12.2	21.2
TOTAL	100.0	100.0	100.0	100.0	100.0	100.0

* Taken from Kreps, op. cit., source: Hearings, Joint Committee on the Economic Report, on January, 1951, Economic Report of the President.
† Totals do not add to 100 per cent due to rounding.

Taxation and the Class Struggle

"THE THIRD FALLACY requiring exposure to facts" observes Kreps, "is the notion that 60 per cent of the people must do 60 per cent of the consumption." As exposure of this tendentious argument in favor of increasing taxes on the lower income groups, in order to restrict consumption and thereby save critically needed materials, he offers the evidence contained in Table VII, submitted by Professor Musgrave in testimony before the Joint Committee on the Economic Report.

Comments Kreps:

> Those getting less than $3,000 (representing 54 per cent of the spending units) buy only 26 per cent of the durable goods, only 27 per cent of the liquor, 28.8 per cent of all goods at retail excepting food, and make only 31.3 per cent of all consumer expenditures.
>
> On the other hand, those getting over $4,000, comprising only 27 per cent of the spending units, buy 54 per cent of all durable goods, 50.5 per cent of the liquor, 51.2 per cent of all goods sold at retail excluding food, and account for 48 per cent of all consumer expenditures. *It is the spending of those getting over $4,000 that must be curbed if a major frontal attack is to be made on the problems of restricting consumption.*" (Italics mine – T.N.V.)

The apologists for the bourgeoisie also like to argue that it is the low-income masses who are responsible for the inflationary pressure generated by excess demand. The masses, they claim, hold the bulk of savings. This "hot" money, they assert, will be used to push up prices unless the tax collector relieves the mass of the population of "huge" savings. Nothing could be further from the truth. The overwhelming portion of personal savings has always been concentrated in the hands of the upper five or ten per cent of the population.

The Permanent War Economy

Writes Kreps:

> Actually, the amount of United States Government bonds and savings and checking accounts held by the majority, that is, the 26,000,000 consumer units getting less than 12,700, is only 27.1 per cent of the total. In so far as there is a 'hot money' problem with respect to E-bonds in 1950 or 1951, it is for the most part a middle and upper-income bracket problem. They are the only groups that have any substantial quantities of E-bonds or other liquid assets left. The lower income groups have for the most part sold theirs.
>
> In 1949 more than half the population failed to save a dime. In fact, on balance, their dissaving has continually increased though, of course, there still remain a minority even in the lowest income brackets that manage to save despite the fact that the majority do not. On the other hand, the savings of the top tenth have increased so much that in 1949 their net savings exceeded the total of all net savings in the country. In other words, on balance, the lowest 90 per cent in the income scale saved nothing.

Moreover, adds Kreps,

> ... since V-J Day, about twelve-and-a-half million spending units have parted with all the savings bonds they owned.... In short, 'hot money' in large amounts is primarily not a mass-income bracket, but an upper-income bracket phenomenon.

The workers and lower middle classes, thus, were not responsible for the orgy of consumer buying following the outbreak of the Korean war. On the contrary, it was the bourgeoisie and upper middle classes, the only ones with the income, savings or credit to permit widespread advance buying and hoarding, particularly of durable goods, who built up private inventories in precisely the same manner as businessmen accumulated huge inventories. While inflation is inherent and permanent under the Permanent War

Taxation and the Class Struggle

Economy, as we have previously demonstrated, the engine of inflation is always and necessarily the accumulation and expenditure of surplus values on the part of the bourgeoisie.

We need not be particularly concerned with Kreps' conclusions, for his position is the traditional one of the liberals and intellectuals. As such, it will receive brief comment below. His case against heavier taxes on mass incomes, however, is most cogently made. It is well to have the data before us when evaluating the position of the various classes with respect to taxation.

> . . . any new tax falling on those getting less than $3,000 will cut production much more than it will cut or divert consumption.

In support of this contention, which is based on the fact that "tens of millions of families have had their budgets so cruelly cut by inflation that minimum standards of health and productivity are being eroded away" Kreps offers the following income analysis, which we present on page 184 as Table VIII.

> To be sure, economic literature abounds in controversies concerning the 'efficiency level' of consumption or the level of 'minimum needs.' Thus, for example, the minimum health and decency budget currently published by the Bureau of Labor Statistics is one so high that even at current high levels of national income, nearly three-fourths of the population fail to attain it.
> Yet in quantitative terms even that budget hardly seems luxurious or excessive. It provides, for example, that a man can buy a top coat only once in ten years, that his wife can have only one new cotton street dress a year; that her wool dress has to last five years. The family can buy a low-priced car only once every 15 or 16 years. Other durable goods such as cook stoves, refrigerators, washing machines, vacuum cleaners, sewing machines, have to last 17 years or longer. In quantitative terms, such a budget level seems a considerable distance removed from luxury consumption, yet at 1950 prices the income estimated by the Bureau of

The Permanent War Economy

TABLE VIII
INCOME RECEIVED AND ESTIMATED MINIMUM INCOME REQUIRED FOR FAMILY MAINTENANCE BY INCOME CLASSES – 1948*
(Billions of Dollars)

Adjusted Gross Income Classes	Adjusted Gross Income Received‡	Federal Personal Income Tax Liability	Income After Federal Income Tax	Estimated[†] Amount Needed for Maintenance	Deficiency (–) or Excess of Income Over Estimated "Minimum Need"
Under $1,000	$4.3	$0.1	$4.2	$11.8	–$7.6
$1,000–$1,499	6.5	0.2	6.3	9.5	– 3.2
$1,500–$1,999	10.5	0.4	10.1	11.5	– 1.4
$2,000–$2,499	14.1	0.7	13.4	12.7	0.7
$2,500–$2,999	16.9	0.9	16.0	13.1	2.9
$3,000–$3,499	17.3	1.0	16.3	11.4	4.9
$3,500–$3,999	15.2	1.0	14.2	8.9	5.3
$4,000–$4,499	13.0	0.9	12.1	6.8	5.3
$4,500–$4,999	9.7	0.8	8.9	4.6	4.3
$5,000–$5,999	12.6	1.1	11.5	5.3	6.2
$6,000–$9,999	17.2	1.8	15.4	5.6	9.8
$10,000 and over	26.8	6.6	20.2	3.0	17.2
TOTAL	164.2	15.4	148.8	104.3	44.5

* Taken from Kreps, op. cit., source: Joint Economic Report, Senate Report No.210, 82ndCongress, 1st session, April 2, 1950, US Government Printing Office. ‡ Statistics of Income 1948, Part I (Preliminary).
† Estimated on the basis of number of families by size groups within each income class multiplied by an estimated minimum income figure needed to sustain a family of a specified size – i.e., $1,000 for each individual living alone; $1,500 for two person families;$2,000 for three, $2,500 for four, $3,000 for five, $3,500 for six, and $4,000 for families of seven or more persons.

Taxation and the Class Struggle

Labor Statistics as necessary to finance this standard of living is $1,630 for a single person, and $2,330 for a married couple.

In order to be highly conservative, the figures in Table VIII have been computed on a basis more than one-third lower than the BLS figures . . . Even on this basis, as the table clearly indicates, the tens of millions of families and single individuals who receive less than $2,000 a year come short by many billions of dollars in obtaining the income necessary for efficiency consumption and productivity. As a defense measure, incomes not higher than efficiency levels ought to be kept inviolate and not further lowered by general sales taxes or general manufacturers' excise taxes.

Table VIII likewise indicates where the money in excess of such, a minimum may be found. Of the total of roughly $44.5 billion in 1948 that may have been available in excess of minimum need, $17.2 billion, or 40 per cent was in the hands of persons with incomes of $10,000 or over; another 22 per cent in the hands of persons receiving over $6,000 but less than $10,000; more than 23 per cent in the hands of persons receiving over $4,500 but less than $6,000; and less than 8 per cent in the brackets below $3,000.

THAT TAXES HAVE BECOME a major arena of the class struggle can be seen from the sharply divergent position of the various classes with respect to proposals for increased taxation and the bitterness that conflicts over taxation have engendered. With taxes taking a steadily increasing proportion of current output in order to finance the war machine and its inevitable bureaucratic apparatus, it is only natural that this should be the case. The impact of taxation in general has become so great that all classes and all income levels feel "hurt in the pocket-book," which is popularly believed to be the severest hurt of all. At any rate, it is a fact that today no major business transaction is consummated or policy adopted without careful examination of the impact on the tax position of the corporation or stockholder involved.

There has likewise been a noticeable trend toward crystallization of opposing and conflicting class positions with respect to taxation policy. Although an element of fluidity

The Permanent War Economy

in class positions and attitudes toward various proposals to increase tax revenues still prevails, we can distinguish sharply among the positions of the more class conscious strata, especially the industrial bourgeoisie as represented by the NAM, organized labor, particularly its left wing as represented by Reuther, and class-conscious socialists. The most fully developed and highly articulated class position is that of the NAM for a uniform manufacturers' excise tax. The NAM position was adopted in 1949 and is presented in its post-Korean form in a basic study entitled *A Program to Combat Inflation by Paying-As-We-Go*, approved by the NAM's Board of Directors on February 21, 1951 and published as Economic Policy Division Series No. 38. Its chief features are put forth in a popular catechism of 34 questions and answers on A Manufacturers' Uniform Excise Versus A Retail Sales Tax, appearing as a special report of *NAM News*, May 5, 1951.

We need not be concerned with the internecine quarrel within the bourgeoisie between the advocates of a Federal retail sales tax and the NAM advocacy of a manufacturers' uniform excise tax. Both are taxes on consumption to be paid by the consumer, i.e., those least able to afford higher taxes. Both are designed to shift the major burden of taxation to the workers and lower middle classes. Advocates of both positions are prepared to accept either method as offering the best prospect of maintaining the wealth and power of the bourgeoisie and still assuring needed support for the capitalist state. Aside from technical differences, the major dispute is one of perspective. Advocates of the retail sales tax, representing less reactionary segments of the bourgeoisie and their supporters, view such measures as "temporary," to be repealed after the "emergency" is over. The NAM, on the other hand, states categorically:

> For the purposes of the long-range future, *this uniform tax at a moderate rate should be regarded* as the basic federal excise, to be carried through into the period beyond the defense period, or even a third war, *as a permanent feature of federal taxation*. (Italics in original.)

The NAM is quite open in its objective. Catechism 5 goes:

> Q. Why has the NAM recommended a uniform excise tax? A. This recommendation is made for two reasons: 1 – TO CORRECT THE

Taxation and the Class Struggle

DEFECTS OF THE EXISTING FEDERAL EXCISE SYSTEM ... A uniform excise tax across the board on all consumer purchases would introduce equality of tax burden in proportion to purchases of consumer goods. It would put all producers on a par in competing for the consumer dollar ... 2 – TO ESTABLISH A BROAD BASE OF CONSUMPTION TAXATION. *The distribution of a part of the total tax load over income as it is spent will make possible the levy of less heavy taxes on income as it is received.* Thus the attainment of the dual objective of high-level production and consumption would be less hampered than by *extreme concentration of taxes on income as received, a policy that would diminish the incentives to work in order to get income.* (Italics mine – T.N.V.)

If the motivation is not entirely clear, we can cite catechism 13. Because of its touching solicitude for the general welfare, and its conscious and unconscious revelation of NAM philosophy, we reproduce it in full:

Q. Would a manufacturers' uniform excise be an unfair burden on the low-income groups?
A. No. The excise or consumption taxes are one of the tax methods which the Government must use in order to keep the defense program on a pay-as-we-go basis. There must be some tax payment toward this cost by all, regardless of the level of their income. *There is not enough income left after present taxes in the middle and higher incomes to pay the bill, even if all of the income after tax were confiscated. The lower incomes must carry a part of the load.* Available figures show that if food, rent, and various services are excluded, as they would be under the NAM program, the relative burden of excise taxes would rise *somewhat* as income increases. In other words, the more one has to spend, the more he is likely to spend, and hence the more excise tax he will pay.
In the financing program which the nation faces there is a choice of evils. If we try to protect too many people against an increase of tax burden, we shall fail to keep on a pay-as-we-go basis. The alternative to this course is

The Permanent War Economy

> inflation, and this would inflict a heavier burden on all consumers than they would have to carry as a tax load. *If we try to balance the budget by increasing income taxes, it will not be possible to shelter the small incomes from this tax.* Excise taxes will be a means of keeping income tax rates lower than they would otherwise have to be, and *thus they become the least of the evils, for the small income groups* and for all taxpayers. (Italics mine – T.N.V.)

It would be difficult to crowd more arrant nonsense and utterly false reasoning in such a short space. The ignorance betrayed on the causes and effects of inflation, not to mention the relationship of taxation to inflation, is equaled by the erroneous statements on the facts of economic life and the evident self-contradictions. In fact, the only correct statement in the entire catechism is that consumer expenditures are related to income. The implication that the lower incomes are relatively untaxed is completely false, as already shown. The statement that even confiscation of income of upper income levels would not raise sufficient revenue to balance the budget is sheer nonsense. As Table VIII demonstrates, in 1948 there was over $20 billion left after Federal income taxes in the $10,000 and over category. In spite of increased taxes (which do not apply to the NAM argument), there is at least that sum available today, and the Federal deficit is never presented, at more than half that figure. There are, in fact, many ways of raising the amount stated as necessary to finance the war program without increasing taxes on incomes under $4,000 by one cent.

The NAM position, taken at face value, becomes the ludicrous one of asserting that higher income taxes are equally bad for rich and poor, and that higher excise taxes, whose burden is admittedly heavier on the mass of the population, will favor rich and poor alike. The sleight of hand by which the majority of the population in the low-income groups is supposed to favor a tax program designed to minimize the tax burden of the upper income groups is matched by the effrontery that attempts to pass off sales taxes as progressive because they are proportional.

In passing, it should be noted that the NAM is not opposed to increasing the yield from the income tax if it be done through reducing the present exemption for dependents from $600 to $500. The important question, however, is at what rate would the uniform excise tax have to be placed in order to achieve the NAM's objective of a balanced budget. And how much of an increase would this bring in the average price level?

Taxation and the Class Struggle

While the NAM carefully avoids such questions in its popular catechism, it provides its own answer in its programmatic statement:

> At current levels of gross national product, a tax base for the uniform manufacturers' excise tax of $90 billion is estimated. With no allowance for the effect of high rates on the volume of consumption buying, a flat rate of 10 per cent would produce $9 billion, and a flat rate of 20 per cent would produce $18 billion, as compared with $4 billion under the present selective system [not true by more than $4 billion as shown in Table I; even if the figure is intended to refer only to excise taxes other than liquor and tobacco, it would be $4.5 billion in 1950 – T.N.V.]. *These rates on the final manufactured price would become equivalent rates of 5-6 per cent, and 10-12 per cent, respectively, in relation to the retail price.* (Italics mine – T.N.V.)

It is clear that maintenance of the war program at NAM-approved levels, would require a uniform excise tax on manufactured commodities other than food of close to 20 per cent. For the working masses, this would raise the cost of living by about 8 per cent. Why direct inflation is any worse than such a tax-legislated inflation is not at all clear. It is clear, however, why the Administration has so far rejected the NAM program as politically unfeasible, and has proceeded to maintain the existing tax structure, by raising income, corporation and excise taxes.

ORGANIZED LABOR'S OPPOSITION to the tax gouge was indicated in the previous article by quotations from statements issued by the United Labor Policy Committee. Its position on the Revenue Act of 1951 is adequately indicated by a CIO press release of September 20, 1951, in which the CIO charged that:

> ... the tax bill under Senate consideration will represent a $1.10 weekly cut in take-home pay for four-member families with incomes of $4,000, and called for a series of six improvements ... : (1) remove the $1.3 billion excise tax increases; (2) eliminate tax increases on incomes under $4,000; (3) close the split income loophole; (4) eliminate alternate methods of computing income tax that benefit the wealthy; (5) retain House-passed provisions on

The Permanent War Economy

excess profits and corporation taxes; (6) levy a withholding tax on dividends and interest.

The CIO estimated that these amendments would provide a net increase in taxes (above what Congress actually passed) of more than $2 billion. And, of course, by closing certain loopholes and eliminating certain regressive features, the CIO's proposal would have resulted in a less reactionary tax system. Unfortunately, in the absence of a united and forcefully expressed position on the part of the trade-union movement, the Administration could afford to ignore the attitude of organized labor.

In relation to the future of the tax question, the last paragraph in the CIO statement is most interesting:

> Of all the raids upon the incomes of workers, farmers, professional and fixed-income persons contained in this bill, the $1.3 billion excise (sales) tax gouge is the most outrageous and, when compared to the split income and alternative tax rate loopholes for the well-to-do, the most immoral proposal in the bill. Moreover, these increases and extensions of excise (sales) taxes must be fought and should be defeated because they are preliminary steps in the campaign led by the NAM in fastening a comprehensive Federal sales tax upon the American people as part of a permanent tax policy.

In the light of the NAM-spearheaded drive to shift a substantial portion of the tax burden from the upper income groups to the lower income groups, and the apparent awareness of the CIO, at any rate, that the fight over sales taxes will become increasingly important as time goes on, the statement of Walter Reuther on taxes of August 8, 1951 (carefully ignored by the press) is of considerable interest. Criticizing the NAM's proposal, Reuther analyzes the shift in tax burden that would result were the uniform excise tax substituted for income taxes to the extent desired by the NAM:

> As of 1948, the NAM's proposal would have reduced by $5 billion the tax burden on families with incomes ranging upward from $5,000 and shifted an equivalent burden onto those with income below $5,000. More than $3

Taxation and the Class Struggle

billion of the savings in the upper brackets would have been gained at the expense of those with incomes of less than $4,000 a year . . .

In terms of its impact on individual families, the NAM proposal as of 1948 would have been equivalent to a wage cut of $133 a year, $2.56 a week, or 6.4 cents per hour for spending units whose breadwinners earn less than $1,000 a year. For those earning $7,500 or more the NAM seeks an income increase averaging $1,760 a year, $33.85 a week or 84.6 cents an hour, on the basis of the 1948 situation.

The interesting part of the Reuther statement, however, is not so much the criticism of the NAM proposals, or the existing tax structure, which largely parallels the material presented herein, especially the position of Kreps, but his proposal to adopt a spendings tax as an equitable anti-inflationary device. To quote from the press release summarizing his statement:

> The kind of tax on spending proposed by Reuther was proposed by the Treasury Department in 1942 after extensive study by the department.
> 'As far as we have been able to determine,' Reuther said, 'the proposal was never given adequate consideration in Congress.'

In describing how the tax on spending would work, Reuther said:

> In essence, the Treasury proposed (in 1942) that spending above specified exemption levels be taxed on a graduated basis. To take a hypothetical example, suppose an exemption of $1,500 per person were allowed. In that case, a family of four would be liable under the spending tax only if its spending exceeded $6,000 a year. For purposes of this example, we can assume tax rates equal to the surtax rates proposed by the Treasury, which were as follows:

The Permanent War Economy

Spending	Tax Rate
Less than $1,000 above exemptions	10%
$1,000 to $2,000 above exemptions	20%
$2,000 to $3,000 above exemptions	30%
$3,000 to $5,000 above exemptions	40%
$5,000 to $10,000 above exemptions	50%
Over $10,000 above exemptions	75%

Thus, a family of four which spent a total of $7,000 would be liable to a spending tax of 10 per cent on the last $1,000 or $100. A similar family which spent $10,000 would have to pay a tax of $1,000. A four-person family spending $25,000 would pay a spending tax of $10,650.

Such a tax would obviously be a powerful deterrent to nonessential spending. Yet if the exemption level were set high enough, no family would be hampered in the purchase of necessities. Every well-to-do family could maintain a high standard of living – only its standard of luxury would be somewhat curtailed. Proper exemptions would assure that only nonessential spending would be taxed. Exemptions would protect large families, who would suffer worst under a sales tax.

While the administrative difficulties in collecting and preventing evasion under a spendings tax would be vastly greater than Reuther is willing to admit, the proposal merits serious consideration, especially if the main emphasis in future tax programs is to be prevention of inflation. Although Reuther indicates that the revenue to be anticipated from a tax on spending along the lines he proposes would be about $10 billion, it is extremely doubtful, given its administrative difficulties, that a spendings tax could be relied on to close the gap in the Federal budget. This is our major objection to the Reuther proposal, for a tax program to be politically effective must point the way toward an end of deficit financing. Nevertheless, if the trade unions show any disposition to espouse the spendings tax, socialists should unhesitatingly give it complete support.

Taxation and the Class Struggle

THE LIBERAL POSITION with respect to taxes has been indicated by the material cited from Kreps. Fundamentally, as exemplified by the ADA, it operates within the present tax structure, concentrating chiefly on eliminating present tax loopholes that benefit the wealthy. Most emphasis is usually placed on removing the split income provision, although Kreps also wants to "regraduate tariffs down to a maximum of 10 per cent." The liberals worry about both "not raising taxes so high as to impair incentives to work" and "placing the main burden on those who can afford to pay it." Their dilemma increasingly reflects a central contradiction of the Permanent War Economy.

The liberal position roughly coincides with that of the Administration, and is quite close to that of the labor bureaucracy. In the popular vernacular, it may be summarized as "Let's have both guns and butter." As civilian standards of living are impaired under the pressure of increasing war outlays, the liberals necessarily make concessions to the position of big capital, which may be summarized as "More guns and less butter."

It is particularly important, however, that all possible forces be united against the bourgeois contention that they do not have the money from which additional taxes could come, even if their incomes were to be confiscated. This palpable falsehood is paraded not only by the NAM, as revealed above, but by every segment of the big bourgeoisie. Their financial and economic writers take particular delight in expatiating on what they mistakenly regard as a basic fallacy in the position of everyone else. Writes Edward H. Collins, chief financial writer of the New York Times, in his column of October 15, 1951:

> The rapidly contracting elbow room left in the upper individual income brackets is illustrated by a segregation of incomes of $10,000 or higher. If all such income were to be taxed at the rate of 100 per cent, according to a recent estimate by Harley Lutz [tax consultant to the NAM - T.N.V.], the yield would amount to only $3.5 billion. And the pending legislation proposes to take one billion of this.

Lawrence Fertig, economist apologist for the bourgeoisie, repeats the same argument in the *New York World-Telegram and Sun* of June 11, 1951, by citing statistics from Treasury Secretary Snyder's report of February 5, 1951:

The Permanent War Economy

Look carefully at these figures. Obviously the raising of three to four billion of extra income taxes will have to come mainly from the citizens of moderate incomes because the steeply progressive income tax has already stripped the higher brackets.

\multicolumn{4}{c}{INDIVIDUAL TAXABLE NET INCOME FOR 1951 (In Billions)}			
Surtax Brackets	Present Tax	Residue	Total Taxable Net
Under $2,000	$12.5	$50.2	$62.7
$2,000 – $4,000	2.3	8.2	10.5
$4,000 – $10,000	2.5	6.3	8.8
$10,000 – $20,000	1.8	2.3	4.1
$20,000 and over	2.8	1.2	4.0
TOTAL	21.9	68.2	90.1

The answer to the canard that there is only $3.5 billion left to be taxed in the over $10,000 income bracket is that the Treasury presents all kinds of tax figures and a certain amount of obvious care must be exercised in using them, as a letter to the editor of the *New York Times* by George W. Hewitt, published on November 22, 1951, reveals. The Lutz-Collins-Fertig-NAM-etc. conclusion that there is practically no money left to be taxed within the bourgeoisie is based, apparently, on Table 13 of Secretary Snyder's report, where the data are based on "surtax net income." The same Treasury report, Table 12, shows that only 7 per cent of "gross income" is in the under-$2,000 class.

The manipulation, to which the Treasury has wittingly or unwittingly contributed, is explained by Mr. Hewitt as follows:

Taxation and the Class Struggle

But there are two departures from previous usual custom found in Table 13 that accentuate this segregation of taxable income in the lower-income brackets and away from the higher brackets, which in our opinion may lead to misunderstanding of the conclusions reached. First, married joint returns are considered as two taxpayers, each with half of the combined surtax net income. Second, amounts subject to the 50 per cent alternative rate on long-term capital gains are excluded from income.

In the great majority of cases it is the husband's income that determines the family status, the wife ordinarily having little or no income. We commonly think of a family in which the husband has a $22,000 salary, for example, as being in the above-$20,000 class as to gross income and slightly below $20,000 on taxable income classification. But in Table 13 viewpoint we will have two incomes, each of which will be classified as under $10,000. As married people making joint returns are 3.5 to 1 in ratio to single taxpayers, this detail should be held definitely in mind when drawing conclusions as to taxable income totals in certain groups. As to exclusion of long-term capital gains from income, we do not see how this can be done logically, when the Government has already set the precedent by including 50 per cent of these gains in adjusted gross income. That much of these sales is surely to be considered as income.

Few persons have reference to Table 13 in the Treasury report. When conclusions are drawn from this table and presented to us it would be helpful to have notations made of the conditions governing the tabulation. But simpler and clearest would be to present surtax net incomes and tax based on adjusted gross income brackets and taxable returns.

In this method of presentation it would be found that in gross income classification of over $10,000 the total taxable income of that group is $28.4 billion and tax is $9.9 billion, the difference between income and tax being $18.5 billion. In gross income classification of over $4,000 the

The Permanent War Economy

total taxable income is $62.4 billion and tax $16.9 billion, the difference between income and tax being $45.5 billion.

Moreover, without reference to the split income feature and the omission of capital gains income, it is obvious that the income of those in the $10,000 and over surtax bracket is also included in all lower surtax brackets. The claim that bourgeois incomes have been virtually confiscated by high income taxes stands revealed as a miserable deception – one that on the part of the professional apologists of the bourgeoisie is either conscious, or they are guilty of gross incompetence in the handling of economic data.

Such chicanery and stupidity have, however, apparently had some effect, for an editorial in the World-Telegram and Sun of October 11, 1951, reveals that a Gallup poll shows 59 per cent of the population in favor of limiting Federal income taxes to a maximum of 25 per cent of anybody's income. It is also revealed that a constitutional amendment for such an income tax limitation has already been endorsed by 25 states. If 32 states go on record for such a limit, Congress will have to reckon with a constitutional barrier to higher income taxes. In fact, such a limitation would reduce existing income taxes, and automatically guarantee adoption of the NAM tax program.

A CAPITAL LEVY is the only rational approach to the current problem of taxation. That is the socialist answer to the NAM tax program and other proposals to make the working masses bear the main burden of supporting the war economy. A levy on capital is not only just since the war economy has as its primary aim the protection of the wealth and power of the capitalist class, but it is the only method of taxation that can readily and easily raise the huge sums that the bourgeoisie claim are necessary to support the capitalist state.

Historically, socialist parties, particularly in Europe, have traditionally mentioned a capital levy whenever the problem of taxation has become acute, but the literature on the subject is rather sparse. In the United States, a proposal for a graduated capital levy was made by former Senator Elmer A. Benson of Minnesota. The Benson proposal was inserted in the Hearings on the Revenue Act of 1942 by Benjamin C. Marsh, representing the "People's Lobby."

Taxation and the Class Struggle

The proposed tax or capital levy would be in effect for 1 year and would be levied on the total value of all property owned by individuals at a graduated rate from 1 to 20 per cent, and the tax would be payable in 18 monthly installments with a 6 per cent discount for payment in advance. Married persons would be given a credit in paying the tax of $500 and single persons a credit of $300.

The Benson capital levy was a naive proposal, whose rates on personal property would run from 1 per cent on $10,000 and under to 20 per cent on all personal property over $1 million. It would have been difficult to collect and would not have raised any great sum, for the major capitalist wealth is owned by corporations. Moreover, there is little point in attempting to assess personal wealth that is not functioning as capital. It is capital that is responsible for the development of the Permanent War Economy and it is capital that should be taxed to provide the finances that the bourgeoisie consider to be necessary.

To keep the capital levy simple and easy to administer, it should at this time be assessed not on all corporations, but on those with assets in excess of $1 billion. There were 58 such billion-dollar companies at the end of 1950, whose combined assets totaled almost $148 billion. A 10 per cent capital levy on corporations whose assets exceed one billion dollars would therefore raise $15 billion. This would be more than ample to balance the Federal budget, even after rescinding the increases provided under the Revenue Act of 1951.

A survey by Alfred F. Connors, copyright by United Press, was published toward the middle of 1951 on the firms with assets in excess of one billion dollars. The list on the following page was taken from the *New York World-Telegram and Sun*, and compares these 58 leading corporations' assets at the end of 1950 with the end of 1945.

The Permanent War Economy

ASSETS OF BILLION-DOLLAR COMPANIES					
(In Millions of Dollars)					
Company	Dec. 31, 1950	Dec. 31, 1949	Company	Dec. 31, 1950	Dec. 31, 1949
Bell System	$11,576	$10,775	Standard Oil (Ind.)	1640	1651
Metropolitan Life	10,338	9,708	Socony-Vacuum	1610	1472
Bell System	8,924	8,325	Consolidated Edison Company	1,604	1,502
Bank of America	6,863	6,250	First National, Boston	1,602	1,528
Equitable Life	5,702	5,269	National Bank of Detroit	1,568	1,366
National City Bank	5,526	5,052	Pacific Gas & Electric	1,513	1,322
Chase National Bank	5,283	4,780	Texas Company	1,449	1,368
New York Life	4,908	4,675	Northwestern Bancorp	1,446	1,352
Standard Oil (N.J.)	4,188	3,816	Massachusetts Mutual	1,395	1,313
General Motors	3,444	2,824	Santa Fe Railway	1,379	1,295
John Hancock	2,960	2,697	Irving Trust	1,360	1,187
Guaranty Trust	2,940	2,731	Gulf Oil	1,344	1,216
U.S. Steel Corp.	2,829	2,556	Ford Motor Co.*	1,343	1,149
Manufacturers Trust	2,773	2,452	Bank of Manhattan	1,320	1,232
First National (Chi.)	2,599	2,461	Bethlehem Steel Corp.	1,314	1,155
Northwestern Mutual	2,594	2,443	Penn Mutual	1,300	1,241
Continental Ill. Nat'l	2,591	2,553	Mutual Benefit	1,299	1,238
Pennsylvania RR	2,345	2,280	General Electric	1,277	1,171
Mutual Life (N.Y.)	2,143	2,075	First Bank Stock	1,273	1,227
Travelers Insurance	1,995	1,879	Marine Midland	1.266	1,199
E.I. du Pont	1,974	1,749	Union Pacific	1.247	1,177
Southern Pacific Co.	1,854	1,760	Baltimore & Ohio	1.243	1,220
New York Central	1,843	1,775	Standard Oil California	1,233	1,158
Bankers Trust, N.Y.	1,838	1,624	Cleveland Trust	1,222	1,120
Sec. First Nat'l (L.A.)	1,824	1,713	Commonwealth Edison	1,194	1,115
Aetna Life	1,812	1,643	C.I.T. Financial	1,174	996
Central Hanover Bank (N.Y.)	1,770	1,592	New England Mutual	1,170	1,083
Mellon National Bank	1,718	1,424	American Trust San Francisco	1,091	992
Chemical Bank & Trust	1,714	1,593	Sears, Roebuck†	1.033	808
TOTAL				147,782	136,730

* Ford Motor reports once annually in September to Massachusetts State Tax Commission. Latest figures given above are for Dec. 31, 1949 and Dec. 31, 1948.

† Fiscal year ended Jan. 31, 1951.

Taxation and the Class Struggle

The 58 largest companies, ranked by their assets at the end of 1950, can be grouped as follows:

Number	Type	Assets (Billions)
15	Insurance Companies	$59.4
20	Banks	48.3
6	Manufacturing	12.2
6	Oil	11.5
6	Railroads	9.9
3	Public Utilities	4.3
2	Miscellaneous	2.2
58	All types	147.8

It will be seen that 35 banks and insurance companies account for $107.7 billion, or almost 73 per cent of the total assets of the leading 58 billion-dollar firms. Thus, if it be objected that a capital levy of 10 per cent on gross assets would create insurmountable difficulties as the banks and insurance companies may not have a 10 per cent equity in their total assets, our proposed capital levy can easily be transferred to a 10 per cent tax on all corporations with net assets in excess of one million dollars.

Such a tax on capital would easily raise more than enough to balance the Federal budget after rescinding the increases contained in the Revenue Act of 1951, for a glance at Table VIII-A of Part III (The New International, May-June 1951) shows that the book net assets of 3,304 leading corporations on January 1, 1950 totaled $101.9 billion. Since that compilation by the National City Bank excluded the banks and insurance companies, there cannot be more than $40 billion of duplication even if there were no

The Permanent War Economy

difference between net and gross assets. The banks and insurance companies, however, should not escape from a capital levy, as of all privately owned institutions they are the most parasitic and are strong candidates for nationalization even under capitalism.

A 10 per cent capital levy on the net assets of all business firms with net assets over $1 million would therefore yield at least $15 billion. Most corporations could pay such a tax out of surplus and undivided profits. Those that could not could either borrow the money or arrange to turn over an equivalent amount in shares of stock to the government, sufficient to pay their capital levy tax liability.

In other words, contrary to the position of the NAM that taxes must be paid out of current income, there is no reason why taxes cannot be paid out of past income by those who have accumulated capital through exploiting the labor of others. To the extent that the workers and lower middle classes own stock in corporations that would be subject to the capital levy, they will gladly reduce their equity in such means of ownership by 10 per cent.

Of course, the rantings of the bourgeoisie and their paid hirelings against a capital levy can easily be imagined. They will cry "socialism," as if that were an argument. Actually, a capital levy is possible only under capitalism, although it might well be a step in the direction of socialism. It is doubtful, however, that a 10 per cent levy on capital would seriously impair the functioning of capitalism. They will also "argue" that a capital levy is inflationary, for corporations "would have to increase the prices of their commodities and services sufficiently to recoup the losses of capital arising from the capital levy." Why this follows would be clear only to those who believe that the rights of property are sacred and at all times to be placed above human rights. In any case, maintenance of price control would prevent a sudden recoupment of the capital that has been taxed away. If anything, a capital levy would be deflationary for capital accumulation is one of the main contributing forces to inflation.

IF THE BOURGEOISIE object to a 10 per cent capital levy as too radical, we can offer them as an alternative the proposals of two of their most eminent spokesmen. We refer first to the late President Roosevelt and his proposal that during World War II a ceiling of $25,000 be placed on individual incomes. If such a proposal possessed validity at that time, as it did, it is surely even more germane to a fight for capitalist survival against Stalinism, which is the underlying raison d'être of the Permanent War Economy today.

Taxation and the Class Struggle

And, if Roosevelt was too radical for the American capitalists, we give them that arch-capitalist, Bernard M. Baruch, who wrote a 500-page book in 1941 called American Industry in the War, the main theme of which is "Take the Profit Out of War." In his testimony on the need for price control, published in the New York Times of September 20, 1941, Baruch amazed his fellow capitalists by stating:

> We have talked for years of taking the profit out of war. Price control is one of the ways to do it. The inflationary process affords an opportunity to many to reap huge rewards, while the average person with a fixed income must tighten his belt . . . America, which has refused to take a foot of territory for its own war profit, should show the way so that its citizens shall not profit from war. I cannot emphasize this too strongly. We have talked about it, we have written about it, we have preached about it, we have radioed about it. Veteran organizations and Congress both have adopted resolutions about it – that there shall be no profits from war. Let us now make good that promise . . . But I must emphasize that no tax program alone can recapture all excessive profits. Profits must also be controlled at their source, which is rising-runaway prices. We must not have a crop of 'defense millionaires' to parallel 1918 'war millionaires.'

Understandably, all that happened was more talk, inequitable controls, and a crop of war millionaires in World War II that far exceeded those produced by World War I. With the Permanent War Economy conducted by the representatives of the big bourgeoisie in their own interests, with the state guaranteeing profits, as we have previously shown, there is no tendency toward any decrease in the number of war-induced millionaires at the present time. We do not question the fact that the problem of incentives and capital accumulation is becoming an ever more difficult one for the bourgeoisie to solve. That is the reason for the NAM drive for a politically unpopular universal sales tax. But the state manages to ease the burden for the patriotic capitalist through five-year amortization of war plants, sizable war contracts and, above all, an economy propped up by huge war outlays.

The Permanent War Economy

The bourgeoisie moan and weep crocodile tears because on the average profits after taxes in 1951 are running 10 per cent below 1950. But, as we have shown, profits in 1950 reached an all-time historic high. They will probably never again be equaled. We can sympathize with the millionaire who finds it increasingly difficult to become a billionaire because of high taxes, but the real impact of high taxes under the Permanent War Economy is to make it increasingly difficult for the ranks of the bourgeoisie to be replenished with new entrants from the working and middle classes. That is why the bourgeoisie so tenaciously hang on to the biggest tax loophole of all, the capital gains tax. This is virtually the only device left whereby a newcomer to the bourgeoisie can amass a fortune and legally retain it. So-called capital gains should definitely be classified as income and taxed at 100 per cent of the value of net gains or profits.

NATIONALIZATION OF WAR INDUSTRIES must be the chief slogan of socialists in the period of the Permanent War Economy. That is the only effective way to "take the profit out of war." And the definition of war industry must not be confined to atomic energy and government arsenals that are already nationalized. It must be extended to every industry whose output goes mainly in a period of all-out war to direct war outlays. In general terms, the war industries are usually defined to include metal mining, oil and gas mining, chemical and petroleum refining, metal fabrication, and contract construction. This is the way they are defined by Simon Kuznets in Our Economy in War, published by the National Bureau of Economic Research. While there may be some difficulty in classifying certain plants whose output is mixed as between war and civilian purposes, and easily interchangeable one with the other, a good working guide would be to declare a company part of a war industry, and subject to nationalization, if 50 per cent or more of its output went for war purposes in 1943-1944.

Nationalizing the war industries as thus defined would place the decisive sections of American capital under ownership of the government. It would exclude small industry, whose output for the most part did not go directly toward support of the war. Above all, it would exclude agriculture and retailing. Should questions arise with respect to firms that were not in existence in 1943-1944, or whose output has radically changed since that time, it would not be difficult to develop workable criteria to determine whether such firms ought to be nationalized. All the industries included under the general definition of war industries by nature require large aggregations of capital. If, under present conditions, they require substantial concessions in rapid amortization of capital investment, they should be nationalized. If the industry as a whole is classified as a war industry, new firms in that industry should be considered part of the general class and subject to the same policy as the entire industry.

If the copper, aluminum, steel, oil and gas mining, chemical, petroleum refining, aircraft, rubber, auto, and contract construction industries were to be nationalized, to name only the obvious, the problem of administering the war economy would be greatly simplified. The bulk of production controls would apply to government-owned industry. Control of capital investment and allocation of resources as between war and civilian purposes would not be subject to the pressures of hundreds of competing capitalists, each seeking a greater share of the market and worried lest his competitor obtain a presumed peacetime advantage. Moreover, assuming the same degree of productivity, the profits of these war industries would go to the government as the owner, thereby reducing the problem of taxation from one of major importance to a secondary problem.

Nationalization of war industries completes in its rounded economic effect the process that would be begun by a capital levy, which is by its nature a limited and temporary measure. Neither nationalizations of war industries nor a capital levy are thinkable as realistic political slogans without the development of an independent labor party. Economic problems under the Permanent War Economy cannot begin to be solved except through political means. The working class is confronted with a host of tasks before it will be in a position to cope with the problems of living under the Permanent War Economy. All of them depend for solution on the ability of the American workers to achieve that political and organizational maturity that formation of an independent labor party would signify.

NATIONALIZATIONS OF WAR INDUSTRIES AND A CAPITAL LEVY are the transitional slogans of the Permanent War Economy that correspond to the needs of the workers and the times. Together with traditional transitional demands that retain validity, such as Workers' Control of Production, they can point the way toward the socialist emancipation of society. American imperialism has no perspective other than to defeat Stalinist imperialism in bloody conflict, risking in the process the atomization of all society.

The Permanent War Economy

The Permanent War Economy has provided capitalism with but a temporary respite, while aggravating every phase of the class struggle. There can be no rational or permanent solution to any of the basic problems that beset mankind so long as capitalism or Stalinism exist. Both require war, war preparations, and the threat of war to maintain their reactionary class rule. If the forces of the Third Camp, upon which the ultimate victory of the socialist revolution depends, appear to be weak and scattered in a world dominated by the clash of two irreconcilable imperialisms, it is well to remember that both the capitalist and Stalinist ruling classes have seen their better days.

Neither offers mankind any hope of progress toward universal freedom and a high standard of living. Aside from the stimulation of war, both serve as an actual brake upon the development of the forces of production. The historic task of the working class is to put an end to the Permanent War Economy without permitting the bourgeoisie and the Stalinists to unleash World War III.

The New International December 1951 — T. N. VANCE

A.A. Berle's Capitalist Revolution

While Berle's *20th Century Capitalist Revolution* (*The 20th Century Capitalist Revolution*, A.A. Berle, Jr. *Harcourt, Brace and Company*, New York City, 1951) has been loudly criticized by all types of critics as a very shallow and superficial study – one which fundamentally repudiates his basic work on the modern corporation which he wrote together with Means in 1939 – it would be a mistake to dismiss his series of lectures as merely a panegyric in favor of the large corporation and state monopoly capitalism. That, of course, it is, but Berle does succeed in raising some very interesting questions even if he cannot provide the answers.

Moreover, in passing and in developing his general thesis, Berle provides some very interesting and useful information. For example, he quotes fairly extensively from a study on concentration of economic power by Professor M.A. Adelman of Massachusetts Institute of Technology, in which it is stated that "135 corporations own 45 per cent of the industrial assets of the United States – or nearly one-fourth of the manufacturing volume of the entire world. This represents a concentration of economic, ownership greater perhaps than any yet recorded in history." Adelman seems to be of the opinion that this is a relatively static situation with little change from year to year. Berle indicates at the end that he is not entirely in agreement. It is clear, of course from the current merger movement that the situation is far from static.

Berle is concerned with the fact that in most industries:

> Two or three, or at most, five corporations will have more than half the business, the remainder being divided among a greater or lesser number of smaller concerns who must necessarily live within the conditions made for then by the 'big two' or 'big three' or 'big five' as the case may be.

In other words, no matter what figures are cited, as Berle says,

> There will be little dispute however, with the main conclusion: considerably more than half of all American industry – and that the most important half – is operated by 'concentrates.' Slightly more than half is owned outright by not more than 200 corporations. This is calculated on

The Permanent War Economy – Commentary

the coldest basis – the amount of actual assets owned by the corporations involved.

There is, of course, nothing new in this brief description of concentrated capital accumulation in the United States. What is new is Berle's assertion that progress in the interests of the entire population, not only of the United States but of the world at large, rests upon these 200 private corporations, who are performing a constructive role in helping to organize the entire process of industrial production and distribution. At one point, Berle puts it this way:

> Mid-twentieth-century capitalism has been given the power and the means of more or less planned economy, in which decisions are or at least can be taken in the light of their probable effect on the whole community.

In other words, Berle has discovered state monopoly capitalism and has declared that the assumptions of multiple competing units that were the foundation of Adam Smith and classical bourgeois economics no longer hold true. Consequently, the "judgment of the market place" is no longer – in Berle's opinion the motive power of the economy.

Berle also perform a useful function in calling attention to the study by the National City Bank on sources of capital accumulation. This study covering the eight years from 1946 through 1953, estimates that a total of $150 billion was spent for what might termed capital expenditures, namely, modernizing and enlarging plant and equipment. Sixty-four per cent of the total of $150 billion came from "internal sources" – that is to say from – surplus and depreciation reserves. Of the total of $99 billion financed through such "internal sources," retained earnings were by far the largest proportion. Of the remaining $51 billion, or 36 per cent of the total, according to Berle, one-half was raised by current borrowing, chiefly bank credit. This accounts for about $25½ billion.

Of the remainder, $18 billion or 12 per cent of the grand total was raised by issue of bonds or notes. Although half of this amount was probably privately placed, Berle

A. A. Berle's Capitalist Revolution

is willing to admit that a large portion of this capital was forced to run the gauntlet of so-called "market-place judgment" The astonishing fact is that

> ... 6 per cent or $9 billion out of a total of $150 billion was raised by issue of stock, Here, and here only, do we begin to approach the 'risk capital' investment so much relied on by classic economic theory. Even here a considerable amount was as far removed from 'risk' as the situation permitted: without exact figures, apparently a majority of the $9 billion was represented by preferred stock. Probably not more than $5 billion of the total amount was represented by common stock – the one situation in which an investor considers an enterprise, decides on its probable usefulness and profitability, and puts down his savings, aware of a degree of risk but hoping for large profit.
>
> There is substantial evidence, which need not be reviewed here, that this is representative of the real pattern of the twentieth-century capitalism. *The capital is there; and so is capitalism. The waning factor is the capitalist. He has somehow vanished in great measure from the picture, and with him has vanished much of the controlling force of his market-place judgment.* He is not extinct: roughly a billion dollars a year (say five per cent of total savings) is invested by him; but he is no longer a decisive force. In his place stand the boards of directors of corporations, chiefly large ones, who retain profits and risk them in expansion of the business along lines indicated by the circumstances of their particular operation. Not the public opinion of the marketplace with all the economic worlds from which to choose, but the directorial opinion of corporate managers as to the line of greatest opportunity within their own concern, now chiefly determines the application of risk capital. Major corporations in most instances do not seek capital. They form it themselves. (Italics mine – T.N.V.)

The Permanent War Economy – Commentary

The existence of what is sometimes termed monopolistic competition or oligopoly or any of the other choice phrases used, does not of course mean that capitalists no longer exist. But Berle is correct in pointing out that capitalism has changed its form considerably during the twentieth century, and capitalism has introduced an aspect of planning which was surely not envisaged by Marx or early Marxists.*

There is, above all, the role of the state which makes present-day capitalism differ qualitatively from nineteenth or even very early twentieth-century capitalism. Berle correctly points out, for example, that

> . . . the development of atomic energy, perhaps the crest of the next great wave in modern development, was not socialist by theory or by design. It was twentieth-century capitalism in respect of which the government played a major part, as it will continue to do.

The role of the state in modern state monopoly capitalism in the United States is not confined to Democratic administrations. There has been no significant change under the present Republican administration either in fact or in theory.

As a matter of fact, even in Eisenhower's Economic Report to Congress of January 20, 1955, which is devoted mainly to assuring the bourgeoisie that everything is fine and there is really very little to worry about, there is a type of recognition of the role of the state which certainly could not have been present in any official document of the last Republican administration. The economic report, after raising various questions concerning the shortness and mildness of the recent economic decline, implies that the government, i.e., the state, is really the factor that is different in the situation today and basically responsible for preventing a severe depression along classical lines. The report states:

> Clearly, many people had a part in stemming the economic decline and easing the readjustment from war to peace. The Federal government also

---

* Actually, Marx wrote a series of articles on the *Crédit Mobilier* scandal for the *New York Tribune* in 1856 which credited the government of Napoleon III (Louis Bonaparte) with contemplating just such a national planning mechanism. (Hal Draper, *Karl Marx's Theory of Revolution*, Vol. 2, pp. 442-451.) EH)

contributed significantly to the process of recovery. It influenced the economy in two principal ways, first, through the automatic workings of the fiscal system, second, by deliberately pursuing monetary, tax, and expenditure policies that inspired widespread confidence on the part of the people and thus helped them to act in ways that were economically constructive.

There can be little doubt that so-called fiscal policy, especially with reference to tax structure, and monetary and credit policy, did enable the state to play a constructive role in so far as helping to maintain general economic equilibrium is concerned. The important word, however, in the passage quoted above is the word "expenditure" for it relates to government expenditures and here we find ourselves face to face with reality. What type of recovery from the so-called recession 1958-54 would have taken place had Federal government not been spending $50 billion or more per year on war outlays? It suffices to raise the question to realize that none of the platitudes of the theoreticians of the bourgeoisie can begin to cope with the recent situation. The economy is maintaining itself and giving an outward appearance of health – although inwardly extremely sick – only because capitalism has entered what we have previously described as the stage of Permanent War Economy.

That is why it is somewhat pathetic to find an outstanding bourgeois economist like Sumner Slichter of Harvard state in the current issue of the *Harvard Business Review* that the old-fashioned business cycle has in effect disappeared. The implication would seem to be that American capitalists have become super-intelligent and can now eliminate depressions. Slichter refers to many points in reaching this rather remarkable conclusion, such as developments in the financing of construction, and the so-called development of individual cycles of different industries. He also refers to the fact that durable goods industries "will at all times have a far higher ratio of unfilled orders to sales and inventories than prevailed in pre-Korean days."

The Permanent War Economy – Commentary

One reason for this, according to the *New York Times* of January 23, 1955, is

> ... the defense program ... [But] ... even if diplomacy in the next few years succeeds in substantially mitigating the vigor of the cold war, I suspect that the volume of unfilled orders in the durable goods industry will be kept high simply as a matter of national policy.

Slichter continues, according to the New York Times, by stating:

> In the unlikely event that a large additional drop in defense spending becomes possible, the country will probably offset the drop in defense spending by a long-term development program.

What Slichter is saying, of course, is that the state will continue to support the Permanent War Economy – and if, in the unlikely event that international economic conditions change so as to render socially unnecessary the large-scale expenditures in the means of destruction, then the state will find other types of investments which will help to maintain the economy. Here he is reverting to a theory which he promulgated about 1930-31 which, had he was right then, would have meant that it would have been impossible for mass unemployment to have developed. Slichter is no more right today than he was in the 1930's. The only socially acceptable large-scale state expenditures are those which do not compete with private capital and those which are absolutely and unmistakably essential to the preservation of the capitalist class. Such expenditures, so far, have only been found in the new third category of economic investment, namely, means of destruction. Yet, we should not lose sight of the fact that one of the essentials of state monopoly capitalism is that there is an unusual degree of state intervention in the economy which permits achieving stability, or relative stability, in many cases that could not have previously been attained. Of course, to do this the capitalists must have the support of other sections of the population, particularly of the labor movement. So far this has not been difficult for them to achieve.

A. A. Berle's Capitalist Revolution

WHAT WILL HAPPEN during the year 1955 and into 1956 as the pressure of mass unemployment constantly grows remains to be seen. Already, there are signs that the leadership is being forced to take cognizance of the fact that there are several million unemployed and that these are not people who are superfluous to the normal functionings of capitalism – but who have been rendered superfluous by the very rapid accumulation of capital which, as Marx pointed out, necessarily brings about a certain increase in the industrial reserve army.

Or, as we have demonstrated previously, under the Permanent War Economy the basic Marxism law of accumulation of capital becomes transformed into a relative decline in the standard of living rather than an absolute increase in unemployment but as we have had occasion more recently to point out, this holds only when there is a steady increase in the ratio of war outlays. At the present time the ratio of war outlays has been declining, if only slightly, so that whereas a year ago it ran around 17 per cent, today it is down to around 15 per cent. The pressures that develop, particularly in basic industries, are apparent in such cities and industrial centers as Detroit, Pittsburgh, etc.

A process of attrition has developed. To revert to our analogy used in our original presentation of the nature and structure of the Permanent War Economy (see Part III, *Increasing State Intervention*, *New International*, May-June, 1951),

> The restoration of the rate of profit could not be followed by an abandonment of state intervention. On the contrary, like a patient who has recovered from an almost fatal illness solely by taking medicine containing habit-forming drugs, the enduring 'health' of capitalism demands the continuation of the 'habit-forming drug' of state intervention. This becomes obvious as the economy of depression is followed by the Permanent War Economy. There are differences, however. Not only is state intervention more expensive, but it is no longer confined to restoring the profitability of 'sick' industries. The most decisive sections of capital are subjected to state control and direction, but the reward is the virtual guarantee of the profits of the bourgeoisie as a class.

The Permanent War Economy – Commentary

To maintain the precarious equilibrium that exists, constantly increasing state intervention is necessary. This is a fundamental law of the present epoch of capitalism – the Permanent War Economy. Not even Old Guard Republicans can defy this law and escape its consequences. Thus, we have the Eisenhower Administration talking about a 100 billion program for road building, and similar measures – most of which will naturally remain confined to paper and which will be trotted out every year around November when elections take place. There will, however, be state intervention in the economy so long as it is within the power of the bourgeoisie to use this new weapon to preserve its own historically outmoded system.

Not all bourgeois economists are optimistic about the outlook for economy as a whole as the official prognosticators in Washington. For example, an article in the *New York Times* under date of January 27, 1955 is headlined, "Economists Wary of Business in '55." The sub-headline is even more to the point: "Their Testimony Casts Doubt on Eisenhower Optimism." There were eight private economists who testified before the Joint Congressional Committee on the Economic Report and not all of them represented the trade-union movement. They all appeared to be worried by what in some quarters is loosely referred to as automation which is simply a high-sounding public relations word for a process which has been going on for many years – even if it is accelerating now in certain industries and results in an increasingly high organic composition of capital. This is inherent in the nature of capitalism and should not cause surprise to those who presumably understand, more or less, how the capitalist system operates. It means that in a situation where business as a whole is good, where the bourgeoisie is making very high profits, there could be mass unemployment amounting very easily to a figure of 5,000,000 at the end of 1955. This gives rise not only to much uneasiness within the labor movement and pressures on the labor bureaucracy to do something about it, so that they in turn begin to exert pressure on Washington, but it also gives rise to such phenomena which are appropriate for this period in the form of renewed promises to investigate the "new trend toward monopoly and the concentration of economic power." There will be, without question, many types of Congressional investigations this field. Whether any of them will add materially to the work of the temporary National Economic Committee remains to be seen, but the New York Times

A. A. Berle's Capitalist Revolution

of January 24 reports that the subcommittee of the Committee of the Judiciary, in a report submitted by its majority, Senators Langer, Kefauver and Kilgore, stated that their hearings had lead them to two conclusions:

> (1) That there is a two-pronged drive by private monopoly to destroy public competition in the power business, and that the Dixon-Yates contract is a part of that drive. (2) The Wall Street domination of the power industry has revived many of the monopolistic holding company evils which Congress sought by legislation to suppress, particularly the extension of monopoly control over very wide regions.

Here we have the makings of a great debate which may very well play an important role in the elections of 1956.

Mr. Berle, however, would answer to all of this that while the large corporation must adopt a conscience comparable to that of the king in feudal days, it is the engine of progress not only in domestic affairs but in international affairs. It is at this point that Mr. Berle, trying to pursue a preconceived thesis, becomes a simple apologist for state monopoly capitalism in its most rapacious form, with its justification of the oil cartels and similar international agreements.

He still, however, manages to flirt with important thoughts when he virtually concludes his essay by stating:

> Corporations still have, perhaps, some range of choice: they can either take an extended view of their responsibility, or a limited one. Yet the choice is probably less free than would appear. Power has laws of its own. One of them is that when one group having power declines or abdicates it, some other directing group immediately picks it up; and this appears constant throughout history. The choice of corporate management is not whether so great a power shall cease to exist; they can merely determine whether they will serve as the nuclei of its organization or pass it over to someone else, probably the modern state.

The Permanent War Economy – Commentary

Since the power of the state should be kept to a minimum, according to Berle and the traditional liberal philosophy, it is obvious that corporate power must be built up and maintained, but the corporate managers should please have a social conscience to that it would really be true for the former president of General Motors to say that "What is good for General Motors is good for the country."

Sermons are interesting to those who like them but only in their proper place, and an essay on the twentieth-century capitalist revolution is hardly the place for Berle's type of propagandistic sermon. His critics, however, have sufficiently well disposed of him so that we can merely state that there has been a type of revolution in the twentieth century but Berle doesn't understand its nature, its causes or its probable results.

The constant decline in factory employment focuses attention on one of the major problems of American capitalism – and one for which there is no solution in sight. PWE (permanent war economy) or WPA (work relief projects) have actually been the only two solutions that capitalism has had to offer for the last 25 years. An entire generation has grown up and come to maturity which can only know from reading, but never from experience, what the old capitalism was like. This does not make the new capitalism less capitalist, but it does mean that some of its laws of motion and methods of operation are different and require analysis and understanding – especially by socialists.

Symptomatic of danger ahead for the economy, is a most interesting article that was published in the *New York Times* of September 20, 1954. The heading was "Per Capita Output Only 1 per cent Above '47." This is an article by one of the New York Times' economic reporters, Burton Crane, and one which is highly recommended to Mr. Berle and to all students of the economy. It is worth quoting from fairly extensively:

> Per capita industrial production in this country has dropped so sharply in the last year that it is only 1 per cent above the average rate for 1947
> . . .
> The question facing the economy is whether industrial production and gross national product can be allowed to fall farther below the normal trend. *Our economy, as observers of all shades of political thought have pointed out, works best when it is expanding. Signs that the dynamism had disappeared*

A. A. Berle's Capitalist Revolution

might discourage investors from risking their capital and dissuade industrialists from expanding their enterprises.

There are warnings that such attitudes may be in prospect. Expenditures for new plant and equipment, expressed in constant dollars and weighted for population changes, in the first half of 1954 were at 113 per cent of the 1947 level. In the two preceding years they had been at 116 and 123 per cent.

What is the normal upward trend in our economy due to growing mechanization and efficiency? Some economists have set it as high as 3.5 per cent for manufacturing production. At that annual improvement factor, per capita industrial production in 1954 should be at 127.2 per cent of 1947 output. It is at 101 per cent. (Italics mine – T.N.V.)

The twentieth-century capitalist revolution is thus not so earth-shaking as would appear from Mr. Berle's panegyric. It has not solved the problem of unemployment. Here is one of the essential contradictions of capitalism under the Permanent War Economy only where, with attrition setting in, some of the basic laws of capitalism begin to reassert themselves. The economy must constantly grow and expand, at least to the point where it can support the 600,000 to 700,000 new entrants into the labor force each year. This it is obviously failing to do. Moreover, the two prime sources of economic infection, the agricultural crisis and the crisis in consumer durable goods (centering in the automobile industry), clearly remain – with no alleviation in sight. Many factors have been responsible for the rapid increase in population, and it is clear that the Permanent War Economy is intimately connected with this sociological phenomenon. The increase in population in turn, however, gives rise to the very correct analysis of Mr. Crane, quoted above, that only a per capita approach becomes meaningful in appraising the economy, its performance and its outlook. The American economy is simply not suited, nor large enough (on a capitalist basis) to provide the constantly expanding market that is required to sustain an expanding capitalism.

We are, therefore, back where we started and Mr. Berle is at least partially aware of this central problem when he speaks of:

The Permanent War Economy – Commentary

A modern corporation thus has become an international as well as a national instrument.... The present political framework of foreign affairs is nationalist. The present economic base is not. The classic nation-state is no longer capable, by itself alone, either to feed and clothe its people, or to defend its own borders. (Italics mine – T.N.V.)

Here, then, is the central fact of the modern capitalist "revolution." Capitalism has visibly, before our very eyes, outgrown its national framework and must burst this integument asunder in one form or another. The only question that history must still answer is the form in which the capitalist national state will be destroyed and the nature of the political organization that will succeed it.

The New International May 1955 T.N. Vance

An Amalgam of Marx and Keynes
John Strachey's View of Contemporary Capitalism

If capitalism (i.e., advanced capitalism such as Britain and America) can through the exercise of non-economic democratic political pressures be reformed or so controlled in its operations that progressively the average standard of living is raised, the capacity of the productive forces increased, and some type of peace maintained, then what is the need for any type of socialist movement? This question insistently intrudes itself after a reading of John Strachey's, despite the fact that at the end of his *Acknowledgments,* the author states: "*Contemporary Capitalism* is the first volume of a projected series of studies on the principles of democratic socialism."

In fact, so many projected studies are indicated in the course of this one volume, that one must wish Strachey an exceptionally long life in order that he may set forth in writing his *magnum opus*. For, despite numerous disagreements that this writer has with many ideas expressed by Strachey, he is discussing questions of fundamental importance in a serious manner. Moreover, Strachey is aware that capitalism through a process of mutation, as he calls it, has changed fundamentally. In addition, while rejecting many of Marx's principles, others are accepted. There are far too few analyses of contemporary society from the standpoint of democratic socialism to ignore Strachey because his economics are based on a curious amalgam of Marx and Keynes or because his politics appear to be acceptable to Bevan.

Contemporary capitalism, according to Strachey, has succeeded in raising the average standard of living' because of trade union and leftist (democratic) pressures. Now, however, with the stage of oligopoly having been reached, there is a conflict between capitalism and democracy. "Capitalism in its latest stage, when it is progressively outgrowing the forms of ownership which were once appropriate to it, threatens to turn upon what was once its own political counterpart, namely, democracy." (p.344) It is the fact that capitalism through ever-increasing centralization constantly undermines the foundations of democracy that necessitates the struggle for socialism, according to Strachey It is his belief that only democratic socialists are the true fighters for democracy. The struggle for socialism is in reality the struggle for democracy. And, despite Strachey's failure to distinguish clearly between democracy and democratic rights and between bourgeois and socialist democracy, it must be admitted that there is much truth in this dichotomy.

The Permanent War Economy – Commentary

If all classes in modern society before capitalist and Stalinist, were prepared to accept indefinitely the absence of democratic rights, then it is theoretically conceivable that a precarious international equilibrium could be maintained indefinitely. The apposition between capitalism and democracy is, in reality, the basic constructive theme of Strachey's work. Among many quotable sentences of the author's thesis is the following

> Thus the continuance of effective democracy depends upon the protection of big capital's control of the media of expression becoming absolute. And upon the continuance of effective democracy in two or three key societies of the world everything else will be found to depend.

It is interesting to note Paul Homan's evaluation of Strachey in a article in the June, 1957 issue of *The American Economic Review*, "Socialist Thought in Great Britain":

> Strachey has now taken time out for reflective thought; his book is a restatement of his philosophical position and a misinterpretation of the process of social change. The title is somewhat misleading, because the book contains very little on the institutional characteristics of contemporary economic organization — in fact, hardly more than a stereotype of oligopoly. What he does, essentially, is to set up two abstract creatures, capitalism and democracy, put them in the prize ring and let them fight it out, while he cheers in the corner of democracy. Capitalism is a sort of brutal monstrosity — the apotheosis of every inhumane, anti-social pursuit of private self-interest. Democracy is the champion of all generous-hearted efforts to attain general well-being and communal interest. The complete victory of democracy, would usher in socialism.

The professor's sarcasm is not well taken for Strachey does have an analysis of the laws of motion of contemporary capitalism. Even if one disagrees with Strachey, which this reviewer does in certain fundamental respects that will be set forth below, the fact

An Amalgam of Marx and Keynes

of the matter is that Strachey in thinking about important problems, which is more than most professors of economics permit themselves to do these days.

Strachey is also to be commended for realizing the importance of theory. He knows that capitalism has altered in certain of its basic characteristics in certain aspects of its functioning. He is not content with superficial description of these structural alterations, important though they may be. He wants to know "why." He wants to be able to predict. In short, he seeks a theory of the latest stage of capitalism that will serve as a guide to action. Again, the fact that Strachey has exchanged his prewar Stalinist theories for his current amalgamation of Marx and Keynes, is hardly justification for rejecting him out of hand. In fact, how immeasurably superior is Strachey's crude analysis of contemporary capitalism to the apologetics of bourgeois professors!

Strachey's beginning is most encouraging, for he realizes that the wholesale modifications of the market that have occurred in recent years have led capitalism into a new stage. As he says:

> The first and decisive reason why an economy of large and few units exhibits new characteristics is because at a certain point in the increase of their size and decrease of their number, the managers of the remaining units begin to be able to affect prices instead of being exclusively affected by them. *It is impossible to exaggerate the importance of this transformation.* (p.22, italics mine – T.N.V.)

While he uses different terms, Strachey is aware of the development of state monopoly capitalism and the era of administered prices that it has ushered in, and to a certain extent of its consequences. For example (p.31):

> Accordingly, the State has come, in the advanced industrial nations, to feel that it must, and can, control such basic things as the pattern of the distribution of income between social classes and individual citizens, instead of leaving that pattern to the consequences of the play of the market.

The Permanent War Economy – Commentary

To examine each and every argument presented by Strachey, both those with which we concur as well as those with which we disagree, as well as to indicate significant areas of omission, would require a book rather than a review article. Suffice it to say that we believe Strachey to be fundamentally correct in his emphasis on the importance of prices now being administered in large measure, rather than determined competitively in the market. The "essence of the mutation," as the author describes it, is (p.39):

> ... the ability of the producers in some, but not in all, of the spheres of production to affect prices, instead of merely being affected by them ... Thus the ability to influence prices will inevitably sap the automatic, self-regulating character of the economy. It will consequently provoke and require more and more State intervention, and will lead to an intensified struggle for the now all-important levers of economic power which will be in the hands of the State ... Thus the characteristics of the latest stage of capitalism both make possible a much higher degree of social control and at the same time make such control imperative.

This is insight and understanding of a high order.

Strachey devotes an important section of his book to value theory in economics. While he accepts Marx's analysis of the centralization of capital, accepting as he does the term "oligopoly" from modern bourgeois economists, he rejects the labor theory of value as faulty and the theory of ever-increasing misery as Marx's cardinal error. Strachey notes that from Ricardo on increasing disparities occurred between the price and value of many commodities. He feels that the labor theory of value has neglected to take into account the role of capital in the determination of prices. He states (p.67):

> *In other words, in real life not only man-hours of socially necessary labor but also a reward of some sort for capital entered into the determination of the points round which prices fluctuated.* (Italic in original)

Why Strachey is under the mistaken notion that Marx ignored the role of constant capital in the determination of the price of production and henceforth of market price

An Amalgam of Marx and Keynes

is a complete mystery, since he merely makes the assertion, whereas Marx devoted large part of Volume III of *Capital* to an explanation of these interrelationships in connection with capitalist production as a whole. The skeptics are referred merely to Chapter I of Volume III, although Kautsky will serve as a good introduction. Consider just the following two paragraphs from the first chapter on Cost, Price and Profit (*Capital*, Kerr edition, Volume III, pp.38-39)

> However, the cost of this commodity to the capitalist, and the actual cost of this commodity, are two vastly different amounts. That portion of the value of the commodity which consists of surplus value does not cost the capitalist anything for the reason that it costs the laborer unpaid labor. But on the basis of capitalist production, the laborer plays the role of an ingredient of productive capital as soon as he has been incorporated in the process of production. Under these circumstances the capitalist poses as the actual producer of the commodity. For this reason the cost price of a commodity to the capitalist producer necessarily appears to him as the added cost of the commodity. If we designate the cost-price by k, we can transcribe the formula $C=c+v+s$ into the formula $C=k+s$, that is to say, the value of the commodity is equal to the cost plus the surplus-value.
>
> In this way the classification of the various values making good the values the capital consumed in the production of the commodity under the term one price expresses, on the one hand, the specific character of capitalist production. The capitalist cost of the commodity is measured by the *expenditure of capital*, while the actual cost of the commodity is measured by the *expenditure of labor*. The capitalist cost-price of the commodity, then, is a quantity different from its Value, or its actual cost-price. It is smaller than the value of the commodity. For since $C=k+s$, it is evident that $k=C-s$. On the other hand, the cost-price of a commodity is by no means a mere heading in capitalist bookkeeping. The actual existence of this portion of value continually exerts its practical influence

> in the actual production of the commodity, because *it must be ever reconverted from its commodity-form, by way of the process of circulation, into the form of productive capital,* so the *cost-price of the commodity must always buy anew the elements of production consumed in its creation.* (Italics in last sentence only mine. – T.N.V.)

How could the originator of the theory of the increasing organic composition of capital ignore the role of capital in the determination of price? Strachey ought to acquire his economics first-hand rather than through the courtesy of Joan Robinson. Implicitly, Strachey has fallen into the common bourgeois fallacy of "productivity of capital" as distinct from "productivity of labor." And, if he thinks he can explain the origin of profit without recourse to the labor theory value, the bourgeoisie have been trying unsuccessfully for a hundred years to develop a theory that would both explain the origin of and justify profit, and at the same time correspond to reality. It might be added that the absence of a theory of profit creates numerous difficulties for Strachey, of which he seems to be totally unaware. He does understand that the accumulation of capital is the mainspring of capitalism (*cf.* Chapter 10), but why capital is accumulated or the laws governing its accumulation he doesn't know because Mrs. Joan Robinson, his mentor, does not know.

It is sufficient to quote the following from p.247:

> What in the world, then, determines the level of investment? Mrs. Joan Robinson, in a striking passage (from her *Accumulation of Capital*), declares simply that we do not know! She writes: '. . . as to what governs the level at which it' (investment) 'gets itself established we know very little . . .'

Mrs. Robinson is here feeling the need of some kind of *summa*, transcending, although including, economics and laying the basis of an inclusive science of human society, a *summa* at which Marxism is at present the sole attempt. She is confronted with the fact that her analysis has led her to conclude that the true prime mover of a capitalist economy – the decision to invest – is determined by causes which are largely outside the scope of economic analysis.

The absence of a theory, even a much-abused Marxist theory, leads to all kinds of difficulties. Above all, if the government, through fear of the electorate or whatever motivation one wants, decides that slumps must be avoided at all costs, and that consequently the decisions to invest (i.e., the determination of the rate and mass of capital accumulation) cannot be left in the hands of profit-seeking private capitalists, and if further this can be achieved under bourgeois democracy or under a "labor" government, then why is there a need for socialism?

Intuitively, Strachey feels that he must reject the labor theory of value, not because he (Strachey) does not understand it, but because he wishes to attribute to Marx an "iron law" or subsistence theory of wages as an out-growth of the labor theory of value, and hence a failure to allow for increasing productivity of labor and consequently to deny the possibility and the actuality of increasing the national product and the average standard of living. The original sin of the labor theory of value thus becomes the source of the disastrous theory of ever-increasing misery.

Strachey puts it this way (p.70):

> *Reckoning in terms of man-hours of socially necessary labor, the total national product is a given figure: all that can really be considered is its division between the social classes.* (Italics in original).

Why this should be so when the amount of socially necessary labor required to produce the means of sustenance of labor or for labor to reproduce itself, i.e., the value of labor-power, is clearly dependent on the general historical and specific geographic environment, is not explained by Strachey. He merely asserts it. It is as if he never bothered to read Marx, for just reading the first few hundred pages of Volume I of *Capital* would have destroyed his entire fallacious attack on Marx's development of the labor theory of value and surplus value.

The Permanent War Economy – Commentary

Let Marx speak for himself (Volume I, pp.189-190):

> The value of labor-power is determined, as in the case of every other commodity, by the labor-time necessary for the production, and consequently also the reproduction, of this special article. So far as it has value, it represents no more than a definite quantity of the average labor of society incorporated in it. Labor-power exists only as a capacity, or power of the living individual. Its production consequently presupposes his existence. Given the individual, the production of labor-power consists in his reproduction of himself or his maintenance. For his maintenance he requires a given quantity of the means of subsistence . . . the value of labor-power is the value of the means of subsistence necessary for the maintenance of the laborer . . . His means of subsistence must therefore be sufficient to maintain him in his normal state as a laboring individual. His natural wants, such as food, clothing, fuel, and housing, vary according to the climatic and other physical conditions of his country. On the other hand, *the number and extent of his so-called necessary wants, as also the modes of satisfying them*, are themselves the product of historical development, and depend therefore to a great extent on the degree of civilization of a country, more particularly on the conditions under which, and consequently the habits and degree of comfort which, the class of free laborers has been formed. In contradistinction therefore to the case of other commodities, there enters into the determination of the value of labor-power a historical and moral element. (Italics mine – *T.N.V.*)

In other words, since, by way of illustration, England is more civilized than, let us say, South Africa, and Strachey is accustomed to a greater degree of comfort than the South African miner, presumably the value Strachey's means of subsistence (or of the British miner) exceeds that of the South African. And the value of the means of subsistence required for Mr. John Strachey today, or the British miner today, clearly is

An Amalgam of Marx and Keynes

far greater than the value of the means of subsistence required for, say, Mr. Lytton Strachey some decades ago or that of a British miner a generation or more ago.

Marx was certainly guilty of many mistakes. He certainly didn't foresee that capitalism would survive decades beyond the point where it clearly outlived its social usefulness. He also could not have been expected to have foreseen the Bolshevik revolution and the Stalinist counter-revolution. But surely before his basic thoughts are twisted and distorted, he has the right to assume that his critics (friendly they may be in the case of Strachey) will at least have made an effort to read and understand his works!

Strachey, however, is not concerned with what Marx wrote. He has a point to make:

> Therefore a subsistence theory of wages has always been, explicitly for Ricardo, explicitly for Marx, an essential part of labor theory of value. *But wages have not* remained at subsistence. Therefore one vitally important commodity namely, labor power, has not even tended to sell at its value. This formidable fact has driven a great hole, not only in the labor theory of but also in the associated Ricardian-Marxian diagram of what the distribution of the national product will be among the classes. *It is the fact of rising real wages which has above all done the damage to the whole schema.* (Italics mine – T.N.V.)

It would be pretty difficult to crowd more errors into one short paragraph than Strachey does in the above. To be sure, the very next two sentences read (p.71):

> Nevertheless we shall find that it has by no means destroyed its importance as an elucidation of would happen unless tireless and drastic steps were taken to prevent. That, I repeat, is one of the reasons why it is still indispensable to master the labor theory of value. (*sic!*)

It is a pity that Strachey has not followed his own advice, for one thing he cannot be accused of is having mastered the labor theory of value.

The Permanent War Economy – Commentary

In passing, it should be obvious Strachey's attributing to Marx on an "iron law" of wages requires him also to ignore the fact that Marx developed the theory of the class struggle. To summarize Marx's central message, as does Strachey (p.102): "This is the statement that wages will in all capitalist societies tend towards what is for that time and phase a subsistence level" – which implies the influence of historical forces upon the determination of wages – and to deny the influence of the class struggle upon the level of wages, is to perpetrate an absurdity. To be sure, the forces of the class struggle cannot drive wages up to the point where for any length of time the profits of the capitalist class disappear without at the same time destroying capitalism.

To assert that Marx ignored the possibility that the productivity of labor could alter or increase is enough to make Marx turn over in his grave. Marx even devotes an entire chapter of Volume I of *Capital* to *Changes of Magnitude in the Price of Labor-Power and in Surplus-Value* (Chapter XVII), wherein he considers as the three decisive forces in determining these changes:

> (1) the length of the working day, or the extensive magnitude of labor;
> (2) the normal intensity of labor, its intensive magnitude, whereby a given quantity of labor is expended in a given time; (3) the productiveness of labor, whereby the same quantum of labor yields, in a given time, a greater or less quantum of product, dependent on the degree of development in the conditions of production. (p.569).

While Strachey pays homage to Marx for being the first to throw light on the business cycle, with his theory of crisis, Marx's basic achievement was to analyze the conditions that led to, and to predict, the centralization of capital. His basic error was to assert the labor theory of value as a law rather than as a tendency. And the thing which destroys Marxism as a valid social theory is that from this labor theory of value, instead of merely asserting a tendency toward a polarization of classes, Marx predicted "ever-increasing misery" for the mass of the population. And it was this "ever-increasing misery" that would lead the masses to the revolutionary overthrow of capitalism.

An Amalgam of Marx and Keynes

Since, according to Strachey, in the advanced capitalist nations, the average standard of living has increased, there is no ever-increasing misery and, consequently, Marxism is outmoded as a scientific basis for socialism. There is, says Strachey, to be perfectly fair to Marx, a tendency under capitalism for the entire increase in production to accrue to the benefit of the capitalist class,

> But this tendency has been overruled, in the advanced capitalist societies, but not elsewhere, by essentially non-economic forces, the existence of which Marx overlooked. (Strachey's emphasis, p.129.)

What Marx meant by the increasing pauperization of labor (a thought which cannot be found in *Capital*, but only in *The Communist Manifesto* and certain propagandistic works) is not quite as simple as Strachey thinks. The evidence would seem to indicate that Marx based this prediction on his basic law of capital accumulation; namely, that an increase in capital accumulation leads to an increase in the industrial reserve army (unemployment). That this tendency still exists, even under the Permanent War Economy, we have shown in our original series of articles on the Permanent War Economy (cf. *The New International*, Vol. XVII). Nevertheless, as we have already demonstrated, the development of the Permanent War Economy stage of capitalism has altered Marx's fundamental law of capitalist accumulation. To this extent, the doctrine of ever-increasing misery is in need of revision. Marx, so far as we can determine, never stated that the standards of living of the employed working class would deteriorate. He expected that the weight of the *lazarus-layers* of the working class (the unemployed) would carry down the average standard of living of the entire working class. Only in this sense is it proper to speak of ever-increasing misery.

And until the last decade, or until the development of the Permanent War Economy, it looked, as Strachey tacitly admits, that Marx was more or less correct. If, however, we are to admit that the average standard living of the employed working class is higher today than, let us say, it was two, three or four decades ago, we might try to include in this total evaluation, for surely it is part of total misery, the casualties of wartime, both in war and peace, and the psychological impact on want satisfactions on

The Permanent War Economy – Commentary

a world that lives under the constant threat of total annihilation. Moreover, as Strachey stresses, the major egalitarian trends that are truly significant occurred mainly during World War II.

As we stated at the outset, if capitalism can progressively raise average standards of living, and at the same time maintain a relatively peaceful international equilibrium, then it is still a viable historical system. We then need neither Marx nor Strachey but it is suggested that before everyone joins the capitalist band-wagon, we wait another decade, or even less to see if capitalism has really solved the problems of economic and political stability and progress.

The real significance of Strachey's present volume is that he recognizes that we have entered a new stage of capitalism, that capitalism no longer is self-regulating, that it is (and must in order to survive) be controlled. He gives Keynes great credit for recognizing that capitalism was no longer self-regulating. What he fails to see is that Keynes was the great bourgeois' economist of the depression. His views on state intervention were acceptable only so long as the Great Depression prevailed. Once World War II and the ensuing Permanent War Economy developed, Keynes went into considerable decline, especially within American governmental circles.

It is interesting to note that *Merchant's View* column in *The New York Times* of August 11, 1957 poses the question:

> Can the national economy be controlled? It would appear that Government officials are experimenting with this problem in ways, perhaps, that appear to be baffling to the average business man.

Apparently, even *The New York Times* is not aware of the fact that *the economy has been controlled for the past decade and more*. The nature of the controls, their success and their impact on capitalism are necessarily subject of a future article. Suffice it to say, that we are of the opinion that under the Permanent War Economy, the capitalist state must control the economy. How long-lasting and successful this type of state intervention will be is a separate question. The permanent peace-and-prosperity school ought to wait a few years before they declare the present precarious equilibrium to be permanent.

An Amalgam of Marx and Keynes

After all, capitalist planning is not the same thing as socialist planning. Moreover, the capitalist world is in a curious dilemma with respect to the Stalinist sector of the world. Capitalism needs Stalinism to help maintain the existing international equilibrium and to provide a socially acceptable *raison d'etre* for the huge war outlays that alone provide the current decisive underpinnings of the entire economic system. Yet, the maintenance of Stalinism can lead to its strengthening, and the further whittling-away of the capitalist market, not to mention the ever-present danger that Stalinist political-military maneuvers will be successful and that, consequence, the physical dimensions of the capitalist world will be reduced still further.

Strachey would like to believe that a marriage of Keynesianism and social democracy can solve the problems of the world. In any event, he rejects any concept of the Permanent War Economy. He states (p.295 *et sequitur*):

> There is another and less palatable reason why it would be a great mistake to dismiss the Keynesian techniques as illusory. As we noted, those Marxians [Stalinists?] who are unable any longer to deny that capitalism in the nineteen-fifties is behaving very differently from what it did in the nineteen-thirties, explain that this is simply due to vast expenditures upon armaments . . .

> The case of these – mainly communist – critics is, briefly, as follows:

> No doubt it is true that *if* a capitalist government supplements the activities of its profit-seeking entrepreneurs by itself spending or investing sufficiently massive sums, it can sustain the economy at a level of full employment. But a capitalist government will be intensely unwilling to do this *for peaceful purposes* . . . Such (military) government expenditure fits into the generally aggressive policies of capitalist governments of the latest stage. It is this kind of government expenditure and this kind alone which the capitalist governments have

The Permanent War Economy – Commentary

> undertaken on a scale sufficient to be economically significant since 1945....
>
> Such an explanation is a crude caricature of the complex realities of the contemporary situation ... The American economy had, it is true, suffered a very shallow depression in 1948-49 ... But the figures show incontrovertibly (they will be given in a later part of this study) that this depression was over and the progress of full employment had been resumed before the outbreak of the Korean war and long before the American rearmament program began.

It is a pity that Strachey does not submit his figures on the American situation in the current volume, for the future of capitalism depends on the United States, not on Britain. This provides us with an opportunity, without any elaborate explanation, to present our latest figures on the relationship of war outlays to total output in the United States during the past ten years of the Permanent War Economy.

While many of our priors actual are herewith revised, the only important change is for the year 1947 where our present figures are considerably lower and the ratio of a war outlay to total production is revised downwards from the previous 13.7% to the present 11.6%. It will be seen that in the year 1950, in the middle of which the Korean war broke out, the ratio declined below 10% to 9.8%. It should be remembered that at that point official unemployment statistics in the United States reached a total of 4,700,000. It was only the rapid increase in the ratio of war outlays to total production that prevented a serious unemployment situation from having far-reaching political effects; and, of course, it was the sharp rise in the war outlays ratio to a peak of almost 17% in 1952 and 1953 that reduced the level of unemployment to politically tolerable and relatively minor levels.

The gradual reduction and leveling off in war outlays in the post-Korean period has brought about a decline in the ratio of war outlays to total production. Attrition begins to set in. The big bourgeoisie demand a halt to inflation, or rather they use the concern of the working classes to prevent inflation as a device for getting the government to raise interest rates to place a squeeze on small and medium-size business.

An Amalgam of Marx and Keynes

	Net National Product	WAR OUTLAYS			Ratio of War Outlays to Total Production; Col. (4) as % of Col. (1)
		Direct	Indirect	Total	
Year	(1)	(2)	(3)	(4)	(5)
1947	218.1	12.3	13.1	25.4	11.6
1948	240.8	11.6	12.9	24.5	10.2
1949	238.9	13.6	13.7	27.3	11.4
1950	264.6	14.3	11.7	26.0	9.8
1951	304.8	33.9	9.3	43.2	14.2
1952	321.6	46.4	8.0	54.4	16.9
1953	336.7	49.3	7.2	56.5	16.8
1954	331.9	41.2	6.9	48.1	14.5
1955	359.5	39.1	7.6	46.7	13.0
1956	378.4	40.4	7.6	48.0	12.7

Direct and Indirect War Outlays, 1947-1956 and Their Relationship to Total Output (Dollar Figures in Billions)

Source: July 1957 *Survey of Current Business* for net national product and direct war outlays. Indirect war outlays calculated as explained in Part I of *The Permanent War Economy* (Jan.-Feb. 1951 issue of *The New International* and the March-April 1953 issue of *The New International*, pp.94-95.

The "battle the budget" has all kinds of political motivations and overtones, but it is already clear that to the extent the government succeeds in halting inflation, the ratio of war outlays will continue to inch downward and unemployment will continue to creep upwards.

That the government is not entirely unaware of the economic implications of reductions in military outlays is graphically revealed by Marc Childs in his widely

The Permanent War Economy – Commentary

syndicated column of August 20, 1957, wherein he comments on *Jobs and Defense* by stating, in part:

> The aviation industry is beginning to feel the effects of cutbacks in competing missile programs and in military aircraft production. *The resulting unemployment* when it is put together with pockets of joblessness, *has raised the fear in the administration that the rising spiral of prices may eventually and sooner rather than later – bring deflation. As a result, Sherman Adams, the assistant to the President, instructed Clarence Randall, White House adviser on trade and economic affairs, to review every government cutback that might adversely affect a plant having more than 5,000 employees.* Randall is confident the economy can absorb this unemployment and continue at the present high level, but there are others not so optimistic. Italics mine – *T.N.V.*)

We belong in the latter group, Strachey presumably would side with the optimists. In any case, it should already be clear (and, if not, it will become increasingly so) that contemporary capitalism, while a new stage (the Permanent War Economy), has achieved only the most precarious of equilibria, both domestically and internationally. The continual production of ever-increasing amounts of the means of consumption depends not only on constantly increasing production of the means of production, but on maintenance of the high level of production of the means of destruction. The impossibility of continuing to expand in all three departments of production will lead to a deteriorating economic situation and in the relatively near future to the beginnings of a first-rate political crisis.

The New International June 1957 T.N. Vance

The Myth of America's Social Revolution

The political economy the United States of America is indeed strange, as has frequently been remarked by analysts with varying points of view in the political spectrum. Moreover, in no other country has public relations and the art of sweeping exaggeration been carried to such refined lengths. This social environment helps to explain why a crude statistical work achieves front page publicity in the *New York Times*.

When the preliminary findings of the Kuznets study (*Shares of Upper Income Groups in Income and Savings*, Simon Kuznets, assisted by Elizabeth Jenks, National Bureau of Economic Research, Inc. 1953) were released early in 1952, the *New York Times* gave them substantial coverage in its issue of March 5, 1952, starting with a front-page headline: "Shift in Income Distribution is Reducing Poverty in U.S." The lead paragraph by economic reporter Will Lissner stated: "The United States has undergone a social revolution in the last four decades, and particularly since the late Thirties." To be sure, the same newspaper, in an article by the same reporter one month later – to be precise on April 3, 1952 – carried an article with the headline: "Living Standards Off 4 per cent Since Korea." This is the conclusion of a study by Dr. Julius Hirsh on the impact of price rises and tax increases on the moderate income city worker's four person family – "the type of family . . . that occurs most frequently in the varied structure of the American urban family."

The "social" revolution apparently was not too profound, or at any rate it proved to be rather short-lived. Perhaps history was rather unkind to the advocates of the American "social" revolution by launching the Korean war before the findings of the Kuznets study were made public, and before the advertising agencies could use these findings to launch a campaign for reduction of taxes on the upper income groups.

What are the Kuznets' findings? Lissner summarizes them with reasonable accuracy in the above-mentioned article, as follows:

As a result of little-appreciated changes in the distribution of a rapidly growing national income, the United States has gone about half the way toward eliminating inequities in incomes. But it has done this, not by leveling down, but by leveling up. These are some of the changes:

> The very poor have become fewer by two-thirds of their 1939 number.
> The poor have become better off. Where three out of four families had

> incomes of less than $2,000 a year in 1939, only one out of three fell into that class ten years later.
>
> The well-to-do and the rich have become more numerous. In the late Thirties one family in about fifty was in the $5,000 and over income class, and one out of 100 was in the $10,000 and over class. In the late Forties, one family out of six was in the $5,000 and over class, and one out of twenty in the $10,000 and over class.
>
> Over the years, the very rich have become poorer because the rise in labor incomes has been accompanied by a decline in property incomes. The share of the upper 1 per cent of income receivers in total income has declined in thirty-five years from 16 per cent to 9 per cent.

The Kuznets study, of course, is concerned primarily with what has happened to the upper income groups — the top one, five or seven per cent of the population. In his article in the May 1, 1953 issue of the *New York Times*, based on release of the entire study, Lissner provides a more up-to-date summary of the major findings of Kuznets' statistical analysis and identifies the source of interpretation of these income changes as a "social" revolution.

> The decline in upper group shares of total individual income was sharpest for the top 1 per cent of income receivers in the total population. This group had per capita incomes of $5,500 and up in 1948 and thereafter, and typical family incomes of $22,000 and up. Its share, before Federal income taxes, dropped from 12 per cent in 1939-40 to 8½ per cent in 1917-48. After taxes, the drop was from 11 to 6 per cent . . .
>
> From 1913 to 1948 the per capita income of the top 1 per cent little more than doubled. The Consumers Price Index rose two-and-a-half times its 1913 level; the upper group failed even to maintain its real income. The per capita income of the mass of the population, the lower 99 per cent group, rose to four times its 1913 level, making a vast improvement in its real income.

The Myth of America's Social Revolution

This was much more than a mere consequence of the shifts in income distribution which have been reducing poverty in the United States, reported in detail in *The New York Times* of March 5. These shifts, called "a social revolution" by Dr. Arthur F. Burns, Economic director to the President and research director, on leave, of the National Bureau would have produced only a moderate proportional decline.

Inasmuch as there have been more profound statistical studies than this, including several by Kuznets – none which has received notice outside the professional journals – one forced to the conclusion that it is label "social revolution" that is largely or exclusively responsible for widespread dissemination of the findings of the present study. And it is not without interest that Burns, also carries the title of Professor of Economics at Columbia University, is now chief economic adviser to the President.

Whether Burns is aware of the meaning of the phrase, "social revolution," we do not know. Certainly Kuznets is not in any way responsible for this remarkable label. He merely presents his findings in a technical manner, hardly intended for the lay reader, surrounds them with the usual caveats and tables of derivatives and substantiation almost without end. The suspicion must remain however, that Burns was well aware of the fact that referring to changes in income distribution as a "social revolution" would result in extraordinary publicity and presumably in support for redistributing the tax burden — a goal that Burns apparently favors. Consider, for example the following paragraph from the first Lissner story:

> He, Arthur F. Burns, who directed an important part of these investigations, concludes that we have about reached the limit of the usefulness of the income tax as a device for redistributing income. To raise the large revenues required for security at home and abroad, the tax must be heavily on the brackets where income in concentrated – moderate-sized incomes.

The Permanent War Economy – Commentary

The "social" revolution thus fades into something far short of the expropriation, or even the impoverishment of the bourgeoisie. It would seem to center around the high individual income tax rates and the reduction in the proportion of national income going to dividends and interest – developments flowing from the development of the Permanent War Economy, The most important development of the Permanent War Economy, in so far as Kuznets' findings are concerned, is clearly the sharp reduction in unemployment.

States Kuznets (p.xxxvii of his *Introduction and Summary*):

> This recent decline in upper group shares, which for its magnitude and persistence is unmatched in the record, obviously has various causes. The most prominent are the reduction of unemployment and the marked increase in total income flowing to lower income groups (particularly farmers and wage earners); shifts in the saving and investment habits of upper income groups which may have curtailed their chances of getting large receipts from successful mature capital and equity investments; lower interest rates; and steeper income taxes. But *conjectures alone are possible*, and the discussion in the report is limited to a statement of facts. (Italics mine – T.N.V.)

It is more than a coincidence that the basic economic program of the Eisenhower Administration is to reverse this so-called "social" revolution by reducing taxes on the upper income groups, raising the rate of interest, stimulating venture capital and thereby encouraging higher dividends, and stimulating a slight case of unemployment so that labor will not be so demanding and wages can be reduced.

Only the exigencies of the class struggle can account for the absolutely unpardonable use of the term "social revolution" in connection with the relatively insignificant changes that have taken place in income distribution since the development of the Welfare State and, more recently, the Permanent War Economy. Nevertheless, it is still

The Myth of America's Social Revolution

of considerable interest to examine the changes that have taken place in the distribution of income.

Of more interest than the findings of Kuznets are the reports of the Census Bureau. These are based on Census surveys and may be considered to be much more reliable than data based on income tax returns, as is true of Kuznets. The Census data are before taxes and limited to wage or salary recipients. Dividing the latter into five groups, we get the following picture in percentages for selected years from 1939 to 1951:

Wage or Salary							
Recipients	1951	1950	1949	1948	1947	1945	1939
Lowest fifth	3.0	2.3	2.6	2.9	2.9	2.9	3.4
Second fifth	10.6	9.7	10.1	10.2	10.3	10.1	8.4
Middle fifth	18.9	18.3	18.7	18.6	17.8	17.4	15.0
Fourth fifth	25.9	25.7	26.2	25.5	21.7	25.7	23.9
Highest fifth	41.6	44.0	42.4	42.8	44.3	43.9	49.3

In other words, so far as wages and salaries are concerned, accounting for about 70 per cent of total income payments to individuals, the middle income groups have gained – not only at the expense of the upper income group, but also at the expense of the lower income group. At any rate, regardless of what interpretation one cares to make of the above figures, there is clearly nothing that can justify the use of the term "social" revolution.

Kuznets, of course, is concerned primarily with the upper income groups. His figures show a higher decline for the top 1 per cent than for the top 5 per cent – and it is clear that no definition of the upper income groups can properly extend as far as the top 20 per cent. But the major decline has taken place since 1940-41, and this is precisely the period in which individual income tax rates have been raised enormously. The

The Permanent War Economy – Commentary

question of the reliability of the estimates is an inevitable one, and Kuznets is greatly bothered by it, spending an entire chapter of 75 pages, including appendix tables, in justifying his methodology. The chapter starts, however, by stating (p.435):

> We cannot measure the probable errors in our estimates directly because our basic data are either by-products of tax administration or products of censuses, subject to all the imperfections of social records. Some defects are obvious and the adjustments discussed in preceding chapters were designed to correct for them as far as possible. But after all these adjustments, errors inevitably remain, and we are faced with the difficult task of appraising them. *This discussion of the reliability of our estimates must necessarily be incomplete and inconclusive.* (Italics mine – T.N.V.)

If it is inconclusive as to whether the estimates are reliable, it may be wondered why the study was made. Kuznets indicates that the choice between using income tax returns and abandoning the study, and he obviously feels that the basic trends revealed by his study are correct. If by this were meant the small relative improvement in the position of the middle income groups, as shown by Census data, empirical evidence would clearly confirm such findings. For the average number of income earners has increased sharply among factory and white collar workers' families as unemployment has decreased and the percentage of women employees has risen to an all-time high. In other words, on *a family* basis there can be little doubt that there has been increase in the average standard of living since 1939. This is also true on a per capita basis, but it is not so pronounced.

When, however, the claim is made that the upper income groups (one per cent or five per cent) have experienced both an *absolute* and relative decline in their income shares, therefore presumably in their standards of living, one should look with a rather skeptical and jaundiced eye on an analysis that depends completely on the reliability of income tax data. After many comparisons and reliability tests, Kuznets refers to a sample audit study of 1948 income tax returns (which show a minimum of 70 out of 100 returns in the $25,000 and over bracket as containing errors) and concludes (p.466):

The Myth of America's Social Revolution

> The audit study, *as far as the recent results go*, warrants an inference that such underestimation is within a 5 cent margin for incomes at the top 5 per cent level, and within a 10 per, margin for incomes in the 2nd through to 5th percentage bands. (Italics mine – *T.N.V.*)

The difficulty is that the results do not go very far. They cannot do justice the extensive legal tax avoidance practiced by the upper income groups as analyzed in some detail in Part VI of *The Permanent War Economy: Taxation and the Class Struggle*, (*cf.* November-December 1951 issue of *The New International*).

Our own private sample study of millionaires (the only reliable method of estimating what has happened to the incomes of the bourgeoisie) indicates that they are managing to survive although the fees to tax accountants and lawyers have increased rather sharply. Mansions costing in excess of $100,000 are still being built – in fact, in larger numbers than in any period during the last 25 years. Of course, vacations are frequently transformed into business trips – or is it vice-versa? Profits are frequently allowed to remain in corporations, in the expectation that the Eisenhower administration will ultimately reduce the surtax rates in the upper income brackets, so that it will "pay" to retrieve the dividends that are waiting to be declared. Some of these factors Kuznets tries to take into account, but the majority (and they are cumulatively decisive) are beyond statistical analysis.

We can only conclude that in a period of high tax rates any analysis of upper income groups based on tax returns is not only necessarily inconclusive, but tends to be unreliable. Kuznets, moreover, bases his analysis on a per capita approach. Aside from certain statistical difficulties in converting income tax returns to a per capita basis, the procedure as a measure of what has happened to upper income *groups* is exceedingly questionable. While the size of families in upper income brackets is smaller than in lower income groups, an upper income group with a large family might well be excluded from Kuznets' array of the data on a per capita basis. If the purpose of the study is to discover something about standards of living, and not just to collect a lot of figures, then the facts of economic life have to be considered. Using the Kuznets approach, a single individual with an income of $25,000 annually would be part of the upper one per cent in 1948, but a family of five with the one income earner admitting

The Permanent War Economy – Commentary

to an income of $100,000 for the year might be excluded since the per capita is only $20,000. Such an analysis overlooks the fact that one mansion is usually sufficient for a family of this type; in any case, five mansions are rarely used. An analysis of *shares* of upper income groups necessarily involves a ratio of two quantities. The numerator, of course, consists of the amount of income going to the upper income groups, however income is defined. And it makes quite a difference as to what is or is not included in income. The Kuznets data necessarily contain a downward bias (probably on the order of twenty to thirty per cent) in the amount of income currently (since 1943) going to the upper income groups. The numerator of the income ratio is thus understated. But the ratio also depends on the size of the denominator. Here Kuznets uses what amounts to his own estimates of national income. This tends to overstate because of its inclusion of income in kind, imputed rent and other such concepts that are clearly not part of any analysis of the performance of a *capitalist* economy. If the numerator is noticeably smaller than it should be, and denominator somewhat larger than is proper for analysis, the resulting ratio is necessarily considerably smaller than it ought to be.

Unfortunately, we do not have available the statistical resources of the National Bureau of Economic Research or the Department of Commerce, but the decline in the shares of upper income groups since 1939 is not nearly as large as reported. Such decline as has occurred, moreover, is principally confined to the period 1929 and not that of the Permanent War Economy. The bourgeoisie have not been destroyed or impoverished. They have succeeded, so far, in preserving their basic wealth, income and property. Nor has there been any diminution in the political power of the American bourgeoisie. What has happened, as we pointed out in the November-December 1951 issue of *The New International* (p.338), is that:

> *The state however, whose function is more and more to protect the rule and the wealth of the bourgeoisie, is being financed in steadily increasing measure by the workers and lower middle classes.* Therein lies the secret role of taxation under the Permanent War Economy, while equality of incomes remains just as much a mirage on the horizon as it ever was. (Italics in the original.)

The Myth of America's Social Revolution

Kuznets has contributed data that may be useful to income analysts. He is the real pioneer in national income data, and as one who justifiably claims to be a scientist in his field, he should blush at the "social" revolution that Burns has produced from his highly qualified data. Above all Kuznets ought to investigate why his data are being used as part of the drive, spearheaded by the NAM to reduce the tax burden of the upper income groups.

The New International, May 1953 — T.N. Vance

Toward a Permanent War Economy?

AS THIS ARTICLE GOES TO PRESS, the *Wall Street Journal* of Jan. 6 carries a lead story which strikingly confirms one of Mr. Oakes' main points: the scope of the planning now going on for World War III. The *Journal's* Washington correspondent writes:

> The State Department is now considering a big post-armistice stockpile scheme. Under this proposal, which has now reached Secretary Cordell Hull, the Government would accumulate a hoard of strategic materials, mostly from imports, over a *period* of some five years after the war. Goods like crude rubber and industrial diamonds would be stored above ground in warehouses; commodities such as tin and petroleum would be amassed below ground in vaults, mines and subterranean reservoirs.
>
> Such a program, say its advocates, would provide a hedge against any future national 'emergency' (presumably, the next war). In addition, it would provide a balance for the large-scale American export program that is in prospect for world reconstruction, offering a way for debtor nations to repay public loans advanced by this country.

The *Journal* also reports that Vice-Chairman Batt of the War Production Board, speaking the same day in Chicago, urged adoption of a similar plan. Indicating the idea has had "more than casual official consideration", Batt suggested it as "a novel means of approaching a balance in our foreign trade picture."
This last argument shows the intimate connection that is coming to exist between war-making and economic stability. The riddle of how the impoverished, relatively backward rest of the world is going to pay for American exports of goods and capital, is neatly solved by importing vast quantities of raw materials and "sterilizing" them, much as the gold at Fort Knox is sterilized, by burying them in stockpiles withdrawn from the market. War and the prospect of war offer the means for performing this useful economic trick. In war modern capitalism has, as this article shows, an economic stabilizer better than pyramids, cathedrals and WPA rolled into one.— ED *Politics* 1944..

AS WORLD WAR II ENTERS ITS CLIMACTIC stage, it becomes increasingly clear that this is not the "War To End All Wars." Already there have been many warnings of the "possibility of another war." A growing cynicism is abroad concerning the prospects of durable peace. World War III is not only a distinct possibility, it is inevitable as long as the

The Permanent War Economy — Appendix

world's social structure remains one of capitalist imperialism. As Dorothy Thompson puts it in her column of December 6, 1943,

> All grand alliances (referring to the Roosevelt-Stalin-Churchill meeting), have existed only as long as it was necessary to win a war, or protect themselves against the aggressions of other powers. Once all enemies are defeated, the only potential enemies left are members of the grand alliance themselves.

In more scientific terms — the contradictions which led to this war have not been eliminated: if anything, they have been intensified.

More revealing than any theoretical analysis concerning its inevitability are the obvious preparations that are now being made for World War III. One may dismiss the psychological preparations, designed to condition the population to accept the inevitability of the next war, as too intangible to evaluate. One may shrug aside the political preparations, which are clearly inherent in the power politics now being played by the leaders of the United Nations, on the ground that this is *realpolitik* in a materialistic world. But it is impossible to overlook the unanimity with which the business community approves the maintenance of a large standing army, universal military service and an air force second to none as preconditions of America's "security" in the post-war world. Disarmament, the utopian pipedream of Geneva, is to be abandoned as a slogan after this war — except for the conquered enemy.

Important as are the above more or less obvious types of preparation, currently concealed economic preparations are decisive. In the United States, this question is intimately bound up with the problems of reconversion. Much more is at stake than the question of what to do with the huge government-owned war plants (estimated at $20 billion by the end of the war). A plan for reconversion, no matter how loose and flexible, must be guided by some indication of the type of post-war world that is desired. If war within the life of the next generation is a probability, then it must be planned for on the basis of the lessons learned from this war.

American imperialism, for example, has no intention of entering another war without adequate stockpiles of all critical and strategic military materials. And so we

Towards a Permanent War Economy? 1944

have Senate Bill 1582 (introduced early in December, 1943 by Senator Scrugham of Nevada) whose stated purpose is:

To assure an adequate supply of strategic and critical minerals for any future emergency by holding intact in the post-war period all stock piles surviving the present war owned by Government agencies and by necessary augmentation thereof primarily from domestic sources.

The "future emergency" is subsequently defined as "a total war of three years' duration, or of any equivalent emergency."

In the case of copper, an article in the National Industrial Conference Board's *Economic Record* (November, 1943) reveals what would be involved.

As current usage of copper probably is at least 1.5 million tons annually, a supply for a three-year war, as proposed in the Scrugham bill, might require 4.5 million tons. This amount is nearly equal to the entire domestic output of new copper in the Thirties, or four years' output at the peak mining rate of 1.07 million tons in 1942.

While the Scrugham bill leaves the question of cost open, it is estimated that the copper program alone would cost well above $1 billion. Clearly, economic preparations for World War III are beyond the stage of informal discussion.

The big question which all discussions of post-war economy try to answer is, of course: How to achieve full employment? The sad experiences following the last war, culminating in the world-wide depression of the 1930s, give the problem an understandable urgency. Public interest in the question is certainly more widespread than ever before. What better tribute to American advertising genius, or what more fitting commentary on the political and economic naivete of the American people, could there be than the $50,000 contest now being held by the Pabst Brewing Company, in commemoration of its 100th birthday, for the best plans to achieve full post-war employment?

The Permanent War Economy — Appendix

There is an urgent political necessity for capitalism to achieve the abolition of unemployment. It is motivated by the inevitable slack in private investment in order to maintain the savings-investment equilibrium.

Assuming, therefore, that my major thesis is correct and that government balancing operations in the future will consist largely of socially sanctioned war outlays, the question arises: how will the future laws of capitalist accumulation differ from the past?

The Future Laws of Capitalist Accumulation

In the past, the dynamics of capital accumulation have caused a polarization of classes. (On the one hand, concentration of wealth in fewer and fewer monopoly capitalists; on the other, a steady increase in the size of the working class, both factory and non-factory, relative to other classes). The war, far from interrupting, has accentuated both these trends — in general, at the expense of the middle classes.

Although this law will still hold true in the epoch of Permanent War Economy, the increased State military outlays (as compared with prewar State expenditures) will have the effect of slowing up the *rate* of class polarization. This is due not so much to the different economic nature of these expenditures as to their *political* character. Their purpose, it must be remembered, is to stabilize the economy; i.e., by State intervention to freeze class relations *and simultaneously the existing class structure*. That is why the post-war size of the labor force and the national income will be considerably below that achieved during the war. Otherwise, the magnitude of post-war war outlays would be at a level so high as virtually to guarantee widespread political opposition on the part of the capitalist class.

The major revision that will have to be made in the Marxian analysis of capitalist accumulation is in the famous law, that an increase in capital means an increase in the industrial reserve army. If the Permanent War Economy succeeds in stabilizing the economy at a high level, unemployment will be eliminated, but only through employment in lines that are economically unproductive. *Thus capitalist accumulation, instead of bringing about an increase in unemployment, will have as its major consequence a decline in the standard of living.*

The decline in the standard of living will be similar in nature to that which is just beginning to take place in wartime. For example, until about the middle of 1942 it was possible for the developing American war economy to support a substantial increase in military production at the same time that a small, but significant, rise occurred in average civilian standards of living. This was due, for the most part, to the fact that in 1939 there was considerable underemployment of both men and resources. Once more or less full employment was attained, however, further increases in military production could only be achieved at the expense of the civilian sector of the economy. Most civilians have not yet felt the full impact of this development because of the accumulation of huge inventories of consumers' goods in the hands of both merchants and consumers. As these inventories are depleted and as consumers' durable goods wear out, the standard of living begins to decline noticeably. If the war continues throughout 1944, with no significant over-all cutbacks in military programs, the decline is apt to become precipitate.

The Permanent War Economy will operate much the same way. At first, of course, there may be a rise in the average standard of living if the levels of national income reached, are reasonably close to those now maintained and if, simultaneously, there is a sharp reduction in total military out lays (inclusive of expenditures for "relief and rehabilitation"). Within a relatively short period, however, assuming that the economy is stabilized at the desired level with a minimum of unproductive governmental expenditures, the maintenance of economic equilibrium will require a steadily rising curve of military outlays. The decline in the average standard of living of the workers, at first relative, will then become absolute—particularly on a world scale as all nations adapt their internal economies to conform with the requirements of the new order based on an international Permanent War Economy. Naturally, the decline will not be a descending straight line; it will have its ups and downs, but the long-term trend will definitely be downward.

Three major assumptions are implicit in the above analysis. *First,* any significant increases in real national income or total product beyond the reconversion equilibrium level are excluded, due to the capitalist nature of production. This ties in with the reasons why continued accumulation of capital is necessary and why these additional increments of capitalist accumulation require more or less corresponding (socially acceptable) economically unproductive State expenditures. *Second,* while a portion of

The Permanent War Economy — Appendix

the State's consumption of accumulated unpaid labor may take the form of public works, for reasons previously stated only a minor portion of such public works will be capable of raising the standard of living; and these will decline in importance as direct war outlays increase. *Third,* the possible effects of alternative fiscal policies (financing through different methods of taxation and borrowing) to support the Permanent War Economy are excluded as not affecting the basic analysis; although certain methods may markedly accelerate the inflationary process, while others may permit American entry into World War III without having experienced a violent inflation.

Capitalist society is forever seeking a "stable and safe" equilibrium—one which eliminates unemployment or, at least, reduces it to negligible proportions ("stable"); and one which is generally acceptable or, at least, politically workable ("safe").

This is, of course, hardly a new problem. Instability has been a dominant characteristic of capitalism particularly since technological advances in industry have become marked, a matter of some fifty to one hundred years. It is only in recent years, however, especially since the Bolshevik Revolution plainly demonstrated that capitalism is a mortal society and can be succeeded by a different set of socio-economic institutions, that the problem has taken on a new urgency. Theoretical analysis indicates, and the observations of capitalists confirm, that capitalism would have great difficulty in surviving a depression comparable in severity to the recent one. This must be avoided at all costs, say the more enlightened members of the bourgeoisie, even if far-reaching structural changes are called for. True, this type of motivation has led to fascism and can easily do so again. It is assumed, however, that the ruling class prefers to stave off the advent of fascism as long as possible, and that there is sufficient evidence to indicate that what I have termed "a Permanent War Economy" is coming to be a much more powerful stimulus than the increasingly-repeated question: "If we can employ everyone in wartime, why can't we do as much in peacetime?" The fact is that the capitalist system cannot stand the strain of another siege of unemployment comparable to 1930-1940. It does not require a far-seeing statesman to picture the revolutionary dynamite inherent in a situation where 10-12 million people are unemployed. And this is a conservative estimate of the size of post-war unemployment, *if the traditional methods, such as those used after the last war, are followed this time.*

Towards a Permanent War Economy? 1944

The traditional methods (consisting essentially of trying to restore the *status quo ante bellum* as rapidly as possible) will not be followed. Whether Roosevelt presides over the transition period or not, too much water has flowed under the bridge to permit an uncontrolled post-war inflation followed by a resounding and catastrophic depression. This much, at least, the better minds amongst the capitalists see. The State will have to intervene. It is a question of how much and in what form.

Here we encounter a problem in semantics. State intervention, as I shall show below, must take the form of maintaining a Permanent War Economy. What is a "war economy"? In an extreme sense, involving the reduction of civilian standards of living to the bedrock minimum in order to permit the maximum expansion of war output, we have not, of course, a war economy today. Russia, since the consolidation of Stalin's dictatorship, and Germany, since the consolidation of Hitler's dictatorship, both in "peace" and in the period of military hostilities, have experienced this type of war economy. They are the only countries in modern times to have experienced a "genuine" war economy, with the possible exception of Japan.

A war economy, as I use the term, is not determined by the expenditure of a given percentage of a nation's resources and productive energies for military purposes. This determines only the *kind* of war economy — good, bad, or indifferent from the point of view of efficiency in war-making. The question of amount, however, is obviously relevant. At all times, there are *some* expenditures for war or "national defense." How much must the government spend for, such purposes before we can say a war economy exists? In general terms, the problem can be answered as follows: *a war economy exists whenever the government's expenditures for war (or "national defense") become a legitimate and significant end-purpose of economic activity.* The degree of war expenditures required before such activities become *significant* obviously varies with the size and composition of the national income and the stock of accumulated capital. Nevertheless, the problem is capable of theoretical analysis and statistical measurement.

Until the present period, in America at least, only one legitimate end-purpose of economic activity has been recognized (in theory) ; namely, the satisfaction of human wants or, less euphemistically, the production and distribution of consumers' goods and services. In wartime, of course, the legitimacy of war expenditures is never questioned, except by those few who question the progressiveness of the aims of the war. We are

The Permanent War Economy — Appendix

now being prepared, however, to recognize as a legitimate economic activity *peacetime* expenditures for war of a sizable nature. Herein lies the real importance of the psychological preparations now under way for World War III.

The state will have to spend for war purposes as much as is required to maintain a "stable and safe" equilibrium. As a result, unemployment will be a thing of the past. Barring the immediate outbreak of World War HI — i.e., within five years of the end of World War II — the size of post-war war outlays is not significantly influenced by the potential utility of such expenditures for war-making. *The decisive consideration is the level of employment that it is desired to maintain.* Based on preliminary estimates of national income and capital accumulation in the interim period between World War II and World War III, the United States will achieve a Permanent War Economy through annual war expenditures of from $10-20 billion. Thus, the inner functioning of American capitalism will have been significantly altered, with profound consequences for all classes of society.

Why these "balancing" expenditures on the part of government must take the form of war outlays rather than public works requires a brief excursion into the past history of unpaid (surplus) labor.

The Problem of Unpaid Labor

The root of all economic difficulties in a class society lies in the fact that the ruling class appropriates (in accordance with the particular laws of motion of the given society) a portion of the labor expended by the working class or classes in the form of unpaid labor. The expropriation of this surplus labor presents its own set of problems; generally, however, they do not become crucial for the ruling class until the point is reached where it is necessary to pile up accumulations of unpaid labor. When these accumulations in turn beget new accumulations, then the stage of "primitive accumulation" (designed to build up the physical stock of the country for immediate consumption' rose purposes) ceases and the stability of the society is threatened. The ruling class *is* impaled on the horns of a most serious dilemma: to allow these growing and mature accumulations to enter into economic circulation means to undermine the very foundations of existing society (in modern terms, depression) ; to reduce or eliminate these expanding accumulations of unpaid labor requires the ruling class or sections of it to commit hara-kiri (in modern terms, the capitalist must cease being a capitalist or enter into bankruptcy). The latter solution is like asking capitalists to accept a 3 per cent rate of profit, because if they make 6 or 10 per cent they upset the applecart and destroy the economic equilibrium. This is too perturbing a prospect; consequently, society as a whole must suffer the fate of economic disequilibrium *unless the ruling class can bring its State to intervene in such a manner as to resolve this basic dilemma.*

Since a class society can support on a relatively stable basis a certain amount of accumulated unpaid labor, the problem becomes one of immobilizing the excess. State intervention is required precisely because no individual member of the ruling class will *voluntarily* give up the opportunity to accumulate further wealth. The State, therefore, acts in the interests of all the members of the ruling class; the disposition of the excess accumulated unpaid labor is socially acceptable, and generally unnoticed by individual members of the ruling class.

Such, for example, was the role performed by pyramid-building in Ancient Egypt, the classic example of a stable economy based on the institution of chattel slavery. In feudal society, based on the accumulation of unpaid labor through the institution of serfdom, an analogous role was performed by the building of elaborate monasteries and shrines. These lavish medieval churches were far more than centers of worship and learning, or even than examples of conspicuous expenditure on the part of the ruling classes; they were an outlet for the unpaid labor of feudal society — an outlet which permitted a deadening economic equilibrium for centuries.

Capitalist society, of course, has had its own pyramids. These ostentatious expenditures, however, have failed to keep pace with the accumulation of capital. In recent times, the best examples have been the public works program of the New Deal and the road building program of Nazi Germany. Both have been accomplished through what is termed "deficit financing." That is, the state has borrowed capital (accumulated surplus labor for which there is no opportunity for profitable private investment) and consumed it by employing a portion of the unemployed millions, thus achieving a rough but temporarily workable equilibrium.

While the Roosevelt and Hitler prewar "recovery" programs had much in common, there is an important difference. The latter was clearly a military program; all state expenditures were calculated with a direct military use in view. As such, they did not,

The Permanent War Economy — Appendix

for the most part, conflict with the direct interests of the capitalist class of Germany who wished to reserve for private capital all opportunities for profitable investment. In the United States, only a minor portion of the W.P.A. and P.W.A. programs possessed potential military usefulness. Consequently, as such expenditures increased, the opposition of the capitalist class rose (this was basically an economic development, although the psychological impetus afforded by recovery from the depths of depression undoubtedly aided the process). The more money the state spent, the more these expenditures circumscribed and limited the opportunity for profitable private investment. The New Deal was dead before the war; the war merely resuscitated its political expression and was, in reality, an historical necessity.

War expenditures accomplish the same purpose as public works, but in a manner that is decidedly more effective and more acceptable (from the capitalist point of view).

In this, capitalism is again borrowing from the techniques employed by the more static class societies of slavery and projects were officially counted among the unemployed. Today, however, not only are those engaged in producing the instruments of war considered to be gainfully employed; even those in the armed forces are classified as part of the employed labor force. It is only necessary to perpetuate into the post-war period this type of bookkeeping which classifies soldiers and munitions workers as "employed," and then war ("national defense") outlays become a legitimate end-purpose of economic activity; a Permanent War Economy is established and socially sanctioned; capitalist society is safely maintained — until the next war.

Capital Accumulation and State Intervention

Perhaps the most distinctive feature of capitalist society — in comparison with earlier class societies, and at the same time that which indicates its superiority over these earlier forms — is the rapidity with which wealth is accumulated. Alternating periods of rising and falling business activity have resulted and have come to be accepted as an inevitable and peculiarly *capitalist* feature of the accumulation of capital. This was, at least, the situation prior to World War II. To understand the basic laws of motion of capitalist society required the application of the fundamental Marxian concepts of the increasingly high organic composition of capital and the falling average rate of profit. With these tools Marx predicted, and one could analyze, the results of

Towards a Permanent War Economy? 1944

capitalist accumulation. The Marxian general law of capitalist accumulation may, for convenience, be expressed as two laws; namely, the inevitable tendencies toward the polarization of classes and the increase in unemployment.

Today, however, this analysis no longer holds good without certain modifications. The new element in the situation is clearly the fact that the entire present period (in the United States, beginning with the advent of the Roosevelt Administration) is one of increasing State intervention. New forces are set in motion and new laws or trends are discernible. The war both obscures and highlights these basic changes in the functioning of capitalism. The role of the State is obviously increased, but the conduct of the war gives rise to the illusion that this is a temporary affair. But the government cannot spend upwards of $300 billion on war expenditures, acquiring ownership of huge quantities of facilities, raw materials and fabricated goods, without having a profound and lasting effect on the body economic. How to dispose of an anticipated $75 billion of government assets at the end of the war is one of the more perplexing questions troubling the best minds among the bourgeoisie today.

If the Republicans are victorious in the 1944 elections, it is conceivable that they might try to restore the *status quo ante bellum.* Reversing an economic trend, however, is far more difficult than reversing a political trend. Destroying or immobilizing $75 billion of government assets is qualitatively a different proposition than the situation which existed at the end of World War I. It would be *impossible* to do this, and at the same time to maintain employment at a high level and to carry through the international plans of American imperialism. Any such Republican experiment will necessarily be short-lived. As for the Roosevelt Administration—it seems to be "sold" on the Keynesian proposition that public investment must take up the inevitable slack in private investment in order to maintain the savings-investment equilibrium.

Assuming, therefore, that my major thesis is correct and that government balancing operations in the future will consist largely of socially sanctioned war outlays, the question arises: how will the future laws of capitalist accumulation differ from the past?

The Permanent War Economy — Appendix

The Future Laws of Capitalist Accumulation

In the past, the dynamics of capital accumulation have caused a polarization of classes. (On the one hand, concentration of wealth in fewer and fewer monopoly capitalists; on the other, a steady increase in the size of the working class, both factory and non-factory, relative to other classes). The war, far from interrupting, has accentuated both these trends — in general, at the expense of the middle classes.

Although this law will still hold true in the epoch of Permanent War Economy, the increased State military outlays (as compared with prewar State expenditures) will have the effect of slowing up the *rate* of class polarization. This is due not so much to the different economic nature of these expenditures as to their *political* character. Their purpose, it must be remembered, is to stabilize the economy; i.e., by State intervention to freeze class relations *and simultaneously the existing class structure.* That is why the post-war size of the labor force and the national income will be considerably below that achieved during the war. Otherwise, the magnitude of post-war war outlays would be at a level so high as virtually to guarantee widespread political opposition on the part of the capitalist class.

The major revision that will have to be made in the Marxian analysis of capitalist accumulation is in the famous law that an increase in capital means an increase in the industrial reserve army. If the Permanent War Economy succeeds in stabilizing the economy at a high level, unemployment will be eliminated, but only through employment in lines that are economically unproductive. *Thus capitalist accumulation, instead of bringing about an increase in unemployment, will have as its major consequence a decline in the standard of living.*

The decline in the standard of living will be similar in nature to that which is just beginning to take place in wartime. For example, until about the middle of 1942 it was possible for the developing American war economy to support a substantial increase in military production at the same time that a small, but significant, rise occurred in average civilian standards of living. This was due, for the most part, to the fact that in 1939 there was considerable underemployment of both men and resources. Once more or less full employment was attained, however, further increases in military production could only be achieved at the expense of the civilian sector of the economy. Most civilians have not yet felt the full impact of this development because of the accumulation of huge inventories of consumers' goods in the hands of both merchants and consumers. As these inventories are depleted and as consumers' durable goods wear out, the standard of living begins to decline noticeably. If the war continues throughout 1944, with no significant over-all cutbacks in military programs, the decline is apt to become precipitate.

The Permanent War Economy will operate much the same way. At first, of course, there may be a rise in the average standard of living if the levels of national income reached are reasonably close to those now maintained and if, simultaneously, there is a sharp reduction in total military outlays (inclusive of expenditures for "relief and rehabilitation"). Within a relatively short period, however, assuming that the economy is stabilized at the desired level with a minimum of unproductive governmental expenditures, the maintenance of economic equilibrium will require a steadily rising curve of military outlays. The decline in the average standard of living of the workers, at first relative, will then] become absolute — particularly on a world scale as all nations adapt their internal economies to conform with the requirements of the new order based on an international Permanent War Economy. Naturally, the decline will not be a descending straight line; it will have its ups and downs, but the long-term trend will definitely be downward.

Three major assumptions are implicit in the above analysis. *First*, any significant increases in real national income or total product beyond the reconversion equilibrium level are excluded, due to the capitalist nature of production. This ties in with the reasons why continued accumulation of capital is necessary and why these additional increments of capitalist accumulation require more or less corresponding (socially acceptable) economically unproductive State expenditures. *Second,* while a portion of the State's consumption of accumulated unpaid labor may take the form of public works, for reasons previously stated only a minor portion of such public works will be capable of raising the standard of living; and these will decline in importance as direct war outlays increase. *Third.* the possible effects of alternative fiscal policies (financing through difference methods of taxation and borrowing) to support the Permanent War Economy are excluded as not affecting the basic analysis; although certain methods may markedly accelerate the inflationary process, while others may permit American entry into World War III without having experienced a violent inflation.

The Permanent War Economy — Appendix

Capitalist society is forever seeking a "stable and safe" equilibrium — one which eliminates unemployment or, at least, reduces it to negligible proportions ("stable") ; and one which is generally acceptable or, at least, politically workable ("safe").

This is, of course, hardly a new problem. Instability has been a dominant characteristic of capitalism particularly since technological advances in industry have become marked, a matter of some fifty to one hundred years. It is only in recent years, however, especially since the Bolshevik Revolution plainly demonstrated that capitalism is a mortal society and can be succeeded by a different set of socio-economic institutions, that the problem has taken on a new urgency. Theoretical analysis indicates, and the observations of capitalists confirm, that capitalism would have great difficulty in surviving a depression comparable in severity to the recent one. This must be avoided at all costs, say the more enlightened members of the bourgeoisie, even if far-reaching structural changes are called for. True, this type of motivation has led to fascism and can easily do again. It is assumed, however, that the ruling class prefers to stave off the advent of fascism as long as possible, and that there is sufficient evidence to indicate that what I have termed "a Permanent War Economy" is coming to be regarded as a feasible, even if temporary, alternative to fascism.

The P.W.E in Action — A Look Ahead

How will the Permanent War Economy operate? Can it achieve the "stable and safe" equilibrium? It is possible to chart the major outlines of the functioning of the Permanent War Economy. The assumptions underlying this projection are listed below in outline form without any attempt at justification. They are grouped under three broad headings, as follows:

MILITARY
1. The European phase of World War II will end late in 1944.
2. The Asiatic phase of World War II will end late in 1945.
3. While some demobilization will take place with the defeat of Germany, the major transition will occur in fiscal 1946.
4. World War III will occur in 1960.

Towards a Permanent War Economy? 1944

INTERNATIONAL

5. Conduct of world affairs in the interim period between World Wars II and III will be in the hands of the United States, Great Britain, and Russia, with American imperialism the dominant partner.
6. No successful proletarian revolution will take place.
7. Stalinism will successfully maintain itself in power in Russia.
8. A form of international "grossraumwirtschaft" will govern economic relations among the major economic regions of the world.
9. There will be a limited restoration of international trade based on direct and open State intervention.

DOMESTIC ECONOMY (all dollar figures in 1943 prices)

10. The national income will vary within the limits of $120-150 billion, averaging around $135 billion.
11. There will be a gross national product of $140-180 billion, with an average of about $160 billion.
12. The dangerous margin of excess capital accumulations (over and above private capital formation) will run between $20-25 billion.
13. Private capital formation will reach about $10 billion in 1947, declining to approximately $5 billion in 1952 and thereafter leveling off at this rate.
14. Government war outlays will average about $15 billion, with probable limits of $10-20 billion the trend will be toward the upper limit as World War III approaches.
15. The national debt in 1946 will be close to $250 billion, increasing thereafter at an annual rate of $5-10 billion.
16. The employed labor force will be stabilized at about 50 million persons; additions, due to the growth of population of working age, are ignored, as it is unlikely that they will be substantial enough to alter the picture.
17. While it is probable that productivity of labor will increase, this factor is omitted from consideration as being too difficult to estimate and, in any case, unlikely to affect the basic analysis.

The Permanent War Economy — Appendix

18. There will be a steady, but somewhat falling rate of interest.
19. The propensity to consume will remain fairly constant.
20. The rate of profit will be sustained at a level comparable to the best prewar years, its tendency to decline being offset by increasing State intervention and a relatively minor increase in the rate of surplus value.

On the basis of these assumptions, the table below of the movement of capital accumulation, government war outlays, the average standard of living and average real wages of the working class under the Permanent War Economy follows logically.

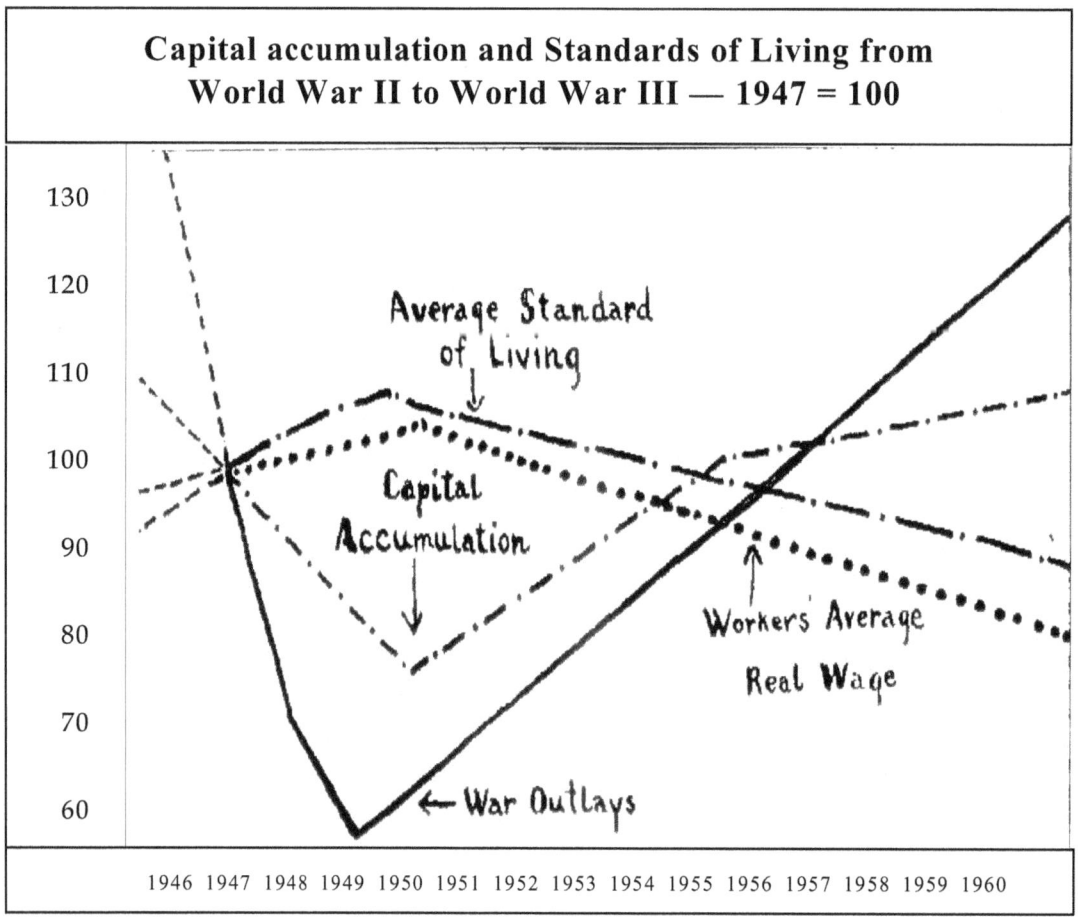

Towards a Permanent War Economy? 1944

1947 is chosen as the base year, for this is assumed to be the first "normal" post-war year. 1946 is considered as a year of transition. The concepts are presented in index numbers in order to show bask trends under the Permanent War Economy. Thus, according to the chart, the critical period will be 1954-1956. It is at this time that the inherent contradictions of capitalism will begin to threaten seriously the newly-found economic stability, pushing society rapidly in the direction of World War

Minor divergences will not materially affect the validity of the assumptions. This Is particularly true of assumptions 19 and 17-20, which are really political and economic generalizations. For example, the analysis still holds true even World War III should take place in 1965 or 1970, rather than, as predicted, In 1960. Assumptions 10 – 16 are of a an entirely different character. Here, substantial differences in magnitude might render the forecasts useless. But 12, 13, 14 and 16 require explanation. The others conform rather closely to most predictions now being made.

The figure stated in assumption 12, taken together with that stated in assumption 13, is only slightly above the estimate made by Professor Alvin Hansen (one of the outstanding authorities in this country on the theoretical aspects of investment policy) of $20–25 billion as the amount necessary to be invested in the post-war period. The level indicated have would be $30 billion, hardly a significant difference. Assumption 13 provides for private capital formation is perfectly consistent with the best prewar years starting with the history of capitalism since it entered the phase of permanent crisis.

Assumption 14 will appear very high to those who view the post-war situation in the same manner as the prewar situation. An interesting confirmation of the estimate made here appears in the October 1943 issue of the National Industrial Conference Board's *Economic Record* in an article entitled *Postwar Budget Prospects: 1945–1948:*

> While all the figures for future years are necessarily speculative, they are particularly so for national defense expenditures in the post-war period. Armed forces numbering 1 million would constitute a smaller number than are assumed in some quarters. *If the size of the armed services should be nearer to 2 million, expenditures of about $7 billion* would seem to be more nearly the level of our peacetime defense expenditures than the $4

billion shown for 1948. *The nature and the extent of equipment* that would be used by our armed forces in the post-war era could account for variations in expenditures of *several billion dollars a year.* (My italics — W.J.O.)

A total military establishment of 2 million appears to be conservative in the light of plans for occupation and policing forces, plus conscription of the youth. Equipment and supplies for this size military force should easily reach $10 billion. Stockpiling and other military outlays, direct and indirect, appear to b quite capable of raising the total to $20 billion, the upper limit in the assumption.

The average of current estimates regarding the probable size of the post-war labor force is about 55 million persons Assumption 16, therefore, is considerably below prevailing estimates; for if the difference of 5 million were to constitute unemployment in any genuine sense of the term, it is obvious that the Permanent War Economy would not be, fulfilling its main function. 50 million is a more realistic figure than 55. It is higher than all prewar records, although it is some 13 million below the current peak o about 63 million (which includes those in the armed forces) The translation of those in the armed forces into active members of the labor force, is subject to shrinkage which depending on battle casualties and related factors, should run between 1 and 2 millions. Net retirements, due to the excess of over-age people leaving jobs as compared with new entrants, should be close to 3 million. The balance of 8 million represents women who are temporary war worker and are expected to leave the employed labor force once the war is over. This figure includes current child labor and is therefore not much higher than generally accepted "guess-timates."

The assumptions upon which the operations of the Permanent War Economy are predicated thus appear to be realistic. *Among the many problems which will remain are two outstanding and closely related ones: can class relations be frozen, and can disastrous inflation be prevented. Each requires a separate article, to be adequately discussed.* The first, as I have indicated, is directly related to the process of capitalist accumulation in the post-war period.

It depends not only on many political factors but on several economic ones, the most important of which is clearly the question of inflation.

Towards a Permanent War Economy? 1944

It is not my belief that the Permanent War Economy will provide an enduring solution for capitalism. But it can work for the period under consideration, and there is likewise no reason why appropriate fiscal policies (from the point of view of the capitalists, which means anti-working class in essence) will not be successful in preventing out right inflation. The national debt, astronomical as it may seem, presents no serious problem. Assuming an annual interest burden of $7 billion, a very generous estimate, this will easily be covered out of current tax receipts. It is the *type,* as well as the amount, of taxes to be levied that will constitute one of the major areas of political and class conflict. The question is made still more acute by the fact that inflation appears to offer the bourgeoisie an easy way out to unload the cost of the war onto the backs of the working masses of the population. A policy of this kind however, cannot be drifted into; it must be adopted consciously. If the die is now, or soon to be, cast in favor of deliberate and uncontrolled inflation, this can only mean that the decisive section of the ruling class is determined to establish fascism as soon as possible. I see no evidence at present, to warrant this belief although, of course, there are many similarities between fascism and the Permanent War Economy. The danger of inflation is not diminished by a Permanent War Economy; on the contrary, it is steadily increased. But it seems more probable that the inflation-fascism sequence is a contender for a prime place on the agenda after World War III than in the post-World War II period.

Labor's Responsibility

It is not likely that the above analysis, necessarily presented in sketchy, outline form, will meet with any enthusiastic reception. For one thing, it runs counter to all currently organized and clearly defined bodies of political thought. Orthodox Marxists (Trotskyists) have convinced themselves that only a successful proletarian revolution can end this war; otherwise fascism will rule the post-war world. New Dealers want to restore "free competition" and make capitalism humane; the only practical note amidst their absurdities is the attempt to win a fourth term for Roosevelt. Social Democrats are still for socialism in theory and capitalism in practice. In fact, all capitalist (and Stalinist) political thought will deny the possibility of a Permanent War Economy, although they will support measures leading toward its establishment.

The Permanent War Economy — Appendix

Moreover, the imagination, courage and capacity of the human mind to project itself forward in an hour of deep social crisis and deal with reality instead of illusion has not been a very noticeable characteristic of the human species. Nevertheless, this war, which has already destroyed so many cherished illusions, will destroy many more before it is consigned to the history texts. The drift of events is toward a Permanent War Economy. What better solution has -3pitalism to offer? And what likelihood of an anti-capitalist solution is there at present? What may now seem fantastic to many will, as the present war draws to a close, appear to be obvious as the evidence piles up.

Upon the shoulders of the labor movement rests the real responsibility for preventing World War III. This universally-approved objective can never be achieved by the Roosevelts, Churchills, Stalins, or Chiang Kai-Sheks of this or the next decade. For the labor movement, especially its socialist-minded sector, to stand a chance to prevent the atomization of society as a result of repeated wars requires much closer and more realistic study of what is actually happening in the world today than has yet been evidenced. The basic strategic aim of socialism as the only rational alternative to capitalism needs no revision except that of modernization. It is in the field of tactics that substantial revisions are needed. A declining standard of living under a Permanent War Economy cannot be successfully fought by a labor movement whose most powerful organizations are trade unions, no matter how powerful these may be. The important battle areas will be abstruse (to the masses) economic questions, such as the size and composition of the Federal budget, taxation and fiscal policy, investment alternatives, and the like, rather than wages, profits and working conditions for specific industries or factories. These latter will still be important, to be sure, but they will largely be determined by the decisions affecting the former. This points to the necessity not only of widespread mass economic education, but of the vital need for an independent political Party of labor. Only a labor party, independent of capitalist political machines, and based upon trade unionists, is capable of coping with the problems of living under a permanent war economy.

Politics February 1944 — Walter J. Oakes

After Korea — What?
An economic Interpretation of U. S. Perspectives

The following essay begins with an overview of the American role in the Korean war. The essay itself is of interest here, not only because it is referred to by the author in his subsequent series of essays, but also because it is a sort of introduction to those essays. It essentially asks "what is happening to the American economy in the context of the cold war?" The opening section, a discussion of the Korean war is not included here since it would be digressive and is, in any case, reasonably accessible in good libraries. (EH)

No better illustration of the significance of the new policy can be found than in what has happened to the Marshall Plan. Although in the interests of American imperialism, and part of the policy of Stalinist containment, it did nevertheless eschew military policies and it had made some progress toward improving standards of living in Western Europe and achieving a more rational and integrated economy. Now all this has been abandoned under the impact of the mobilization program. As *The New York Times* correspondent, Michael L. Hoffman, expresses it in his dispatch published on October 13:

> Time and again in the past few weeks this correspondent has heard European economic officials of various nationalities say with an actual or figurative shrug of the shoulders that *as the United States seemed to have lost interest in everything except rearmament, each country had better start looking out after itself in economic matters.* (My italics — T. N. V.)

In fact, the article was headlined "Europe's economy edges to autarchy."

The political reception that the new American policy has received in Europe and Asia, especially Asia, is anything but favorable. But it is its economic causes and effects that are the key to the shape of the world after the end of the Korean war.

THE IMMEDIATE ORIGIN OF THE economic pressures that have pushed American imperialism into its new course, which is without historical precedent for a democratic capitalist nation, lies in the phenomenal expansion of the productive forces during World War II and the virtual maintenance of this level of production during the last five years. This development has not only been contrary to the expectations of the bourgeoisie but also, let us admit, unexpected by most Marxists. Here our analysis will he helped by making reference to some statistical measures, even if they are considered as but crude approximations.

The Permanent War Economy — Appendix

We start with the fact that production increased about 12 per cent a year during World War II, from 1939 to 1945. In other words, total output was some 72 per cent higher when the war ended than when it began. This can be seen by examining the figures for national income and national product of the Department of Commerce as published in the *Survey of Current Business* and reproduced below (the latest revisions are contained in the issue of July 1950).

National income and product figures are, of course, estimates, but they are the only dollar figures that attempt to portray the productive performance of the economy. Without entering into current controversies among the national income specialists, and granting that important conceptual and statistical problems are involved, we are

WARTIME GROWTH OF OUTPUT (Millions of Dollars)				
	1939	1945	% Increase current dollars	% Increase Constant Dollars*
National Income	$17,532	$182,691	%152	%84
Net National Product	83238	202800	144	78
Gross National Product	92339	215210	136	72
*Calculated by deflating the 1945 current dollar figures by the rise in the BLS wholesale price index, which rose from 77.1 in 1939 to 105.8 in 1945 — a rise of 37.2 per cent yielding a deflator of 27.1 per cent.				

concerned only with basic trends which are not altered even if the margin of error in the figures is sizable. Fundamentally, gross national product is larger than net national product by the inclusion of capital depreciation and depletion. That is, the net value of current production ought not to include the consumption of capital as this is already reflected in the final prices of commodities on the market. Net national product is larger than national income chiefly due to the inclusion of indirect business taxes and

After Korea — What?

liabilities, i.e., sales and excise taxes, etc., thus affecting the evaluation of government services.

We have based our conclusion about the wartime growth of output on gross national product because, while the BLS wholesale price index is the best single indicator of price changes throughout the economy, it undoubtedly understates to some extent the degree of wartime inflation. A sounder procedure would have been to deflate separately each component of gross national product, but the work involved would not be justified by appreciably greater accuracy in the results. And for our purposes it is of relatively minor importance whether real output increased by 60 per cent, 70 per cent or 80 per cent during the war.

As a matter of fact, the Federal Reserve index of industrial production, which is based on physical volume, tends to confirm our analysis. This index, by far the most comprehensive of all industrial production indexes, rose from 109 in 1939 to 203 in 1945, a rise of 86 per cent. The Federal Reserve index, however, definitely overstates as a measure of total output in wartime because of the relatively large weight assigned to war industries in its composition.

We are therefore content to rest with the figure of 72 per cent as the wartime increase in total output. How was this huge increase in production achieved? Initial impetus, of course, was provided by the availability of significant quantities of idle resources, including over nine million unemployed. There then occurred a surprising increase in the total employed labor force which, including both the civilian and armed force sectors, rose from over 45 million in 1939 to about 64 million in 1945, a rise of roughly 40 per cent. Even without the armed forces of almost 12 million, the employed civilian labor force still rose by about seven million workers, who worked for longer hours and whose productivity was increased by a huge expansion in productive capacity largely as a result of the enormous government expenditures for plant and equipment. In other words, the wartime expansion in real output was made possible essentially by an increase in capital accumulation and in the supply of labor power, in roughly equal proportions.

Had the wartime increase in the total labor force largely evaporated with the cessation of hostilities and had the wartime increase in capital been totally unsuited for

The Permanent War Economy – Appendix

peacetime use or, to the extent that it was unadaptable, had it not been substantially replenished by new, peacetime accumulations of capital, the level of activity of the economy would have reverted to prewar output, with consequent depressing effects. This did not occur, contrary to many expectations, because government expenditures were maintained at high levels, partly for war purposes, and American imperialism decided to support the recovery of the economies of Western Europe as part of the policy of containment of Stalinist imperialism and as a means of increasing the market for the products of American capitalism. The entire process, of course, was nourished by the backlog of accumulated consumer demands in the domestic market which, in turn, were supported by the tremendous level of private savings.

THE SAME PROCEDURE THAT WAS used to calculate the wartime increase in output shows that postwar output is currently almost at the levels achieved at the end of the war. It is true that our calculations yield an 18 per cent decline in real output in the last five years, but the decline in the last four years is only 5 per cent. In other words, more than two-thirds of the relatively small decline that has occurred took place in 1946, in the first postwar year before the menace of Stalinist imperialism became apparent to the leaders of the American bourgeoisie. Perhaps a planned reconversion would have averted the decline of 1946 but it must be remembered that the dominant elements within American capitalism at that time were basing all their plans and policies on a return to the status quo ante bellum.

It must be emphasized that the achievement of these extremely high levels of production occurred prior to the outbreak of the Korean war. For example, the Federal Reserve index was at 201 in July 1950 compared with 203 in 1945. Since then it has risen sharply, but at that level it is 14 per cent above 1949 and 5 per cent above 1948, the previous postwar peak. The labor force data show that the wartime peaks have been equaled. For June 1950 the employed civilian labor force was estimated (September 1950 issue of *Monthly Labor Review*) at 61,482,000. When the derived armed forces figure of 1,311,000 is added to this figure, the total employed labor force becomes 62,793,000 or close to the 64 million figure reached in wartime. There is, of course, the vast difference that the wartime figure included 12 million in the armed forces whereas the current pre-Korean armed forces figure is only slightly over 1,300,000. In other words, more

After Korea — What?

than 9 million have been added to the employed civilian labor force since the end of World War II. These figures help to explain why Washington is so concerned about manpower shortages as the mobilization program unfolds, but they also reveal, in spite of the shorter work week, a goodly portion of the reason why postwar output has been maintained at almost wartime levels.

The other part of the postwar story of high level production and employment is to be found in the extremely rapid rate of private capital accumulation, the figures for which are even more pregnant with meaning for the future than the manpower data. The following tabulation, based on the Department of Commerce data, graphically reveals the picture:

POSTWAR CAPITAL ACCUMULATION (Billions of Dollars)			
Year	Gross Private Domestic Investment	Net Foreign Investment	Total Gross Private Capital Formation
1946	28.7	4.6	33.3
1947	30.2	8.9	39.1
1948	43.1	1.9	45
1949	33	0.4	33.4
1950 est.*	46	-2	44
Postwar Total	181	13.8	194.8
*Based on estimates for first and second quarters of 1950 as contained in August *1950 SURVEY OF CURRENT BUSINESS.*			

Thus, in the five postwar years American capitalists have accumulated on a gross basis about 195 billion dollars, or an average of 39 billion dollars annually. This represents about 16 per cent of the postwar annual gross national product, a truly staggering percentage, especially when we remember that this growth in capital accumulation occurred with the economy already operating at peak levels due to the war.

The Permanent War Economy — Appendix

If we wish to measure the net additions to private capital formation (i.e., the net additions to plant, equipment, construction, and business inventories, or constant capital as Marx would have put it), we have to subtract the postwar consumption of capital from gross private domestic investment. This is a field in which the experts always disagree as it involves depreciation, treatment of business reserves and accounting practices. It is clear that the maximum it can be, using the Department of Commerce figures, is the difference between what is termed "net national product" and "gross national product," or about $83 billion. This would mean an average postwar annual capital consumption of over $16 billion, which appears to be excessive, and is accounted for not only by the rapid amortization that was permitted of wartime plants but by the inclusion of "statistical discrepancies" and other uncertain quantities in the figures. It is noteworthy, however, that even on a net basis without any adjustment the annual rate of capital investment in the postwar period is 10 per cent, a rate that has not taken place in peacetime since the 1920's. With proper adjustments, the percentage of net capital formation to net national product would appear to be about 12 per cent annually, which even exceeds the period 1919-1923, the five years following World War I.

All current reports testify to this unprecedented accumulation of capital, the material base for American imperialism. For example, a report of the Securities and Exchange Commission for the second quarter of 1950, which is summarized in *The New York Times* of October 12, states "that the net working capital of United States corporations reached $73,800,000,000 at the end of June." No wonder, then, that a National Association of Manufacturers analysis of the postwar financing of business, the findings of which are summarized in *The New York Times* of October 16, is able to state: "Retained earnings were an important source of new capital," although this admission is then qualified, "but this resulted from a relatively low level of dividends rather than from high profits." We would not expect the N.A.M. ever to admit that business is making "high profits," but without passing judgment on current arguments between management and stockholders as to the proper distribution of profits, the fact of the matter is that American business has never accumulated such profits as it has in the postwar period.

After Korea — What?

IT IS PRECISELY THE RECORD ACCUMULATION of capital that makes so interesting the figures for the "net foreign investment" component of national product. Net foreign investment represents the net changes in claims against foreign countries and is affected principally by the net private balance of foreign trade and the net flow of long-term capital abroad. Thus, in the words of the August 1950 *Survey of Current Business*,

> The negative balance of net foreign investment—arising from the substantial excess of Government grants over the current export surplus—remained (for the second quarter of the year) at approximately $2 billion, at an annual rate.

While perhaps too much significance should not be attributed to the absolute figures, the trend—rapidly accelerating after the end of the war through 1947 and rapidly reversing itself from 1948 to the present—portrays the entire tragedy of modern capitalism in the constriction of the world market and a paucity of opportunities for profitable foreign investment of surplus capital. The most recent figures on the net outflow of private long-term capital show the pathetically low levels to which American imperialism has sunk (from the September 1950 issue of the *Survey of Current Business*):

In other words, a mere 642 million dollars represents the total net export of capital by American imperialism during the past year. For the same period, the net outflow of Government long-term capital amounted to $162 million, or 25 per cent of the private total. Even on a gross basis, discounting the total inflow of capital into America from abroad, the private total for the past year is only $1,434,000,000.

With capital accumulation proceeding at the all-time record rates described above, it is clear that the point where the American economy would be choked by surplus capital was rapidly being approached. The Point Four program, in particular, has been designed to establish a climate favorable to the investment of American capital abroad, but Truman has turned out to be just as fortunate as Roosevelt in the matter of having an aggressive foreign imperialism turn up at just the right time to make all sections of the American bourgeoisie unite in supporting an expanding "national defense" program.

The Permanent War Economy — Appendix

War outlays will more than substitute for the inadequacies of the Point Four program. They will relieve a number of economic and political pressures, although in turn creating others. Just how high they will go remains to be seen, but Secretary of the Navy Matthews is reported in *The New York Times* of October 13 as saying, "the cost of operating the national military establishment alone next year might exceed this year's entire national budget. That would be more than $42,000,000,000." There will, of course, be differences of opinion within the ruling class as to the degree of preparation that is required. And it makes quite a difference to many industries and many sections of the capitalist class whether, say, 10 per cent or 25 per cent of the national product is devoted to direct war outlays.

An interesting statement of the perspective involved was made recently by Francis Adams Truslow, president of the New York Curb Exchange, as reported in *The New York Times* of September 26:

> This war, or time of preparation, is not a specific all-out effort, but is perhaps almost a *new way of living which we must endure indefinitely.* (My italics — T. N. V.)

It should not escape our attention that this "new way of living" will operate on a world scale and that it is only another name for what we have called the Permanent War Economy. Its nature and impact are of the greatest importance, but will require a separate article or articles to analyze in any meaningful form.

The New International November-December 1950 — T. N. VANCE

For the Common Defense
A Plea for a Continuing Program of Industrial Preparedness

DURING the last two years we Americans have facers learning in the hardest of all schools—the school of bitter experience—in which many of the key textbooks, unfortunately, were written by our enemies. We are paying a stiff price for that knowledge and will continue to pay until the last life, the last sacrifice, and the last dollar have been entered in the ledger. That will not be in our time. Twice in one generation this has been our common experience. The first time we flunked the course I think it is fair to say that the reason we are here tonight is not only to honor the Army Ordnance Medalists for their past achievements but to survey once more the circumstances that have made those achievements necessary and to build upon them, if possible, a structure of peace and preparedness that will prove more durable.

In the preamble to the Constitution of the United Stares we may find our text in these words "We the people . . . in order to provide for the common defense . . ." That is a highly important fragment of a great document—one which our enemies have never understood. We tend to forget it ourselves until we are thrown into fighting for our lives. This is the people's war—all of them, all of the time—not just the Army's, or the Navy's, or labor's, or industry's war. We know now that industrial and economic wealth does not of itself mean military strength. It becomes striking power only when it is organized and directed. When that organization and direction are too long delayed, we pay a tremendous price, which is a sort of discount in blood to penalize us.

Make no mistake—I think we have done a magnificent job in the last two years, We have learned in the hard school of war how to make the utmost use of the energy, the resources, and the intelligence with which God has blessed us. My quarrel, and yours, is with that bloody discount, exacted from us as a people because we mistakenly thought that a simple desire to remain at peace would be adequate protection against war-mad aggressors.

I should like to frame what follows in three sections: first, to review briefly some aspects of this war and the way we are fighting secondly, to draw a few lessons from that review, and, finally, to put before you a program that I hope you will consider in principle, rather than form.

The enemy set the opening date for our war. That has always been the fate of a democracy which prefers peace, and we must accept it as standard practice. The Axis

The Permanent War Economy — Appendix

nations stole a march on us in the matter of industrial mobilization and hail their economies geared to war long before we awake to our danger. They made lavish display of munitions and equipment in the war's early stages while we trained troops with stovepipe cannon and wooden rifles.

In our painful humiliation we overlooked the fact that they were equally far ahead of us qualitatively. They had better, as well as more, weapons, That is not to say that we did not carry on research and development in military fields because we did. I shudder to think what might have happened to us these last two years if it had not been for the intelligent, patient, and devoted work done in the years of peace by Army Ordnance officers, among others. But the scale was small, the thoughts of the Nation were elsewhere, and the improvement of our means of defense received, between the last war and this one, a pitifully small part of the country's scientific and engineering attention.

From our earliest days, the fundamental training in engineering and tactics provided by West Point and the Naval Academy has been of the best, but we have not made really adequate provision to keep our services abreast of the swift advances in science and technology. The truth is that peace is our business — not war. Our skills have been aimed at a better life, not better weapons of death.

General Campbell has declared that our armament program began two years before Pearl Harbor. He and all of us are proud of the fact that never once has our production been out of step with battle requirements. However, during the transition period from the production of peacetime articles to wartime devices there were costly delays. I am convinced — and hope to document this as we proceed — that not only could those delays have been prevented by an intelligent preparedness program, but such a program might itself could have acted as a deterrent. The Industry-Ordnance team, with its endless production of weapons, blasted the hopes of our enemies in the last war; it is repeating the performance for the German and Japanese military leaders in this one.

THE outstanding features of this war, after the sweep of the German war machine over Europe and that of the Japanese over eastern Asia, have been the dogged courage of the British people, the heroic stand of Russia, and the flood tide of America's war production... The influence of top management, and its importance in getting results, cannot be overestimated. With all modesty, and in the name of the thousands of

For the Common Defense

management experts throughout America who literally have accomplished miracles in spite of technical difficulties and insufficient and inadequate equipment, I am in accord with their policies. But has it ever occurred to you that really good managers, in government or business would never have allowed their own businesses to operate as haphazardly and spasmodically as has the business of defending the United States against its enemies?

In industry we chart our sales and orders and keep a weather eye on material sources and market trends from year to year. Even the company that keeps my fuel-oil tank supplied can tell me ahead of time when I will need oil. Yet when it comes to the vastly important and tragic business of war, we shut our eyes and stop our ears until it is so late that top management has to perform miracles, and men die while waiting for them.

It might pay to look at some examples. Our armed services went to war with a good line of communication equipment which had been designed for them by about five of the larger manufacturers. None of these companies carried on any market-research or development on military products — for the very good reason that the services were so restricted as to procurement or equipment that no manufacturer could risk his stockholders' money that way.

As war approached, these manufacturers were given orders and presently had to expand their facilities and develop subcontractors. These steps should have been taken earlier. They, in turn, would have speeded the stoppage of domestic production. Finally, the large engineering companies were asked to take on research and advanced engineering projects. These companies responded all too slowly, because their minds were not on war problems and because the military people were not too sure what equipment might be required. The net result of these developments is an industry producing $250,000,000 in electronic equipment a month, with amazing progress still going on. But there *had* been a costly delay. Consider for a moment the time, and money that could have been saved and the perils that could have been averted if the antisubmarine devices now available had been ready in the summer of 1940.

HERE is another example: Nothing was more critical than the machine-tool industry from 1939 through 1940. Most of the tooling for war production was hated on the feeds

The Permanent War Economy — Appendix

and speeds of high-speed steel tools. With the single exception of the shell-production program, most armament materials that had to be machined were worked with outdated tools that subsequently were discarded at great expense. To achieve a stipulated production under this arrangement, too many machine tools were needed—sometimes twice the number that would have been required with carbide tools. When the latter were substituted, the plants produced far more than their expected capacity. The reason for this situation was that not enough Ordnance officers had had an opportunity to keep abreast of modern metal-cutting practices.

So much for examples. The blame, such as it is, lies not with specific services, or contractors, but with our approach as a people to war.

When we look ahead toward future security for our country, we realize that simply to prepare for the mass production of military goods is not enough. It can be terribly costly to let a potential enemy get the lead in the production of weapons: it is costly, and demoralizing, to let him get the lead in research and development which precede production.

The war economy that harnesses all of a nation's immediate strength for conflict must also harness its scientific and engineering knowledge and ability far in advance. The research that gives us qualitative superiority over an enemy can never again be left to the time when war has arrived, considering the terrible acceleration which science has given to this conflict. It must be a continuing process in peace.

It is an ironic comment on modern society that much of our truly significant scientific and technological progress occurs in wartime, The irony is not averted by the fact that subsequently the new knowledge is translated into peace-time advantages. For instance, we have been twenty years converting the raw, telescoped electronic developments of the last war into things like broadcasting and ultraviolet therapy and X-ray inspection. Under the pressure of war men move fast and dig deep. They are not always aware of what they find because there is no time to examine it. But when normal times return, the research, development, and testing is transferred to peacetime objectives. Compulsion is removed, What had been everybody's business is quickly resigned to the few who concern themselves with military and naval matters. This is natural because science operates in a vacuum rarely invaded by politics and economics.

For the Common Defense

It does not concern itself so much with ends as with methods. But, in any case, the inevitable tendency is for science and engineering to progress the fastest in those fields remote from the Army and Navy.

IT is obvious that this process will repeat itself unless we readjust the machinery somehow. I hope and pray that when this war has been won we shall lay the foundations for an enduring peace. I hope and pray that we shall have the good sense to build on that foundation, so that the dreadful curse of war does not descend upon us again after two or three decades. But hope and prayer are not enough in an uncertain world. We must have insurance against disaster. The development of new weapons and new instruments of terror and destruction must never again be the field in which the men who want to gain by war outstrip the men who dream of a world at peace.

Perhaps it is time for some fresh thinking on this matter of war and peace. Instead of looking to disarmament and unpreparedness as a safeguard against war — a thoroughly discredited doctrine — let us try the opposite: full preparedness according to a continuing plan. The thought may be unpleasant, but through the centuries war has been inevitable in our human affairs. We have yet to learn that hard truth.

I am not proposing a doctrine of aggression and brutality — simply a realistic point of view that the tendency to war is inevitable, just as the human tendency to disease is inevitable. But we do not sit and wait for the latter to strike us down. Perhaps we should even abandon that false phraseology of a "war economy" and a "peace economy." We do not have, individually, a "sickness economy" and a "health economy" in respect *to* the care of our bodies. One of the acknowledged glories of our age is preventive medicine.

It is interesting to apply this thinking to weapons. Take poison gas, one of the most disturbing and terrifying weapons of the last war. It was almost the first to be outlawed by international agreement, but none of us stopped there. For once we were practical, and, as a result, every country in the world assigned its chemists to the study of gas and its defensive complements. Actually, we believe today that gas is minor weapon, relatively ineffective — but, as a result of this intensive attention, gas has yet to he used, except for isolated instances, in this war. No practical person attributes this to moral or humane reasons.

The Permanent War Economy — Appendix

The experience of two years has shown conclusively that industry, cooperating with the Army and the Navy, makes for a very effective combination, a combination that should he extended into the postwar period to the end that we might maintain at all times leadership in the technical and operational superiority of the implements of war. Should the world know that we were in that position, that we were determinedly keeping the fires of scientific and developmental effort burning and that *we* were ready to shift our industry quickly to the production of these thoroughly tested superior weapons, the probabilities of another Mussolini, Hitler, or Tojo undertaking to conquer the world will be much more remote.

Certainly this production front, which today has some twenty million people in its command — approximately twice the number we have its uniform — is as deserving of a continuing general staff operation in peacetime as the Army and Navy. More than that, it demands such continuity if the services themselves are to be kept effectively ahead of their job. Once war is imminent, it is too late to draw full and immediate benefits from our civilian research, engineering, and production techniques in the creation of war products.

First, we must learn what is needed to cope successfully with our enemies. Almost at the same time we must develop and produce equipment which will be superior to theirs. Good planning would anticipate this situation, so that when an emergency arrives we should only have the problem of increased production of equipment already developed and proved. As part of this program there would always be, in the hands of the Army and Navy, a sufficient amount of this equipment so that a nucleus of our forces would have been trained in its tactical use.

I am indebted to Mr. R. E. Gillmor, president of Sperry Gyroscope Company, and a Navy man himself, for the pertinent observation that over since the days of Mahan, our country has recognized the principle of a "fleet in being," as an instrument of national policy in both peace and war. What is more natural and more logical, in view of the increased mechanization of war and in view of the fact that the scientist and the mathematician are the ones who put our fighting planes in the sky and plant our shells in the hearts of enemy cities, than that we should henceforth mount our national policy

For the Common Defense

upon the solid fact of all industrial capacity for war and a research capacity for war that is also "in being." It seems to me that anything less is foolhardy.

Consider, if you will, what is involved in the development and production of a plane or ship, of an automatic turret, a fire-control device, an electronic-detection system. Think of the long years of trial and error, approximating a quarter of a century, that gave us the turbo supercharger . . . . Given only a layman's knowledge of the weapons involved in the present conflict, of their intricate and ingenious design, and their terrible capabilities, how can we help but be appalled at the thought of the weapons which the next war, if and when it comes, will bring forth, The power to destroy will he greatly magnified, the time to prepare an adequate defense will be tragically shorter than it was in this war. Perhaps there will be no time. Where will that leave our vaunted power to perform miracles of development and production on short notice?

The leaders of industry are as much the leaders of their country as are the generals, the admirals, the legislators and the chiefs of state. Their responsibility for postwar preparedness is certainly no less. The burden is on all of us to integrate our respective activities—political, military, and industrial—because we arc in world politics to stay, whether we like it or not. Any latent ability we may have to procure for our children a durable peace will not be impaired by our ability to wage war victoriously and at a moment's notice. I am well aware that sentiments such as these have traditionally been met by the cry of 'Warmonger!' I know, as you do, that the revulsion against war not too long hence will be an almost insuperable obstacle for us to overcome in establishing a preparedness program, and for that reason I am convinced that we must begin now to set the machinery in motion while it is still possible for us to measure the cost of any other course. The peaceful temperament of the American people is well known. We can possess the mightiest and deadliest armament in the world without becoming aggressors in our hearts, because we do not have that intoxicating lust for blood and power which periodically transforms the German military caste.

I HAVE no hesitancy in submitting the following rough outline of *a* program. It is meant as a challenge, or an invitation to action. Certainly the details are open to argument and change. If they serve no other purpose than to stimulate and arouse all of us to our intelligent and patriotic duty, they will accomplish their purpose. I sincerely hope that there are those among you who will exert yourselves, if you agree with me, to see that the proper administrative and legislative groups are not kept in ignorance of our sentiments,

As a preliminary to even these tentative suggestions, I would like to make some general observations which apply, it seems to mc, to whatever form such a plan might take. First of all, such a program must be a responsibility of the Federal Government. It must be initiated and administered by the Executive Branch — by the President as Commander in Chief — and by the War and Navy Departments. At a somewhat secondary level, it is obvious that the Labor and Commerce Departments would also be vitally interested. Of equal importance is the fact that this must be, once and for all, a *continuing* program, and not the creature of an emergency. In fact, one of its objects will be to eliminate emergencies so far as possible.

The program must be insured and supported by the Congress — in the beginning through resolution or perhaps even through legislation; later, by regularly scheduled and continuing appropriations. Industry's role in this program is to respond and cooperate. Industry must be allowed to play its role. By that I mean that it can act only on request or authorization of government. In the execution of the part allotted to it, industry must not be hampered by political witch hunts, or thrown to the fanatical isolationist fringe tagged with a "merchants-of-death" label, Let us make this 3-way partnership permanent and workable, not just an arrangement of momentary convenience.

Next, it is apparent that the proposed program falls into two parts: *research* and *production*. Both have the ultimate objective of continued preparedness, but the methods and resources of each vary considerably. It will be most convenient to consider these functions separately.

Some of us have been particularly aware of the operations *of* the Office of Scientific Research and Development. under which science has been so ably mobilized during the present emergency. Although the work of the OSRD has been secret in nature, certain aspects of the organization recommend themselves as worthy of consideration for a long-range program. For one thing, existing, facilities in industry and in universities are employed for research projects. The work is directed by a board composed of both civilians and Army and Navy officers. with the result, as the *New* York *Timer* reported, that "the natural conservatism of the Army and Navy is offset by the more imaginative approach of physicists and engineers who never smelled gunpowder in action — men who know what science can do when given half a chance "

THE points worth stressing and recommending for a long-range plan are these: Use existing facilities and bring together at some level the research activities of both civilian and service groups. We already have a number of good governmental institutions in operation--the Naval Research Laboratory, the laboratories of the Army and Navy Air Forces, the Army and Navy Ordnance laboratories and proving grounds, the Research and Development Division of the Quartermaster Corps, the Chemical Warfare Service, the Bureau of Standards, and others. These should certainly be kept up. Their usefulness might be increased and their outlook broadened if they were equipped with committees of competent, responsible civilian advisers, appointed by some such agency as the National Research Council for regular 3-year periods, with one-third retiring each year. One of the responsibilities of such a committee would be to keep its assigned institution in close liaison with industry and with the other Government laboratories.

Finally, the chairmen of the various institutional committees, together with high-ranking officers of the Army and Navy, would compose a general committee for continuing postwar research and development. This would not only maintain contact between industrial laboratories, schools, and Government institutions but would guard against compartmentalism and departmental secrecy among service branches. Such a group could formulate and recommend developmental contracts or research projects between Government and various industrial or college laboratories, wherever the best facilities presented themselves. It would be unwise to attempt any consolidation of Government research institutions, since the definite responsibility which each has in its own held is a real stimulus. The general committee would correspond to a small staff group.

Let us leave the research half of the program at this point, and briefly examine the production phase of the problem. In a sense, production is the more critical element, since it entails far more people and Facilities at its peak usefulness and must be readily

The Permanent War Economy — Appendix

expandable. Suppose the largest suppliers of war goods (the exact number to he determined by a study of the present program) were each asked to designate a permanent liaison man, generally familiar with war-production requirements and with his own company's developments and capabilities. Such a man would keep ready at all times a broad plan for converting and reequipping his company, setting up subcontractors, assuring material supply — in short, doing everything that he or his prototype is doing today as an emergency assignment in the country's best run businesses. The services might insure his added interest by commissioning him a colonel in the Reserve which would bind him closer to them and give him added stature within his company in peacetime. Out of this group of "colonels" there might be chosen an industrial coordinating committee to serve in conjunction with the principal procurement officers of the service branches. This committee would parallel the general research committee. Both would be permanent and continuing, although the personnel would change, perhaps, and either group, or both, would meet or regular occasions with designated. legislative and administrative representatives at the President's behest.

What we have here, of course, is a consultative group which carries into peacetime the Combined Chiefs of Star idea which is proving so successful in wartime. Each participant draws inspiration, information, and advice on which to act — not as a member of the committee but in his own capacity as a Congressional committee chairman, as an industry representative, as a Cabinet member, as a scientist with access to research facilities. The staff is clothed with no separate powers; it draws its power from the individuals who make it up.

This is about as far as it is possible to go with respect to organization. I would like to conclude with some footnotes which seem appropriate.

It is my feeling that both branches of the service should keep their technical officers in closer touch with manufacturing plants through assigned tours of duty. The Navy has been the leading exponent of this practice, I believe. It is not a costly thing to do.

In respect to Government research projects, the remuneration for scientists on the Government pay roll should be so substantial as to attract leading men and the positions sufficiently recognized as to keep them. Industry has set the pattern here.

For the Common Defense

As for Government-owned plants, some of these undoubtedly should be retained in stand-by condition for future use. But we must bear in mind that little is to be gained by reserving and maintaining huge plants for the production of highly specialized weapons and equipment, because they will almost certainly turn into the whitest of elephants. So long as warfare is global in character no man can foresee the nature of future weapons, which tend to grow out of the demands of a particular theater of war. It would be preferable to authorize a steady flow of educational orders for small amounts of new equipment so that those companies which would have to swing into volume production might keep their hands in and be ready for expansion. This would be a natural by-product of the general postwar staff operation.

All this has largely been a somewhat documented elaboration of one word — cooperation — between Government and industry. It is the kind of cooperation we are getting now but continued with the expensive peaks leveled off and much of the headache eliminated. No bureaucratic structure has been proposed which would in any way limit or modify the will of the people as expressed through the Congress and executed by the Administration.

We have learned that our country has the strength and brains to do anything it needs to do, provided that it brings the strength and brains together and makes the proper use of them. As we love peace and long for its continuance, it is our responsibility to make sure that America's strength and brains, its craft and knowledge, are kept forever ready — not just ready *for* action but *in* action.

I do not know, and it is not my place to advocate, whether or not we need a huge armament program. But the high importance of this plan of keeping scientifically and technologically ready for war lies in the fact that it does not involve the maintenance of large armed forces. Nor would this program be very expensive. It would not depend upon universal military service, although that offers many advantages, or upon large-scale production of military goods. It can fit into our peacetime way of living without difficulty. I believe with all my heart that it would *guarantee* that way of life.

Army Ordnance Vol. XXVI, No. 143, March-April 1944 — Charles E. Wilson

Index

In addition to the index by subject matter and name, we have added, at the end, an index of the tables which make up a significant part of the work.

20th Century Capitalist Revolution ...205

Acheson, Dean ...112
Adams, Sherman
Adelman, M. A. ...205
American Federation of Labor ...146, 150
American Economic Revue ...70, 218
Americans for Democratic Action ...193
Army Ordnance Association...ii, iv, 271 ff.
Atlee Government ...iii
Atomic Eneregy Commission ...12
Axis, the ...271

Baruch, Bernard M. ...201
Batt, William L. ...243
Benelux ...124
Benson, Senator Elmer A. ...196-7
Berle, A. A ...205 ff.
Bevan, Aneurin ...217
Bolshevik Revolution ...225, 248, 256
Bonapartist tendencies ...24, 105, 142-3, 157, 208
Bourgeoisie ...51-2, 99
Bureau of Agricultural Economics
    Source of data on farm population ..47
Bureau of Internal Revenue ...159, 175
Bureau of Labor Statistics...32-4, 35, 37, 50, 166, 185, 264-5
Bureau of Standards ...279
Bureaucracy ...iii, 23, 66, 72-3, 75, 77, 100, 105, 137, 143, 146-7, 149-51, 153, 163, 193
Bureaucratic Collectivism ...125
Burns, Dr. Arthur F. ...235, 241
Business advisory Council ...149

Campbell, General William Beverly ...272
Carroll, J. J. ...177
Census Bureau ...19, 42, 114, 167, 237-8
Childs, Mark ...231
Civilian "Generals" and
    Military "Captains of Industry" ...143
    279-80
Chamber of Commerce ..34, 149
Chemical Warfare Service ...279

Churchill, Winston ...244, 262
Clay, Gen. Lucius D., Jr. ...144
Collins, Edward H. ...193-4
Commerce Department....3-5, 12, 27-8, 31, 33-5, 49, 59 82, 85-6, 114, 116, 118, 137, 139, 164, 173, 177, 240, 264, 268, 278
Committee of the Judiciary ...213
Congress of Industrial Organizations (CIO) 146, 189-90
Connally, Senator Tom ...112-3
Conners, Alfred F. ...197
Consumer's Price Index ...32-37, 59, 234
Cook, L. D. ...170
Crane, Burton ...214-5
Crédit Mobilier ...208

Denmark ...124
Democracy ...24, 112, 145, 157, 217-8, 223, 229, 271
Dixon-Yates Contract ...213
DuPont ...161

E bonds ...58, 151, 155
ECA (Eonomic Cooperation Administration aka the Marshall Plan) ...112-3, 121, 123
Economic Stabilization Administration 106, 148
Eisenhower, President Dwight D. i, ii, 125, 208, 212, 236, 239
    Economic Message to Congress ...45
England ...124, 131, 155, 224
Equality of Sacrifice ...45
Export-Import Bank loans ...12, 120, 135

Fair Deal ...41
Farmers' Union vs. Farm Bureau ...46
Farming class ...45-6, 50-2, 54-6, 150, 164
Federal Reserve..49, 57, 116, 154, 167, 265-6
Federal Income Tax...48-9, 57, 80-1, 92-3, 151, 163-4, 166, 168, 173-9, 188-190, 194, 196, 234-9
Fertig, Lawrence ...193-4
Foster, William C 112, 123

The Permanent War Economy

Franc, L. ...170
France ...119-120, 124, 126, 142, 155

Gallup poll ...196
Geneva, Treaty of ...244
Gillmor, R. E. ...276
Gould, Jay ...158
Gray Report .. 12, 107, 109, 128-130, 134-6
Great Depression ...14, 54, 65-7, 72-3, 77, 79, 107, 116-7, 131, 137, 139, 142, 154, 164, 168, 208-9, 211, 228, 230, 245, 248-50, 252, 256
grossraumwirtschaft ...257

Hansen, Alvin H. ...70, 259
Harris, Seymour E. ...67-8, 70
Harvard Business Review ...209
Hewitt, George W. ...194
Hinshaw, Randall ...116
Hirsh, Julius ...233
Hoffman, Michael L. ...125, 263
Homan, Paul ...218
Hook, Sidney ...144
Hull, Cordell ...243

Inflation ...6, 14, 24, 28, 34, 37, 54, 56, 59 60, 63, 69, 72, 81, 83, 101, 104, 124, 139 146-7, 150-155, 163, 172, 180-3, 186, 188-9, 191-2, 200-201, 230-1, 248-249, 255, 260-1, 265
International Labor Organization (ILO) 111
International Association of Machinists 146
Italy ...119, 124

Japan ...8, 119, 121, 156, 249, 272
Jenks, Elizabeth ...233
Johnson, Professor Chalmers ...ii
Johnston, Eric ...148
Joint Congressional Committee
 on the Economic Report ...180-1, 184, 212
J. P. Morgan & Co. ...65, 128

Kefauver, Carey Estes ...158, 213
Kennedy, John Fitzgerald ...iv
Kennedy, Paul P. ...111-113, 123

Keynes, John Maynard ...67-68, 70, 154, 217, 219, 228-229, 253
Kilgore, Senator Harley Martin ...213
Korean War ...iv, 1, 8, 12, 19, 37, 39, 75, 80, 107, 111, 1117, 119, 124, 133, 142, 155, 182, 186, 209, 230, 233, 263 ff.
Kuwait ...133
Kuznets, Simon
 National Production in Wartime ...9
 Our Economy in War ...202
 Shares of Upper Income Groups in Income and Savings ...233-241
Labor Bureaucracy ...146-7, 149-151, 193, 212
Labor Department ...167
Labor Management Relations Act ...149
Langer, Senator William ...213
Leffingwell, R. C. ...65, 128, 130
Lenin, V. I. ...22, 65-6
Lewis, John L. ...146
Lissner, Will ...233-5

MacArthur, General Douglas ...75, 144
Marsh, Benjamin C. ...196
Marshall Plan ...12, 70, 112, 118, 120-123, 263
Marx, Karl ...4, 9, 17-18, 41, 56, 60, 62-3, 70, 84-5, 89, 90, 96-7, 106, 142, 152, 208, 211, (and Keynes) 217 ff., 246, 252-254, 261, 263, 268
Military-Economic Imperialism ...24, 107 ff.
Melman, Professor Seymour ...ii, iv

Middle class ...iv, 45-7, 50-1, 53-6, 62, 86, 150, 155, 164, 171-2, 179, 182, 186, 200, 202, 240, 246, 254
Military-Industrial Complex ...i, iv
Military Kenesianism ...iv, 79
Morrison-Knudsen ...144
Musgrave, R.A. ...170, 181
Mutual Defense Assistance Program .12, 122
Mutual Security Program ...122-3

National Bureau of Economic Research
 177, 202, 233, 240
National City Bank ...94-6, 98, 135, 198-9, 206
National Debt ...12-13, 30, 153-, 257, 261
National Economic Committee ...212

Index

National Income Supplement ... 1, 137, 164
National Industrial Conference Board .. 245
National Research Council ... 279
National Tax Journal ... 170
Naval Academy ... 272
New Deal ... iii, 16, 22, 41, 65, 79, 137, 139, 154, 164, 251, 252, 261
New York Curb Exchange
    (American Stock Exchange) ... 270
New York Stock Exchange ... 92-3
Norway ... 124

Oakes, Walter J.
    pen name of Edward Sard ... iii
Office of Scientific Research and
    Development (OSRD) ... 278

Pabst Brewing Company competition .. 245
Peabody, Fred S. ... 178-9
People's Lobby ... 196
Permanent War Economy
    Bonapartist tendencies ... 24
    Decline in the Standard of Living .. 22-3, 27-63, 152, 195, 212
    Effect on "general law of capitalist
        accumulation ... 18
    Effect on personal savings ... 48
    Foreign aid included in ... 9
    general law of accumulation ... 27
    growth of "Military-Economic
        Imperialism" ... 24
    increased taxation ... 23, 57, 101, 241
    increased dependence on foreign
        sources of raw materials ... 114 ff.
    inflation generated by ... 6, 14, 24, 28, 37, 56, 59-60, 63, 69, 72, 83, 101, 104, 139, 146, 150-5, 163, 172, 180-3, 186, 188-9, 191, 230, 248-9, 255, 260-1, 265
    new stage of barbarism ... 24
    The Problem of Unpaid Labor ... 15, 250
    State Intervention increases .. 23, 65 ff., 100, 102-7, 139, 143 ff.
    Transformation of capitalist economy 1
    Undermines independence of labor 147-150
    Veterans' Administration ... 9

Voice of America ... 10
What is excluded ... 10
Planned Ecomomy ... 99, 124, 206, 244, 266
Point Four ... 12, 134-6, 269, 270
Poison Gas (benefits of research on) ... 275

Public Works Programs ... 16, 135, 248, 250-252, 255
pyramid-building ... 16-7, 243, 251

Railway Labor Executives Association .. 146
Randall, Clarence ... 232
Reconstruction Finance Committtee ... 5
Reconversion ... 244, 247, 255, 266
Research and Development Division of the
    Quartermaster Corps ... 279
Reuther, Walter ... 186, 190-192
Rockefeller Report ... 107, 109, 133-4, 136
Robinson, Joan ... 222
Roosevelt, Franklin Delano ... 16, 65, 141, 145, 200-1, 244, 249, 251, 253, 261-2, 269

Sard, Edward
    see T.N. Vance, Walter J. Oakes ... iii, iv
Sarnoff, David ... 143-4
Scrugham, Senator James Grave ... 245
Securities and Exchange Commissnion (S.E.C) ... 92-3, 268
Snyder, John W.,
    Secretary of the Treasury ... 176, 193-4
slavery ... 17, 251-2
Slichter, Sumner ... 209-210
Somervell, Gen. Brehon Burke ... 143-4
Sperry Gyroscope ... 276
Stalin, Josef and Stalinism ... iv, 1, 12, 24, 55, 73, 75, 107, 109, 111, 114, 120, 124, 125, 127, 129, 142, 155-157, 200, 203-4, 218-19 225, 229, 244, 249, 256, 261-263, 266
Standard of living ... 22-23, 27-8, 30-32, 34-5, 37, 40-44, 46, 49 ff., 72, 150, 167-8, 193, 211 ff., 246-9, 254-5, 257-8, 262
Strachey, John .. 217 ff.
strikes ... 54, 145, 149, 151, 160
Survey of Current Business ... 5, 12, 116, 118, 131, 137, 164, 167, 231, 264, 267, 269

285

Taxation ... 23, 30-1, 44, 48-9, 53, 56-7, 60, 66, 69, 72, 77-84, 92-6, 100-1, 147, 149, 151, 155, 159, 161, 163 ff., 209, 233 ff., 248, 255, 261-2, 264, 265
   as instrument of US foreign policy 126, 128-9, 135-6
Teapot Dome ... 158
Temporary National Economic Committee (TNEC) ... 49
Tennessee Valley Authority ... iii
Third Camp ... 24, 107, 127, 204
Third World War ... iv, 9, 39, 142, 204, 243-5, 248, 250, 255-9, 261-2
Thompson, Dorothy ... 244
Trotsky, Leon ... iii, 142-3
Trotskyists ... 261
Truman, Harry S. ... 6, 44, 99, 109, 135, 141, 147, 153, 159, 160-1, 175, 180, 235, 269

Ultraviolet technology (and war economy) ... 274
United Kingdom ... 124
United Labor Policy Committee ... 146-8, 150, 189
United States Navy ... 5, 152, 270-1, 275-6, 278-80
UNRRA (United Nations Relief and Rehabilitation Administration) ... 5, 120

Vance, T. N.
   pen name of Edward Sard ... iii
von Mises, Ludwig
   need for governmental control ... 100-2

Wage Stabilization Board ... 147
War expenditure
   as percent of total expenditure ... 4
West Point ... 272
Williams, Senator John J. ... 161
Wilson, Charles E. (Edward)
   Author of phrase "Permanent War Economy"? ... ii
   Chairman of General Electric ... ii
   "Electric Charlie" ... ii
   Economic rivalry with Russia . 108-9, 124
   Labor attack on ... 149
   Need for governmental control ... 99
   Salary of ... 63
   September 1951 report on inflation 152
   Speech to Army Ordnance Assn. .. ii, 271
   Vice-Chair of War Production Board ii
Wilson, Charles E. (Erwin)
   "Engine Charlie" ... ii
   Salary of ... .63
   "What is good for General Motors ..." ii
Works Progress Administration (WPA) 214, 243
Working class
   Make up of ... 46
   Variations in income ... 47
World Bank ... 136
World War I ... 118, 154, 201, 253, 268
World War II ... 1, 8-10, 38, 40, 56, 73, 89, 91, 103-4, 106, 114, 118, 120, 122, 139, 147, 154, 156, 163, 200-1, 204, 228, 243, 250, 252, 256, 258, 281, 263-4, 267
   changes balance between federal and local government expenditures ... 139
World War III ... 9, 39, 142, 204, 243-5, 248, 250, 255-9, 261-2

X-Ray technology (and war economy) .. 274

Yalta Conference ... 244

Index of Tables

Part I
 Table A — RELATIONSHIP OF WAR OUTLAYS TO TOTAL OUTPUT, 1939-1953 ...4
 Table B — DIRECT AND INDIRECT WAR OUTLAYS. 1939-1953
   AND THEIR RELATIONSHIP TO TOTAL OUTPUT ...11
 Table C — UNEMPLOYMENT, 1939-1950 ...18
 Table D — RATIO OF UNEMPLOYMENT TO TOTAL LABOR FORCE, 1939-1950 ...21

Part II
 Table I   — CIVILIAN OUTPUT OF CONSUMER GOODS AND SERVICES. 1939-1953 ...29
 Table II   — PERSONAL CONSUMPTION EXPENDITURES. 1939-1953 ...36
   — RELATIVE DECLINE IN CONSUMPTION OUTPUT
     COMPARED WITH TOTAL OUTPUT ...38
 Table IV — PER CAPITA AVERAGE STANDARD OF LIVING. 1939-1953 ...42
 Table V   — TOTAL PERSONAL INCOME, PERSONAL TAX AND NON TAX PAYMENTS,
     PERSONAL SAVINGS, AND
     PERSONAL CONSUMPTION EXPENDITURES. 1939-1953 ...48
 Table VI — PER CAPITA STANDARDS OF LIVING BY CLASSES 1939-1953 ...51
 Table VII — INDEXES OF AVERAGE & CLASS
     PER CAPITA STANDARDS OF LIVING, 1939-1953 ..52
 Table VIII — RATE OF SURPLUS VALUE. 1939-1953 ...61

Part III
 Table I — RELATIONSHIP OF GOVERNMENT INCOME TO CURRENT PRODUCTION
     AND SURPLUS VALUE 1939-1950 ...71
 Table II — RELATIONSHIP OF GOVERNMENT EMPLOYMENT TO
     TOTAL EMPLOYED LABOR FORCE, 1939-1950 ...74
 Table II-A — COMPOSITION OF GOVERNMENT EMPLOYMENT, 1939-1950 ...76
 Table III — COMPOSITION OF GOVERNMENT EMPLOYMENT, 1939-1950 ...78
 Table IV — RATES OF CORPORATE PROFIT. 1929-1950 ...82
 Table V — CORPORATE AND NONCORPORATE RETAIL, WHOLESALE,
     AND MANUFACTURING SALES. 1939-1950 ...86

 Table VI — AVERAGE RATE OF PROFIT FOR ALL INDUSTRY 1939-1950 ...88
     COMPOSITION OF CAPITAL 1939-1950 ...93

 Table VII — MASS AND RATE OF PROFIT OF LISTED MANUFACTURING
     CORPORATIONS. ACCORDING TO SEC SURVEY, 1938-1947 ...93
 Table VIII-A — MASS OF PROFIT OF LEADING CORPORATIONS IN 1950
     COMPARED WITH 1949, ACCORDING TO NATIONAL CITY BANK OF NY...95
 Table VIII-B — RATE OF PROFIT OF LEADING CORPORATIONS IN 1950
     COMPARED WITH 1949. ACCORDING TO NATIONAL CITY BANK OF NY ...98

Part IV
 UNITED STATES PRIVATE LONG-TERM FOREIGN INVESTMENTS 1924-1930 ...115
 OUTFLOW OF UNITED STATES PRIVATE LONG-TERM CAPITAL, 1948-1950 ...116
 FOREIGN AID BY COUNTRY July 1, 1945 Through December 31, 1950 ...119
 AMERICAN EXPORTS AND MEANS OF FINANCING, 1948-1950 ...132

The Permanent War Economy

Part V
PERCENTAGE DISTRIBUTION OF GROSS NATIONAL PRODUCT 1929-1950	...138
RATIO OF GOVERNMENT PURCHASES OF GOODS AND SERVICES TO GROSS NATIONAL PRODUCT, 1929-1950	...140
NATIONAL DEBT FOR SELECTED YEARS	...153

Part VI
Table I — MAJOR TAX COMPONENTS, 1929 and 1939-1950	...165
Table II — MONEY INCOME RECEIVED BY EACH FIFTH OF FAMILIES AND SINGLE PERSONS, 1935-36, 1941, 1948 AND 1949 (Percentage of Money Income)	...167
Table III — TOTAL TAXES IN 1938-39 AS PERCENTAGE OF PERSONAL INCOME, BY INCOME CLASSES	...169
Table IV — 1948 TAX PAYMENTS AS PER CENT OF INCOME BY INCOME BRACKETS	...170
Table V — TAX EVASION IN 1946	...177
Table VI — IMPACT OF REVENUE ACT OF 1951 ON SELECTED INDIVIDUAL INCOME TAXES	...178
Table VII — ESTIMATED DISTRIBUTION OF CONSUMER EXPENDITURES FOR 1948 (In Per Cent of Total)	...180
Table VIII — INCOME RECEIVED AND ESTIMATED MINIMUM INCOME REQUIRED FOR FAMILY MAINTENANCE BY INCOME CLASSES – 1948	...184
Spending vs. Tax rate	...192
INDIVIDUAL TAXABLE NET INCOME FOR 1951	...194
58 Largest Companies Ranked by Assets	...198
Assets of Billion Dollar Companies	...199

An Amalgam of Marx and Keynes
Direct and Indirect War Outlays, 1947-1956 and Their Relationship to Total Output	...231

The Myth of America's Social Revolution
Wage or Salary	...237

After Korea — What?
WARTIME GROWTH OF OUTPUT WARTIME GROWTH OF OUTPUT	...264
POSTWAR CAPITAL ACCUMULATION	...267

www.ingramcontent.com/pod-product-compliance
Lightning Source LLC
Chambersburg PA
CBHW081831170426
43199CB00017B/2700